THE SPANISH
ARMADA

THE GREAT ENTERPRISE AGAINST ENGLAND 1588

OSPREY
PUBLISHING

THE SPANISH
ARMADA

THE GREAT ENTERPRISE AGAINST ENGLAND 1588

ANGUS KONSTAM

First published in Great Britain in 2009 by Osprey Publishing, Midland House,
West Way, Botley, Oxford OX2 0PH, United Kingdom.
443 Park Avenue South, New York, NY 10016, USA.
Email: info@ospreypublishing.com

A CIP catalogue record for this book is available from the British Library.

ISBN-13: 978 1 84603 496 1

Page layout by Myriam Bell Design, France
Index by Alan Thatcher
Typeset in Centaur MT
Originated by PDQ Diginal Media Solutions, Suffolk
Printed in China through Worldprint

09 10 11 12 13   10 9 8 7 6 5 4 3 2 1

FOR A CATALOGUE OF ALL BOOKS PUBLISHED BY OSPREY MILITARY
AND AVIATION PLEASE CONTACT:
NORTH AMERICA
Osprey Direct, c/o Random House Distribution Center, 400 Hahn Road, Westminster, MD 21157
E-mail: uscustomerservice@ospreypublishing.com

ALL OTHER REGIONS
Osprey Direct, The Book Service Ltd, Distribution Centre, Colchester Road, Frating Green,
Colchester, Essex, CO7 7DW

E-mail: customerservice@ospreypublishing.com

Osprey Publishing is supporting the Woodland Trust, the UK's leading woodland conservation charity,
by funding the dedication of trees.

www.ospreypublishing.com

Front cover image: Detail from *Defeat of the Spanish Armada, 8 August 1588* by Philippe-Jacques de Loutherbourg,
1796 (BHC0264 National Maritime Museum, Greenwich, London, Greenwich Hospital Collection)
Back cover image: *Elizabeth I, the Armada Portrait* attributed to George Gower, c.1588 (© The Gallery
Collection/Corbis)
Cover background © istockphoto

Contents

✥ Introduction

High in the mountains, some 30 miles north of Madrid, is El Escorial, a monastic eyrie which had been turned into a royal palace. It was from here that King Philip II of Spain (1527–98, reigned 1556–98) ruled his transatlantic empire, and plotted the overthrow of the English state. His palace lay at the centre of a vast intelligence network, fed by ambassadors, spies and informers, and it remained the heart of a Spanish bureaucracy which was the envy of Europe. King Philip's palace was also the hub of the Spanish military machine, with orders and reports coming and going from every corner of the Spanish Empire. Of all King Philip's endeavours, he is probably best remembered for a failure – a great military and naval enterprise designed to change the political map of Europe, and to force a regime change which would remove any challenge to Spain's domination of two continents.

On paper the plan looked simple enough. An 'armada' (fleet) of some 170 ships would gather in Lisbon, and from there it would launch an invasion of England. It would carry an invasion force of 55,000 veteran soldiers, including cavalry, artillery and engineers, plus all the stores this army would need as it marched on London. The amphibious landing would be carried out using specially built galleys – forerunners of the landing craft of the mid-20th century. These Spanish troops were the most experienced soldiers in Europe, and once ashore then victory was all but inevitable. However, like so many military operations, in so many wars, someone decided to cut a few corners. That penny-pinching resulted in too many compromises, and as a result the plan became fatally flawed. What had once been a daring and innovative enterprise had turned into a plan where victory depended on the enemy doing exactly what was expected of them. In the great naval campaign that followed the English proved less than obliging, and fought the invaders in their own novel way.

Posterity records the defeat of the Spanish Armada as the triumph of a small maritime nation which took on a mighty world empire and won a glorious victory. It was seen to mark the beginning of an Elizabethan 'golden age' of exploration, naval glory and overseas colonization. The Spanish defeat preserved the Protestant Reformation, established England as a leading sea-force and caused the first cracks in the bastion of Spanish world power. Today the pantheon of Elizabethan 'sea

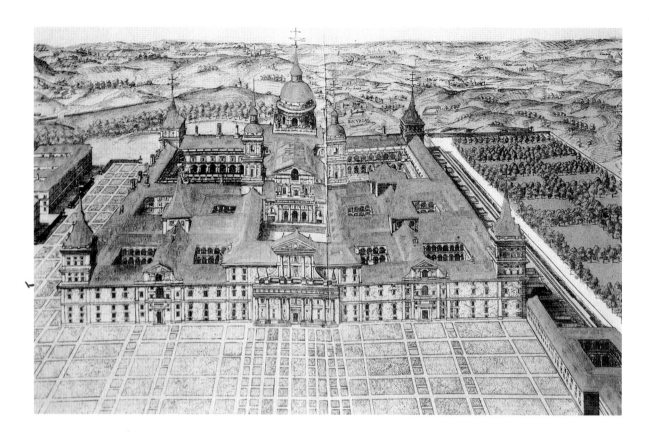

The Escorial Palace outside Madrid served as the headquarters of King Philip II of Spain during the planning and execution of the Spanish Armada campaign. Philip ran his empire from a small suite of rooms in the palace, but maintained a network of contacts and messengers who kept him in touch with European affairs (Biblioteca Marucelianna, Florence).

dogs' who participated in the campaign have become the creatures of legend. Drake, Hawkins, Frobisher and Raleigh are symbolic of a romanticized view of Elizabethan England, set on patriotic pedestals by centuries of historians. In fact the naval battle was a much closer-run thing than the history books often tell us, and with a bit more Spanish luck, or if the English commanders had made one wrong move, the tide of European history could well have flowed the other way.

The participants themselves certainly didn't realize that they lived in a 'golden age'. The 'Good Queen Bess' of popular legend was in reality a shrewd political manipulator, assisted by a powerful police and intelligence service. Decades of religious persecution and xenophobia in England had done much to harden her people against the Spanish, and this strong feeling played no little part in the success of the English sailors. After all, they realized the high stakes they were fighting for. As for the Spanish, Philip II of Spain saw his 'Great Enterprise' as a solution for most of the ills that afflicted Spain. These included a vicious and costly revolt in the Netherlands, the arrival of European interlopers in the New World and revenue from the Americas which seemed to be decreasing a little every year. Philip was at least the political equal of Elizabeth, and the campaign was the climax of two decades of political one-upmanship, in which the stakes were becoming higher and higher. For Elizabeth in 1588, her very survival depended on the actions of her 'sea dogs'.

The Spanish Armada campaign ranks as one of the most fascinating maritime engagements of all time. Two powerful fleets fought a series of battles that transformed naval warfare. In the 16th century no firm tactical doctrines had been established, so the campaign became a test bed for two conflicting theories of war at sea. Although much has been made of the English superiority in gunnery, the English fleet was unable to break the tight defensive formation of the Spanish fleet until a fire ship attack scattered the Spanish ships. For their part the Spanish showed great resolution and bravery throughout the fighting. It is also apparent that the Spanish Armada almost succeeded. England was saved less by her 'sea dogs' than by eight fireships, poor Spanish communications and a storm which took everyone by surprise.

The historical ramifications of a Spanish victory are almost too huge to comprehend. As historian Geoffrey Parker put it, with no English colonies in America and India, 'the Empire of Philip II on which the sun never set would have remained the largest the world had ever seen'. Above all, the Spanish Armada was a naval campaign, fought for the highest possible political stakes, using technologies which were in their infancy. Both sides placed their faith in the superiority of their ships over those of their rivals. In fact, the campaign became a clash between two types of warships, and two very different fighting methods.

The Spanish relied on their superb soldiers to win their sea battles for them, secure in the knowledge that their troops were the elite soldiers of Europe. For their part the English placed their faith in gunpowder, and the emerging 'black art' of naval gunnery. By using speed and agility they could keep their distance from the Spanish ships, and pound them with their superior firepower. This clash would not only decide the political fate of Europe – it would also establish the way sea battles would be fought for the next 250 years. This all meant that when the two fleets first sighted each other off the Devon coast that summer, nobody could really predict what would happen next.

✤ The Road to War

Love and Marriage – Tudor Style

It all began with a king's infatuation with a beautiful young woman. Actually, the story reaches a little further back than that, to the day in November 1501 when Arthur, the eldest son of King Henry VII of England, married a Spanish princess. His bride was Catherine of Aragon, the daughter of Ferdinand and Isabella, the joint rulers of a united Spain. It was later claimed that the teenage couple never consummated their marriage, and just five months later, in April 1502, Arthur, Prince of Wales died of a sudden illness. His Spanish-born widow was just 16 years old. The death of his older brother meant that the 12-year-old Henry – the future King Henry VIII – became next in line to the English throne.

The reason his father Henry VII had arranged a marriage between his eldest son and a Spanish princess was to strengthen political links between the two countries. England was still recovering from a brutal dynastic struggle – the Wars of the Roses – while Spain was a country on the road to greatness. In 1492 Christopher Columbus had discovered the New World, and claimed this as yet unexplored territory in the name of Ferdinand and Isabella. A year later the Borgia pope, Alexander VI, declared that all lands to the west of the Azores now belonged to Spain. The ruling was challenged by the Portuguese, and the result was the Treaty of Tordesillas (1494), which established the boundary as a line drawn between the poles, cutting the Atlantic in two. All new lands to the east, including Brazil and the Indies, belonged to Portugal, while the Spanish were left in firm control of everything to the west. This 'line' meant that the Spanish regarded themselves as the rulers of the Americas.

In 1495 Ferdinand and Isabella completed the *Reconquista* – the Christian reconquest of the Iberian Peninsula from the Moors. This, along with the Treaty of Tordesillas, transformed Spain's fortunes. While Spanish explorers, adventurers and settlers began probing their way along the coastlines of the New World, Spanish soldiers and sailors began the business of expanding Spanish territorial boundaries and Spain's sphere of influence in Europe and the Mediterranean. By

Opposite
Mary I of England and Philip II of Spain, an oil painting by Hans Eworth, c.1555. This union between the crowns of Spain and England led to the suppression of the Protestant faith in England, but failed to produce any lasting military or political results (National Maritime Museum, Greenwich, London).

the following decades England became a staunch bastion of the reformed faith. Henry married again – his next wife being Jane Seymour, whom he wedded ten days after Anne's execution. The following year she gave Henry the son he wanted – Prince Edward – but died days later from septicaemia. Still, it looked as if Henry's Tudor dynasty was secure.

Henry VIII died in January 1547, an obese and gout-ridden man of 55. His nine-year-old son Edward, Prince of Wales, succeeded him, becoming King Edward VII. Like his elder half-sister Elizabeth, Edward had been brought up a Protestant, and he proved a vigorous supporter of the Protestant cause, and consequently a potential enemy of Emperor Charles V. However, in late 1552 Edward fell ill, and the teenage king died the following summer. Before his death his advisors tried unsuccessfully to secure a Protestant succession, but instead the crown passed to Edward's eldest half-sister Mary, the daughter of Catherine of Aragon. The future of England would now take a very different course.

Queen Mary I of England had been raised a Catholic, and she set about restoring the old religion. However, to achieve this she needed an ally – one with military as well as political muscle. She found one in Charles V's only son Prince Philip of Spain – the future King Philip II. The couple married in July 1554. He was 27, and she was 38. If the couple could produce a healthy male heir then the temporary political union of England and Spain would become a permanent arrangement. While they set about undoing the work of the Protestant reformers, they also tried – and failed – to produce the necessary child. After a false pregnancy, Philip made polite excuses and returned to Spain.

The burning of Protestant martyrs in Stratford in East London during the reign of Queen Mary I of England. Her death in 1558 marked a dramatic shift in policy, and her half-sister Elizabeth proved to be a staunch advocate of the Protestant faith (Stratford Archive).

Although the principal aim was to form a political union against France, the marriage also strengthened Mary's position against the Protestants within her own kingdom. Relations between the consort and the queen's subjects soured rapidly, particularly with the widespread and unpopular persecution of Protestants by 'Bloody Mary'. This was blamed in part on the Spanish, as was the waging of an unpopular war with France, where English troops fought alongside Spanish ones. By early 1558 it became clear that Mary was unwell, and so the question of her successor became a crucial matter of state. Philip and his Spanish advisers found themselves in a precarious situation. He was just a consort, and consequently had no claim to the throne. The main contenders were Mary's Protestant half-sister Elizabeth, and the Catholic Mary Queen of Scots. As Mary was a former French queen, Philip reluctantly supported the 'heretic' Elizabeth's claim, considering her the lesser of two evils. Better a Protestant than a French puppet. He would soon regret his decision.

Mary I of England died in November 1558, and on her deathbed she acknowledged the claim of the 25-year-old Elizabeth as her successor. The young princess was duly crowned Queen Elizabeth I of England in January 1559. Much has been written about Elizabeth, and her own Tudor propagandists depicted her as the natural successor of Henry VIII, and a defender of the Protestant cause. In fact, as the daughter of a shamed queen, she had been declared illegitimate, sidelined by the court of her father and brother, and even threatened with execution by her half-sister. Her path to the throne had been an unsteady one, and so she was determined to maintain control of both her crown and her kingdom. With the benefit of hindsight we could argue that conflict between Elizabeth and her brother-in-law was inevitable. If so, then it was a war which was another three decades in the making.

Neighbours and Cousins

Elizabeth's mother – Anne Boleyn – had been a fiery, hot-tempered young woman, with striking looks, and an intelligent, calculating mind. Anne's daughter inherited her mother's brains more than her looks, but with the Boleyn hot-headedness came the ability to make measured decisions, to seek wise counsel, and above all to be patient. As a Protestant she encouraged the strengthening of the reformed English Church, and became its supreme governor. All English officials swore allegiance both to the new religion, and to the queen as its head – strengthening the bond between reformed church and the state. However, she also avoided the worst religious pitfalls of her sister Mary, and took steps not to antagonize Catholics unnecessarily, whether at home or abroad. It was a tightrope, made all the more difficult to walk when religion became a matter of international allegiance.

When Elizabeth Tudor succeeded to the English throne in late 1558 she pursued a policy of neutrality in European affairs, and re-affirmed her wish to live at peace

This Dutch satirical cartoon from the 1570s depicts King Philip II of Spain sitting astride a sacred cow, which represents the Spanish Netherlands. While Queen Elizabeth I of England and the French are feeding the animal at one end, the Dutch Prince William of Orange is depicted tormenting the beast from behind (Hensley Collection, Ashville, NC).

Opposite

The Sea Beggars' 'hell-raisers' attacking the Schelde Pontoon Bridge, 1585.
In 1566 the Dutch revolted against Spanish rule, and by 1572 the revolt had spread throughout the Netherlands. In 1578 the veteran Spanish Army of Flanders led by the Duke of Parma launched a fresh offensive which succeeded in recapturing most of the cities in the Spanish Netherlands. In 1585 Parma laid siege to Antwerp, and linked his siegeworks by constructing a massive pontoon bridge across the River Schelde. The only hope for the defenders was to destroy the bridge and cut off the Spaniards on the northern bank from the rest of the army. The Sea Beggars, Dutch maritime raiders who were already disrupting Spanish sea communications, undertook the job of destroying the bridge. On the night of 5 April 1585 they sailed a fleet of fireships towards the bridge. Each 'hell-raiser' was packed with combustible materials and explosives, timed to explode at intervals. As Spanish troops including Parma watched from the shore and their comrades tried to save the bridge, several fireships exploded, causing utter confusion. An outer defensive boom was cut, and one of the largest 'hell-raisers' drifted against the bridge and detonated. The bridge was blown to pieces, and 800 Spaniards were killed or wounded by the explosion. This reconstruction shows the final moments of the bridge, when even the best soldiers in Europe were unable to protect themselves from this unorthodox form of attack (Angus McBride).

with Spain. She politely turned down an offer of marriage from Philip of Spain in 1559, and while her advisors embarked in lengthy marriage negotiations with Philip's cousin — Archduke Charles of Austria — it became clear that Elizabeth was reluctant to embark on any alliance which would place the sovereignty of England in jeopardy. In effect she was willing to use marriage — or rather the prospect of a dynastic union — as a tool of foreign policy.

This policy of neutrality was relatively short lived. During the 1560s a series of events took place which set Elizabethan England at odds with Catholic Spain, and inevitably this led to a deterioration in international relations. Even then she remained reluctant to commit herself to a path which would lead to war, preferring to rely on diplomacy and negotiation to resolve disputes rather than force of arms. Ironically, the slide from uneasy neutrality towards an undeclared 'cold war' began in 1566, when the ailing Emperor Charles V abdicated the imperial throne. His empire was divided between his brother Ferdinand and his son Philip. Ferdinand gained control of Austria, and became the new Holy Roman Emperor, while Philip became ruler of Spain, the Spanish Netherlands, and the New World.

As a Spaniard, Philip spoke neither Dutch nor French, and had little empathy for his Northern European subjects. He appointed Margaret, Duchess of Parma, as his governor in the Netherlands, but neither ruler nor governor was able to stem the rising tide of religious unrest in the region. Soon iconoclasm and religious dissent turned into a widespread popular uprising, where the Dutch were united by their religious opposition to both Spanish rule and the Catholic faith. The 'Dutch Revolt' began in August 1566, marking the start of a war of independence which

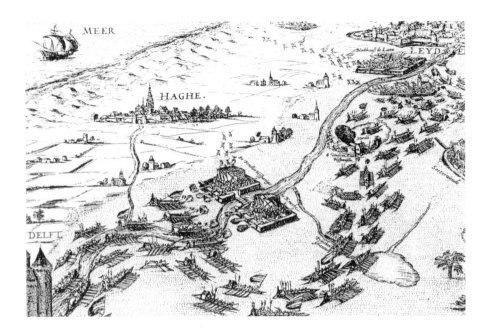

When the Spanish army laid siege to the city of Leiden in 1574, the Dutch rebels flooded the land surrounding the city. This allowed the 'Sea Beggars' to sail to its relief in shallow-drafted galleys. The same craft were then used to drive the Spaniards from their siegeworks. Copy of a hand-coloured engraving, c.1586 (Stratford Archive).

would last for more than four decades. The Spanish quickly sent veteran troops to the region, who became the Army of Flanders, led by the Duke of Alba. The revolt was brutally suppressed in a matter of months, the ringleaders were executed, and the inhabitants of the Low Countries simmered with resentment.

The Duchess of Parma scathingly referred to the rebels as 'beggars', and so the phrase 'Long live the beggars' became a rebel slogan. A fresh revolt flared up in 1572, supported in secret by Elizabethan England and Huguenot France. In April a group of Dutch privateers known as the 'Sea Beggars' seized the tiny Dutch port of Brill, and declared themselves as supporters of the Protestant rebels. They used this foothold and the surrounding coastal and estuarine waters of Zeeland as a base for attacks on Spanish shipping and isolated garrisons. The Sea Beggars' preferred craft was a shallow-draughted Dutch coastal ship with one or two masts known as a 'flyboat' (*vlieboot*), the largest of which could displace 500 tons. Many of these early rebels were former pirates or smugglers who took advantage of the conflict to increase the scope and scale of their activities.

They were led by William, Baron de Lumey, who obtained official support from William of Orange and the rebel Dutch government, although the Spanish regarded him as nothing more than a pirate. The Sea Beggars' campaign continued through the year, with several more coastal towns falling to the rebels. The Spanish forces were stretched too thinly to protect the entire coast, and as their supply convoys fell prey to the rebels, they were forced to divert ships, men and money to counter the attacks. During 1573 the Sea Beggars were reinforced by English volunteers, arms and equipment, and by the following spring they were prepared to step up their campaign of harassment.

The Dutch were besieging the coastal city of Middelberg, and the Sea Beggars intercepted and destroyed every relief force and supply convoy the Spanish sent to the beleaguered city. A final relief attempt was foiled in January 1574 off Bergen-op-Zoom, and consequently the starving Spanish garrison had little option but to surrender. Similarly, the Spanish siege of the rebel city of Leiden was lifted when the Sea Beggars flooded the countryside around the walls, and then sailed in supplies, attacking the Spanish siege works as they did so. These activities consolidated Dutch control of the territories north of the River Schelde, which for the rest of the rebellion would mark the front line between Dutchman and Spaniard. The rebellion also began to spread south of the river, amongst the largely Catholic towns and cities of what is now Belgium. Within four years of the capture of Brill the rebel leader William of Orange had successfully carved out a Protestant enclave in Holland.

In 1578, in an attempt to stop the spread of the rebellion, King Philip II appointed a new commander of the Army of Flanders, Alexander Farnese, Duke of Parma, a highly skilled diplomat and military leader. The bankrupt Spanish treasury was unable to support offensive operations for several years, and the duke paid for much of the army's expenses out of his own pocket. However, within two years he had regained control of most of Flanders and was poised for an attack on

The execution of Mary Queen of Scots in February 1587 shocked the Catholic world, and hardened the resolve of King Philip II to remove the Protestant Elizabeth I from her throne. A 17th-century watercolour of the Dutch school (Scottish National Portrait Gallery, Edinburgh).

the key Protestant strongholds in Brabant. By 1580 he had consolidated his control of the region south of the River Schelde, and in early 1581 he threatened to launch an invasion of the territory held by the Dutch rebels.

Parma regarded Antwerp as the key to the rebellion. If the city was captured, the inland rivers and waterways beyond would be cut off from the sea. This, together with strong coastal garrisons and a secure land-based supply route, would prevent the Sea Beggars from influencing the campaign any further. Parma began to encircle the rebel-held city of Antwerp in early 1585 by building an 800-yard pontoon bridge over the River Schelde to the west of the city, protected by shore batteries, booms and guard boats. It allowed his men to surround the city with their siege lines, and the duke referred to the engineering feat as his 'sepulchre, his pathway into Antwerp'. The Sea Beggars were far from beaten. In April 1585 they launched a flotilla of explosive fireships on the ebb tide which floated down on the bridge, blowing apart first the protective boom, then the bridge itself. Despite the loss of 800 troops, Spanish discipline reasserted itself and prevented any follow-up attack, and Antwerp fell to the Spanish in August.

The war stagnated as both sides required time to regroup and replenish their coffers. Increasingly, the Spanish realized that as long as England remained free to supply the rebels, the rebellion would continue. Three days after the fall of Antwerp Queen Elizabeth openly sided with the Dutch, sending English troops to assist the rebels. At the same time, her 'sea dogs' took the offensive at sea: Walter Raleigh attacked the Spanish fishing fleets off Newfoundland and Francis Drake sailed for the Spanish coast intent on causing whatever damage he could. A 'cold war' had suddenly become very hot.

Another flashpoint between Elizabeth and Philip was Mary Queen of Scots. The daughter of King James V of Scotland and his French queen, Mary was also able to trace a direct line to the English throne through her English grandmother Margaret Tudor, the eldest sister of Henry VIII. While Henry VIII legislated against any succession by his great-niece, it was felt by many that Mary had a stronger claim to the English throne than did her cousin Elizabeth. Mary was raised in the French court, and in 1558 she married the French Dauphin, who succeeded his father the following year to become King Francis II. He died just over a year later, and in 1561 Mary returned to rule her native Scotland.

She spoke only French, surrounded herself with French advisors, and made a series of rash decisions which increasingly alienated her people. She had also returned to a country which had only recently undergone a Reformation. Therefore Mary's Catholicism was at odds with the religious views of her subjects. She married a nobleman — Lord Darnley — and produced an heir, but soon afterwards Darnley was murdered, and the finger of suspicion fell on the Earl of Bothwell, a man who subsequently 'abducted' Mary for her own safety, and whom the queen subsequently married. Many considered her an accomplice in the murder.

The union between Mary and Bothwell proved too much for a group of leading Protestant noblemen known as 'The Lords of the Congregation', who rose in rebellion. Mary was captured by the rebels, and imprisoned. She was also forced to abdicate in favour of her infant son, who became James VI of Scotland (and eventually also James I of England). In May 1568 she escaped from captivity, and raised an army. When it was defeated she fled across the border into England, where she threw herself on the mercy of her cousin Elizabeth, who promptly imprisoned her. She remained Elizabeth's prisoner for another 19 years.

Most Catholics regarded Mary's imprisonment as an outrage, and it helped unite Catholic feeling against Elizabeth and her Protestant realm. In other words, the imprisonment of Mary Queen of Scots greatly increased the religious and political tension in Europe. Mary soon became a political rallying point for Catholics in England and abroad who wanted to overthrow Protestant power in England. In 1569 an uprising was planned by a group of noblemen from the north of England. Their objective was to free Mary, and marry her to Thomas Howard, Duke of Norfolk, the leading Catholic in England. However, the plot was exposed, Mary remained imprisoned, and the Duke of Norfolk was executed.

The rebellion was exposed by Elizabeth's spymaster Sir Thomas Walsingham, who subsequently uncovered other plots designed to place Mary on the English throne. These included the Ridolfi Plot of 1571 and the Babington Plot of 1586, as well as several lesser schemes which were hatched and exposed during the intervening years. This last plot was engineered by Walsingham to root out any potential enemies of the state, and involved Babington – a young Catholic nobleman, a Jesuit priest and papal spy – and another priest, whom Walsingham had 'turned' into a double-agent. Mary was directly implicated in the planning, and after the plotters were arrested she was placed on trial as an accomplice. The result was inevitable, and, faced with such a direct challenge to her rule, Elizabeth was in no mood to be lenient. Mary Queen of Scots was duly executed in February 1587. By that time Philip II was already assembling his Armada.

Elizabeth's 'Cold War'

The imprisonment of Mary Queen of Scots in May 1568 was seen as an outrage by most Catholics, and Elizabeth hardly eased the tension later that summer, when her officials confiscated five Spanish royal ships which had been forced to seek refuge in English ports during a storm in the English Channel. They contained pay chests for the Spanish Army of Flanders, and Elizabeth kept both the ships and the money. As if this weren't bad enough, this coincided with the first English excursion 'beyond the line', into the Spanish waters of the New World. Strangely enough, this English 'interloper' came to trade, rather than to attack Spanish settlements.

John Hawkins was a Plymouth merchant and slave trader who transported a cargo of 300 slaves from West Africa to the Spanish Main. Although trade with interlopers was forbidden by the Spanish authorities, Hawkins hoped that many local governors would turn a blind eye to business with the English. He arrived off Hispaniola in early 1563 and connived with a local Spanish army officer to sell all of his slaves. This first voyage to the Spanish Main was a resounding financial success, making Hawkins the richest man in Plymouth. The investors who supported his plans for a second voyage included the queen, who even leased him a ship, the aged *Jesus of Lubeck*, a 700-ton warship.

This time the Spaniards were more reluctant to deal with him, but after being turned away from Margarita, Hawkins sold his human cargo at Borburata in Venezuela and Rio Hatcha in Colombia, having threatened to turn his guns on the towns if the local authorities refused to trade with him. This may have been an excuse contrived by both parties to justify the trade to the Spanish government if

Taken from the 1588 edition of *The Mariners Mirrour*, the deckhand (left) wears the typical attire of a seaman operating in a cold climate. A knitted woollen hat, a long overcoat, and breeches hanging loose to the ankle mark him as a seafarer. Armed only with a 'kidney' dagger, his primary focus was to sail rather than fight, though this would inevitably change with the prospect of plunder. A highly-skilled individual, master gunners (right) were always in demand, and this status is reflected in his outfit. The carved wooden linstock bearing the head and jaws of a crocodile would have held the burning taper used to fire the guns, allowing them to be fired from a safe distance. As on land, naval officers were armed and outfitted as their means and personal preference dictated. The officer here (centre) is based upon a portrait of Martin Frobisher (Richard Hook).

Previous page

John Hawkins' fight at San Juan
de Ulúa, 1568.

John Hawkins was an English
merchant who tried to break into the
Spanish trade monopoly with their
New World colonies. In September
1568 Hawkins was forced to run for
shelter into the Spanish harbour of
San Juan de Ulúa. The Englishmen
and their five ships outnumbered
the local garrison, and took over
the Spanish defences facing their
anchorage. Moored by their bows to
the island, the English ships had little
room to manoeuvre. A few days later
the annual Spanish treasure fleet
arrived, and moored beside the
English ships. An uneasy peace
prevailed for a few days, until the
Spanish launched an assault on the
nearest English ship (the *Minion*),
using an adjacent derelict hulk for
cover. The English on the island were
overrun by Spanish soldiers as they
tried to fight their way back to their
ships. English sailors counter-attacked,
turning the *Minion* into a battlefield.
Hawkins then ordered his ships to cut
their moorings and drift away from
the dock, running the gauntlet of
Spanish fire from the shore batteries
and warships. After a six hour battle,
only two English ships escaped,
Hawkins' *Minion* and the *Judith*,
commanded by Francis Drake. The
scene shows the last moments of the
English defenders on the shore, while
fighting swirls over the deck of the
Minion out of sight, to the left of
Hawkins. On his flagship the *Jesus of
Lubeck*, Hawkins is depicted peering
anxiously towards the island to see if
their shore parties can fight their way
back to their ships, judging if he can
cut and run for the open sea (Angus
McBride).

they found out about it. Hawkins returned to Plymouth in late 1565 with even
greater profits than before, prompting the Spanish ambassador to lodge an official
complaint at court. A third voyage was planned.

In early October 1567, Hawkins sailed for the West African coast in the *Jesus*,
accompanied by another royal ship, the *Minion*, and four smaller vessels, plus a
pinnace (launch). The African part of the voyage was a disaster. An initial and
unsuccessful slaving raid near Cape Verde left eight sailors dead, killed by poisoned
arrows. Other raids produced a mere handful of captives until Hawkins reached
Sierra Leone. There he allied himself with two local chieftains who wanted to attack
a rival town. In a bitterly fought struggle Hawkins and his allies captured the town
of Conga and the English slave decks were filled.

By early June 1568 the English expedition had reached the Caribbean. A hostile
welcome at Rio Hatcha resulted in a skirmish with the local garrison, and, after
seizing the town, Hawkins was forced to withdraw with little profit to show for his
efforts. At Santa Marta the governor arranged to put up a token resistance before
being 'forced' to trade with the interlopers. The next port was Cartagena, and when
the governor refused to have anything to do with Hawkins, he retaliated by
bombarding the batteries defending the port. It was clear that the Spanish authorities
had clamped down on trading with Hawkins after his first two voyages. He sailed
north, but in September his fleet encountered a hurricane off the western tip
of Cuba.

Although none of his ships were lost, they were all damaged, so Hawkins decided
to put into the Spanish port of San Juan de Ulúa for repairs. San Juan was the
port for the Mexican coastal city of Vera Cruz, where Mexico's silver was collected
by the annual treasure fleets, which sailed between Seville and the New World. The
English fleet entered the harbour at dawn under false colours on 16 September
1569, and seized the port's defences before the small garrison could react. It
appeared that Hawkins would be able to repair his ships in relative security, but the
situation drastically altered the following morning. The treasure fleet arrived, 12
ships commanded by Admiral Francisco Luján. The Spanish sent assurances that
they would leave the English in peace, and Hawkins allowed them to dock next to
his own ships.

The uneasy peace was shattered on the morning of 23 September when the
Spaniards launched a surprise attack on the interlopers. The English garrison on San
Juan de Ulúa was quickly overrun, and Hawkins pulled his ships away from the
dock. The Spaniards promptly manned the shore batteries and a prolonged artillery
duel followed, with the English getting much the worst of the exchange. Hawkins
had no option but to try to run through the gauntlet (and the unmarked offshore
reefs) and break out into the open sea. Only two ships escaped: the *Minion* with
Hawkins on board and the small *Judith*, commanded by Francis Drake. Almost a
third of the 300 Englishmen were killed or captured during the battle. With almost

no provisions left, just under 100 sailors requested to be put ashore, where they were captured by the Spanish. The remainder sailed for England, but disease and starvation took their toll, and the *Minion* arrived in England with fewer than 20 crewmen left alive, including Hawkins.

Although only a relatively minor incident, the engagement at San Juan de Ulúa significantly altered Anglo-Spanish relations. Francis Drake was determined to make the Spaniards pay for his defeat in Mexico, and from 1570 until 1573 he launched annual raids against the Spanish Main. Little is known of his activities in 1570, but in the following year he cruised off the coast of what is now the isthmus of Panama in the 25-ton *Swan*. Operating in conjunction with French corsairs, he captured Spanish shipping on the Chagres River and off the treasure port of Nombre de Dios, returning to Plymouth with 'forty thousand ducats, velvets and taffeta, besides other merchandise with gold and silver'. Even after the plunder was divided between his partners and backers, Drake's fame and fortune were assured.

In the summer of 1572 he returned to the Caribbean with three ships, two English and one French. In late July he attacked Nombre de Dios, landing on a nearby beach and storming the town, where the raiders were repulsed from the city after a vicious fight with the militia garrison in the town's central square. Drake himself was wounded in the struggle. The Englishmen withdrew up the coast to lick their wounds while the French set off in search of easier prey. Drake's next allies were the *cimarrónes*, half-castes or escaped African slaves. Using their new allies as scouts, in February 1573 the English attempted to ambush a mule train carrying silver from Panama to Nombre de Dios. The ambush failed as the Englishmen were discovered

The English warship *Griffin*, a privately owned armed merchant vessel of 200 tons. It is typical of the dozens of smaller vessels which formed the bulk of the English fleet. Copy of an engraving by Claes Jansz Visscher (Stratford Archive).

by a Spanish scout, and Drake retreated back to his ships. Drake cruised off the Central American coast for another three months, attacking Spanish coastal shipping.

In April he allied himself with Guilliaume le Testu, a Huguenot corsair, and together they felt strong enough to launch another attack on the spring mule train. This time Drake's attack was a resounding success, so much so that there was simply too much treasure to carry. Le Testu was wounded in the fight, so Drake left him with a guard and the silver while his men transported the gold back to their ships. When they returned, they discovered le Testu had been killed by a Spanish patrol, and the silver recaptured. The booty was split with le Testu's crew and Drake sailed for home, arriving back in Plymouth in August 1573, where he received a hero's welcome.

In December 1577 Drake set sail from Plymouth on his most ambitious project yet. In the four years since his return he had become a favourite at court, and the queen secretly backed his plan for a piratical cruise along the coast of Peru. His

Francis Drake's attempt to ambush the Panama silver train, 1573. Following his participation in Hawkins' defeat at San Juan de Ulúa, Francis Drake declared an unofficial war against the Spanish. From 1570 to 1572 he launched raids on the Spanish Main, the first undertaken by an English 'sea dog'. In 1572 he sailed for the Darien Peninsula (now the isthmus of Panama), where he hoped to intercept the annual mule train carrying silver from Panama to Nombre de Dios. The trail used to cross the isthmus was undefended, as was Nombre de Dios, which Drake captured in a night raid. In February of the following year he returned to lay an ambush along the trail at the head of 50 men, including local *cimaróne* (half-caste) scouts. Drake split his men into two groups, one to ambush the head of the mule train and the other to prevent its escape, but as the Spaniards passed the first group a drunken seaman named Robert Pike was spotted by a Spanish scout, who raised the alarm. Most of the mule train escaped, and Drake and his men were subsequently hounded through the jungle by Spanish troops and dogs. The Englishmen reached their ships more dead than alive, and Drake sailed off, only to return with French reinforcements to attack the mule train a second time, on this occasion with more success. This reconstruction depicts the ambushers waiting on the sides of the road at the moment when Pike was spotted by the Spaniards. Most of the Englishmen and *cimarónes* are armed with arquebuses and muskets, as well as cutlasses and machetes. Note that most have adapted their clothing to suit the tropical climate of the Darien Peninsula and they wore white shirts over their clothing as a form of recognition sign (Angus McBride).

flagship was the 200-ton *Pelican* (later renamed the *Golden Hind*), and it was accompanied by four smaller ships. He sailed down the African coast capturing several prizes before crossing the Atlantic bound for South America. In late June he reached the Straits of Magellan, where he put down a potential mutiny and burned two of his ships before continuing. A storm sank one vessel and forced another to return to England, leaving only the *Golden Hind* to continue the expedition. By December he was off the Chilean coast, where he sacked Valparaiso, then repaired his ships. By February 1579 he was cruising off Peru, and on 1 March he encountered a treasure ship, nicknamed the *Cacafuego*. It surrendered after a single broadside, yielding a fortune in silver and gold.

Drake elected to return home via the Pacific, and sailed westwards from California in July. The *Golden Hind* visited the Spice Islands of Indonesia before crossing the Indian Ocean, rounding the Cape of Good Hope and sailing north up the African coast. The ship arrived in Plymouth on 26 September 1580 after completing a three-year voyage of circumnavigation. Drake returned a national hero and a wealthy man, and Queen Elizabeth was delighted by his exploits, calling him 'my pirate'. He was knighted the following year, signalling a change in national policy. By rewarding a 'pirate' who had openly attacked the Spanish, the queen indicated that she was openly opposed to the Spanish, making war all but inevitable.

By this stage Philip II had lost patience with the English, and was willing to endorse counter-raids against Elizabeth's realm. In 1580 Philip supported an Irish Catholic rising against English rule, and transported 'papal volunteers' to Smerwick Bay, in south-west Ireland, in Spanish ships. These volunteers had been trained, armed and financed by the Spanish crown, and were led by Sebastiano di San Giuseppe, an Italian general in papal pay. Like the 'Bay of Pigs' operation almost four centuries later, the super-power organizers of the expedition maintained a degree of distance from the proceedings, and so maintained some form of diplomatic deniability if it all went wrong.

The English response was swift. First a naval force blockaded the harbour, preventing any escape. The volunteers fortified their camp, but made no move to escape, as they hoped to encourage a general uprising. They were still there when English troops arrived, under the command of Grey de Winton. Guns were landed

Francis Drake's English privateer *Golden Hind*, shown in battle with the Spanish treasure ship *Nuestra Señora de la Concepción*, fought in the Pacific Ocean on 1 March 1579. In fact the Spanish were surprised at being attacked in friendly waters, and they surrendered without much of a fight. Engraving by Theodore de Bry, c.1590 (Stratford Archive).

A Victorian depiction of the knighting of Francis Drake on the deck of his vessel *Golden Hind*, after his voyage of circumnavigation, and his capture of a Spanish treasure ship. Elizabeth's open support for this 'pirate' enraged the Spanish ambassador (Hensley Collection, Ashville, NC).

from the fleet, and used to batter the fort into submission. After three days Sebastiano di San Giuseppe surrendered, and though he was spared most of his Spanish, Italian or Irish soldiers were not. Not only was the expedition a costly failure, it also increased diplomatic tension between England and Spain to breaking point. The 'cold war' was about to become a full-blown war.

One final element in this ratcheting up of tension was the blitzkrieg-like Spanish invasion of Portugal in 1580, masterminded by the Duke of Alba. As well as conquering an old rival, Philip gained control over Portuguese territories in Brazil, Africa and the Indies. He also took over the Portuguese navy. Until now, most of Spain's naval efforts had involved fighting the Muslims in the Mediterranean, or safeguarding the treasure fleets of the New World. Now she had the nucleus of an ocean-going fleet.

The only part of the Portuguese Empire which still defied Spain was the Azores. There the Portuguese governor had formed an alliance with the French, and so in June 1582 a fleet of 60 French ships arrived off the islands, led by the Florentine nobleman Filippo Strozzi. Philip II ordered the Spanish to retaliate, and so a 36-ship fleet was built around the Portuguese galleons. Its commander, Don Alvaro de Bázan, the Marquis of Santa Cruz, flew his flag in the former Portuguese galleon *San Martín*. Making up numbers were a collection of Spanish and Portuguese armed merchantmen, under the command of Don Miguel de Oquendo.

The Spanish fleet made landfall in the Azores in late July, where they found the French fleet lying off Punta Delgada. A lack of wind prevented battle being joined, but on 26 July the breeze returned, and Strozzi made his move. He fell upon the

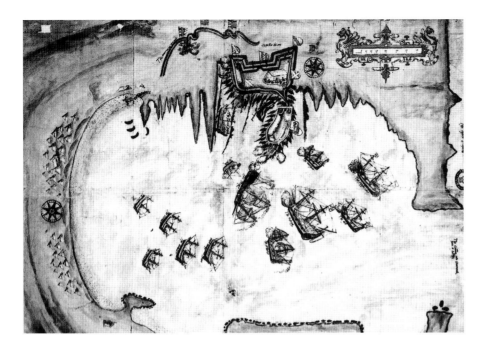

In November 1580 the Spanish launched an ill-conceived and poorly executed invasion of Ireland. This small Spanish expeditionary force was besieged in Smerwick Bay on Ireland's west coast, and eventually forced to surrender. This contemporary map shows naval guns being used to bombard the Spanish defences (PRO, London).

galleon *San Mateo*, but it held on long enough for the rest of the Spanish fleet to come to its rescue. First to arrive was de Oquendo, who 'handled his ship as a cavalryman handled his horse.' By then the fighting had turned into a general mêlée, although the French rearguard of 30 ships was becalmed, and unable to join in the fighting. At close quarters the Spanish could rely on their soldiers to win the battle for them.

When Don Alvaro arrived he attacked Strozzi's flagship, which was still battering the *San Mateo*. The *San Martín* fired a broadside, then the Spanish troops boarded the enemy in the smoke. By the time the fighting ended the French flagship was in Spanish hands, and Strozzi was killed. By then it was apparent that Don Alvaro had won a spectacular victory in the naval battle of São Miguel, capturing or sinking ten French ships for the loss of none of his own. While this did little to directly increase tension between England and Spain, it gave Philip II and his commanders a belief in their own abilities. If Spain could defeat a French fleet twice its size, what could it achieve against Elizabeth's English Navy Royal? The final act in this war was the signing of the Treaty of Joinville in 1584, where the Spanish agreed to support French Catholics against their Protestant rivals. It was clear that Philip II was on a crusade. After dealing with the French and the Dutch, he would surely turn his attention to the English.

Open Conflict

The fall of the port of Antwerp in August 1585 marked a turning point. Elizabeth and her advisors felt that they could no longer stand by and watch the Duke of Parma's troops crush the rebellion in the Netherlands. Until then the

Portuguese carracks off a rocky coast, an oil painting in the style of Joachim Patinir, c.1500. These early carracks were the forerunners of the Portuguese galleons which distinguished themselves during the Spanish Armada campaign – a vital evolutionary link in the development of this iconic type of warship (National Maritime Museum, Greenwich, London).

English had offered covert aid in the form of arms, supplies and money. Now Elizabeth felt she had to offer direct help, or risk losing her staunchest Protestant ally on the European mainland. The result was the Treaty of Nonsuch, signed in late August, in which Elizabeth offered the rebels the support of an 8,000-man force of English troops, and a substantial annual subsidy. Robert Dudley, 1st Earl of Leicester, was named as the commander of the force sent over in December 1585, and the Dutch ports of Ostend, Brill and Flushing were handed over to his control, to be used as English bases.

Philip II saw this treaty as a declaration of war. The 'cold war' of the previous three decades had suddenly become very hot indeed. Although diplomats still sought a way to end the hostilities, preparations were made for an invasion of England, the largest maritime and amphibious operation of the period. Meanwhile, the English had a brief chance to take the war to the enemy. On 14 September 1585, less than a month after England had actively sided with the Dutch rebels against the Spanish, Sir Francis Drake sailed from Plymouth with 25 ships and 2,300 men, effectively declaring war on Spain in the process. Drake's expedition was a private venture, sponsored by a group of investors, one of whom was the queen.

Four of the ships were royal warships, including Drake's flagship, the *Elizabeth Bonaventure*, and the *Golden Lion*, commanded by his deputy, William Borough. Drake's orders were to 'prevent or withstand such enterprises as might be attempted against Her Highness' realm or dominions'. In effect, Drake had a free hand to take the war to the enemy and secure a profit for his investors in the process. Drake cruised off northern Spain before sailing for the Cape Verde Islands. In November the English assaulted and captured the port of Santiago before crossing the Atlantic, bound for the Spanish Main. In late December the fleet lay off Santo Domingo, the capital of Hispaniola, one of the richest cities in the Caribbean islands.

A New Year's Eve bombardment was followed by a land assault. Drake's stratagem of landing 1,000 troops who circled round and took the city from the rear worked perfectly, as the Spaniards were distracted by the bombardment. The garrison fled and the city fell to the English. 25,000 ducats were extorted in ransom after Drake burned parts of the town, but the haul was far less than had been expected. In late January the English fleet sailed away to the south, bound for Cartagena. Drake anchored his ships inside the outer harbour, then landed 600 troops led by Christopher Carleill under cover of darkness. They secured the narrow spit of land separating the outer harbour from the sea, stormed through the outer defences of the city and forced their way into the city in the teeth of tough Spanish opposition. Martin Frobisher provided supporting fire from a squadron of shallow pinnaces.

After some brief hand-to-hand fighting the Spanish panicked and ran, and the city fell to the attackers. Once again, the city yielded less money and treasure than had been anticipated, although the haul amounted to over 107,000 ducats and dozens of bronze guns. Drake's plan to use the city as a base from which to attack

The *San Mateo* at the Battle of the Azores, 1582.

The battle fought off the Azores in 1582 was probably the first major naval engagement in history to be fought out of sight of land. When Spain conquered Portugal in 1580, the only portion of the Portuguese overseas empire to resist the Spanish was the Azores. In 1580 the French crown sent a fleet under the command of the mercenary Admiral Filipo Strozzi to help defend the islands. This action resulted in the Spanish sending their own fleet to the Azores, under the command of the veteran Captain-General Don Álvaro de Bazán, Marquis of Santa Cruz. The two fleets met some 18 miles south of the island of Saõ Miguel on 26 July (the battle is sometimes named after the island's port, Punta Delgada). Strozzi had 40 warships at his disposal, and Bazán 21. In addition, each fleet contained a squadron of transports. The French opened the battle by engaging the Spanish rear with half of their fleet. Although the Spanish were outnumbered two to one, Bazán managed to bring the rest of his fleet into battle, to give him parity in numbers. The brunt of the French attack was borne by the Portuguese-built galleon *San Mateo*, a vessel of 750 *toneladas*, armed with approximately 30 guns. Although simultaneously boarded by several French ships her soldiers held their ground, and repulsed all attacks. They then took the fight to the enemy, boarding and capturing two French vessels before the battle ended. Bazán won a stunning victory against superior odds, capturing ten enemy ships in all and driving the French from the Azores. The islands were captured by Spanish troops the following year. The plate shows the *San Mateo* at the height of the fighting (Tony Bryan).

other ports was thwarted by disease, which decimated his crews. He abandoned plans to attack Panama and instead he sailed for home in mid-April 1586. His ships failed to encounter the Spanish treasure fleet off Havana, so instead he sailed north up the Atlantic coast of Florida and attacked St Augustine. His motives were more strategic than mercenary, as the settlement posed a threat to Raleigh's embryonic settlement at Roanoake in Virginia. The town was captured after brief resistance and was burned, along with the fort guarding it. Drake supplied the colony in Virginia, then sailed for home, arriving in Plymouth in July 1586.

The expedition was a financial failure, but Drake had little time to brood over his losses. Secret negotiations between England and Spain had broken down, and the Spanish were preparing an Armada with which to invade England. On 11 April 1587 Drake sailed for Spain in command of a fleet of 23 ships, including six royal warships. The queen had second thoughts, but the wily Drake was already at sea when the cancellation of his orders arrived in Plymouth, claiming that 'the wind commands me away'. Eighteen days later Drake and most of his ships arrived off Cadiz, where preparations for the Armada were well underway. Half-armed ships filled Cadiz roads, blocking the fire of many of the shore batteries.

Drake attacked immediately and captured or destroyed 24 Spanish ships lying in the outer harbour. Spanish reinforcements manned the town and the shore batteries, preventing him from continuing into the inner harbour, but the blow to the Armada was a severe one. The queen's orders to 'singe the king of Spain's beard' had been carried out to perfection. Drake left Cadiz on 1 May, and the Spanish could only guess where he would strike next. He captured Sagres in southern Portugal and blocked communications between the two main Armada staging areas of Cadiz and Lisbon for a month before sailing home via the Azores. He failed to intercept the homeward-bound treasure fleet, but did capture a straggling treasure galleon, which he took into Plymouth in July. The Cadiz raid cost the Spanish 24 ships, and the Armada's preparations were delayed by several months. However, Drake could not prevent the inevitable; as the Duke of Parma readied his army in Flanders and Santa Cruz prepared the invasion fleet in Lisbon, the English could do little other than prepare for the Spanish onslaught.

The Spanish Grand Design

By that stage the plans for the invasion were well underway. As early as 1584 the Marquis of Santa Cruz was appointed Admiral of the Ocean Sea, charged with all operations in the Atlantic Ocean. Even before his appointment he had drawn up suggestions for invasion plans. Following Elizabeth's alliance with the Dutch in 1585, King Philip II wrote to Santa Cruz and the Duke of Parma, asking for detailed plans for an invasion. In the spring of 1586 they both submitted their proposals, which offered remarkably different solutions to the problem.

The Marquis of Santa Cruz favoured an amphibious operation on a hitherto unimagined scale. A naval force of around 150 major ships would be gathered in Lisbon and transport an army of 55,000 men direct from the Iberian Peninsula to England. It would include all artillery, engineering and logistical support the army needed. Once it sailed, the Armada would retain a tight defensive formation, preventing the English from disrupting the fleet's progress to its destination. On reaching the landing site, 200 specially constructed boats would ferry the army ashore, supported by an inshore squadron of 40 galleys and six galleasses which would accompany the Armada. Once the army was ashore it would advance rapidly to crush the English. The marquis did not specify a landing site, probably for reasons of secrecy.

The Duke of Parma realized that it would be impossible to keep the plans a secret, so he advocated an unsupported lightning dash across the Channel. A force of 30,000 foot and 500 horse would be transported in invasion barges, landing at a point between Dover and Margate. He estimated the crossing would take between eight and twelve hours. If the English were taken by surprise, he felt the invasion would stand a very great chance of success. If the English fleet blocked the way, Parma expected that a naval force sailing from Lisbon could divert the English from the invasion route to allow a crossing. Once ashore, he had no doubt that his troops could drive on London and brush aside any English opposition.

Philip II reviewed the two plans with his military adviser, Don Juan de Zúñiga, and on 2 April 1586 he ordered the marquis to gather together the ships and supplies he needed. Zúñiga then proposed launching both invasions at the same time. The Armada would land a force of around 30,000 men in Ireland, and while the English were diverted, Parma should make his dash across the Channel.

A depiction of the coast of the English county of Dorset, c.1588, viewed from the north. Portland Bill is the peninsula shown in the top right of the engraving – the scene of some of the fiercest fighting of the campaign. The view also shows the beacons which were used to transmit news of a Spanish landing (British Library, London).

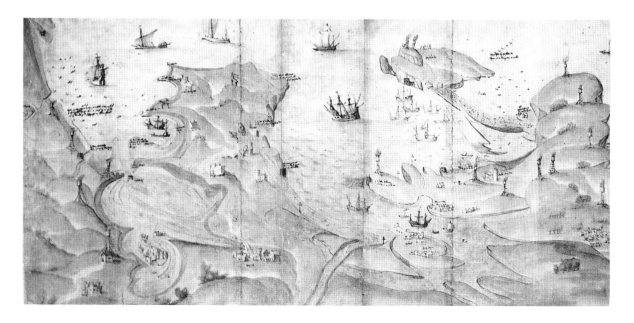

Reinforcements would then be brought up from Spain to support the beachheads. Parma vigorously opposed this plan, claiming that the cross-Channel resources should not be wasted on the Irish venture.

Drake's attack on Cadiz in April 1587 forced Philip to alter the plan. Ireland was abandoned, and, as fewer troops were available in Spain, the Armada would have to rendezvous with Parma, and then escort his invasion barges. Their orders were to 'sail in the name of God straight to the English Channel and go along it until you have anchored off Margate Head, having first warned the Duke of Parma of your approach'. In effect, the Armada and its troops would support Parma by keeping the crossing areas clear of enemy ships. The Armada was reduced to 130 ships, 30 of which would be small craft displacing under 100 tons. They would transport a force of 17,000 soldiers, and would unite with Parma's invasion force of 17,000 soldiers and 120 barges.

Francis Drake's raid on St Augustine, 1586.
In 1585 Drake launched a devastating series of raids against the Spanish Main. Leading a force of 25 ships, the English raider captured Santiago in the Cape Verde Islands before crossing the Atlantic and attacking Santo Domingo in late December. In February 1586 Drake raided Cartagena, where he extorted a substantial ransom and burned the town. Disease prevented any further attacks on the larger Spanish settlements, but on his voyage home he attacked the fledgling Spanish settlement at St Augustine in Florida. A strip of sand dunes separated the river from the sea, and the sandbar prevented large ships from entering the protected anchorage formed by the river mouth. Drake's men came under fire from the palisade fort across the river and, unable to launch a direct attack until it was silenced, the English commander landed a battery of naval guns. Their fire silenced the Spaniards in the fort by dusk, but a surprise attack in the sand dunes by the Spanish garrison and their Indian allies kept the English occupied during the night. English musket and arquebus fire drove off the Spaniards. The next morning Drake realised that the fort and the settlement further upriver had been abandoned in the night. As the English searched for plunder they came under sniper fire from the woods beyond the town, and Drake's lieutenant, Anthony Powell, was killed. Drake ordered the settlement and fort put to the torch, then the sailors returned to the ships with whatever small haul of booty they found. The scene is set during the Spanish night attack, and Drake is shown directing the fire which repulsed the Spanish and Indian assault. Note that the English sailors are exceptionally well equipped with firearms (Angus McBride).

This was a bad compromise, and the king's plan left many questions unanswered, the most important being how the Armada would co-ordinate movements with Parma. It also presumed that the Spanish fleet could keep its position in the waters between Dunkirk and Calais for the time it took Parma's men to cross. Furthermore, it failed to suggest what the Armada would do next, apart from anchor in the Thames and wait for the army to crush the English on land. Above all, it relied on the English reacting as the Spanish planners hoped, and left no leeway for anything going wrong.

The English Defensive Strategy

While all these plans were being drawn up, the English were looking to their own defences. It was clear that the main line of defence would be at sea – the fleet itself. As Sir Walter Raleigh wrote after the campaign: 'An army to be transported by sea ... and the [landing] place left to the choice of the invader ... cannot be resisted on the coast of England without a fleet to impeach it.' This neatly summed up Elizabeth's problem: too few experienced troops and too many places to defend.

During May 1588, the month preceding the invasion, Drake persuaded Charles Howard, 1st Earl of Nottingham, who commanded the Tudor fleet, to move the

The English beacon system in Kent, reproduced from William Lamarde's *Beacons in Kent* manuscript, c.1588. This was the region earmarked for the landing of the Duke of Parma's army (British Library).

Embarkation of Spanish troops, an oil painting by Andries van Eertvelt. Five *tercios* (regiments) of Spanish troops were embarked on the ships of the Spanish Armada in Lisbon, while another 18,000 waited for it to arrive off the coast of Flanders. Scenes like these would have greeted the Duke of Medina Sidonia's envoys as they reached the Flemish ports where the Army of Flanders had begun the process of embarking on its invasion transports (National Maritime Museum, Greenwich, London).

bulk of the English fleet from the Downs to Plymouth, leaving behind a screening force under Lord Henry Seymour, commander of the Narrow Seas Squadron, to prevent any attempted 'sneak' invasion by the Duke of Parma. Because of the prevailing westerly winds, a fleet gathered as far west as possible could follow the Armada from windward and harass it all the way down the Channel, rather than simply contesting the Dover Straits (between Dover and Calais).

By 3 June the fleet had gathered in Plymouth and the force of 105 ships included 19 royal warships and 46 large, armed merchantmen. Drake also advocated a preemptive strike against La Coruña in Spain, and consequently 60 ships sortied from Plymouth on 4 July. However, bad weather and contrary winds forced Howard and Drake to abandon the enterprise, and the fleet returned to Plymouth. They were still in port on 29 July when news came that the Spanish Armada lay off the Cornish coast.

England's land defences were hastily improvised. A third of all the militia of the southern counties were brought to London, where they formed an army of approximately 21,000 troops, charged with safeguarding the queen. On 6 July a reserve army was formed at Tilbury in Essex. Commanded by the Earl of Leicester, this force of 17,000 men consisted of militia stiffened by about 4,000 regular troops recently brought back from Holland. A further 29,500 militia guarded the Channel coast from Cornwall to Kent. Of these, just under 9,000 were stationed in Kent itself.

In theory, as the Armada advanced east up the Channel, these county militias were meant to follow it along the coast, so that wherever the Spanish landed, the local militia would be reinforced.

A system of warning beacons was set up to convey news of the Armada's progress. In reality, when the Armada passed by, most county militiamen simply returned home. A further 8,000 militia were available from the northern counties, and a similar number from Wales and the Midlands. In the event of a Spanish landing, they were to march and join the main army at London or Tilbury. However, it soon became apparent that the militia were reluctant to fight, particularly in Kent, and thousands deserted during the campaign.

Most militia had little or no training, and inadequate weapons. For example, 10,000 raised in London were issued with bows, although no archery practice had been enforced for almost a century. Above all, they had had no military involvement, and even the regulars were seen as inexperienced. By contrast, the Spanish soldiers of the Army of Flanders were hard-bitten veterans, and the Spanish soldiers carried in the Armada had military experience. As the historian Geoffrey Parker surmised, with inadequate coastal defences, a poorly trained and ill-equipped army and ineffective generals, the English would have been hard pressed to put up much opposition to the Spanish if they had managed to land. Parker estimated that Parma could have captured Kent and London in two weeks, and even without further campaigning could have forced Elizabeth to sign a humiliating peace treaty.

The return of a Spanish expedition, an oil painting by Andries van Eertvelt. This harbour scene gives some indication of what Lisbon's waterfront might have looked like as the Armada prepared to sail. Troops, supplies and guns would have been ferried across the harbour, amid scenes of great activity (National Maritime Museum, Greenwich, London).

✤ Chronology

1580

August   The Spanish capture Lisbon, and the Portuguese galleon fleet.

Siege of Smerwick.

1581

January   The Spanish Army led by the Duke of Parma launches its offensive to reconquer the Netherlands.

April   Francis Drake knighted by Queen Elizabeth I.

1582

June   The French send a fleet to the Azores, still ruled by Portugal, pre-empting a Spanish invasion of the islands.

Subsequent Spanish victory in the naval battle of São Miguel.

1584

June   Marquis of Santa Cruz appointed as Spain's 'Admiral of the Ocean Sea'.

December   Treaty of Joinville signed between Spain and France.

1585

May   Philip II places an embargo on all trade with England.

August   Antwerp captured from the Dutch rebels by the Duke of Parma's army.

September   Drake leads expedition to Spanish Main.

November   Drake attacks Santiago in the Cape Verde Islands.

December   Elizabeth I sends the Earl of Leicester with troops to assist the Dutch rebels.

1586

January   Drake sacks Santo Domingo, the capital of Hispaniola (now in the Dominican Republic).

Philip II orders plans for the invasion of England.

March   Drake captures Cartagena on the Spanish Main.

April   Philip II reviews two invasion plans, and adopts a compromise version.

July   Invasion plan approved and sent to the Duke of Parma.

November   Preparations start; ships and supplies are gathered.

1587

February   Mary Queen of Scots is executed on the orders of Elizabeth I of England.

April	Drake 'singes the King of Spain's beard' by attacking Cadiz.
May	The Armada begins to assemble in Lisbon.
June	Drake captures a Spanish treasure galleon off the Azores.
July	Philip II and the pope agree on the government of a Catholic England.
	Elizabeth restricts the traffic of English merchantmen, and orders their conversion into armed merchantmen.
September	Santa Cruz arrives in Lisbon to supervise preparations.
	Final revisions to invasion plan are made.

1588

9 February	Marquis of Santa Cruz dies in Lisbon.
26 February	Duke of Medina Sidonia reluctantly accepts command of the Armada.
1 April	Final orders sent by Philip II to both Parma and Medina Sidonia.
9 May	Armada inspected by Medina Sidonia and deemed ready to sail.
28 May	The Spanish Armada sails from Lisbon.
3 June	The English fleet gathers in Plymouth.
19 June	Bad weather forces Armada to put into La Coruña in north-west Spain.
4 July	English fleet sails to launch pre-emptive attack on Spanish fleet.
5 July	Dutch fleet blockades Parma's invasion force at Dunkirk.
19 July	The English fleet returns to Plymouth due to bad weather.
21 July	Spanish Armada sets sail from La Coruña.
25 July	Galley squadron is forced to put into French port.
29 July	The Armada is sighted by an English scouting vessel.
30 July	The Spanish Armada sights the Lizard on the Cornish coast.
	Medina Sidonia holds a council of war with his senior commanders.
	Word reaches Lord Howard of the Spanish approach, allegedly during a game of bowls.
	That evening the English fleet puts to sea from Plymouth.
31 July	Opening shots – battle off Plymouth.
	Both the *San Salvador* and the *Nuestra Señora de Rosario* are damaged.
	Drake abandons the fleet to pursue the damaged Spanish vessel *Rosario.*
1 August	The Armada re-forms off Start Point.
	English ships capture the *San Salvador.*
2 August	Battle off Portland.
	Word of the Armada's progress reaches the Duke of Parma.
	The English replenish their stocks of ammunition.

Theatre of Operations, 1588

The Armada's primary mission was to rendezvous with the Duke of Parma's invasion force stationed in the Spanish Netherlands. While a screen of veteran troops watched the Dutch rebels, Parma's troops would cross from Flanders to Kent, protected by the ships of the Armada. Once the Armada was forced away from the Flemish coast on 8 August, contrary winds forced it to return to Spain around the British Isles. Scotland was neutral (though Protestant), while Catholic Ireland was occupied by English troops. The inset shows the disposition of troops in Flanders, Kent and Holland during early August, 1588.

3 August	The English reorganize their fleet into four divisions after Council of War.
	The Spanish Armada approaches the Isle of Wight.
4 August	Battle off the Isle of Wight.
	The Armada is now committed to anchorage off Calais.
6 August	Armada anchors off Calais, and word of its arrival is sent to the Duke of Parma.
	Lord Howard calls on Seymour's squadron to join the fleet.
7 August	Fireship attack planned.
	Medina Sidonia learns that Parma's invasion force is not ready.
8 August	Fireship attack off Gravelines scatters the Spanish Armada.
	Galleass *San Lorenzo* captured off Calais.
	Battle off Gravelines – most decisive battle of the campaign.
9 August	Armada forced to abandon rendezvous with Parma.
	Council of war held on Spanish flagship elects to sail home around Scotland.
10 August	Army of Flanders ready to embark, but the invasion is cancelled.
	Main English fleet pursues the Spanish Armada northwards.
	Seymour's squadron returns to the Downs.
13 August	Armada now level with the Firth of Forth in Scotland.
	English fleet abandons the pursuit of the Armada.
19 August	Elizabeth I addresses her troops at Tilbury.
20 August	Armada passes Orkney and Shetland and enters the Atlantic.
21 August	Medina Sidonia sends messenger to Philip II with news of his failure.
31 August	Parma abandons his invasion attempts and resumes war against the Dutch.
14 September	Storms lash the Irish coast; start of two weeks of bad weather.

21 September	Height of the 'Armada storm'; numerous shipwrecks on Irish coast.
	Medina Sidonia arrives in Santander.
24 September	Philip II told of the failure of his 'Grand Enterprise'.
30 September	Worst of the storm passes to the north of Ireland.
	Shipwreck survivors scattered throughout Ireland are rounded up by English.
28 October	De Leiva drowned during shipwreck of the galleass *Girona* off Ireland.
10 November	Full extent of tragedy revealed to Philip II, who prays for death.
12 November	Spanish decide to continue the war against England.
24 November	Queen Elizabeth attends a service of thanksgiving in London.

1589

May	English blockade Lisbon.
	English fleet launches attack on Spanish ports of Vigo and La Coruña.
June	English expedition to the Azores proves fruitless.
August	Assassination of King Henry III of France, and succession of Protestant King Henry IV.
	Spain declares war on France. France allies with England and Holland.

1591

April	English Fleet sails for the Azores.
August	Last fight of the *Revenge*.

1595

August	Drake and Hawkins lead expedition to the Caribbean.
November	Attack on San Juan. Death of Sir John Hawkins.
December	Drake's failed attack on Panama.

1596

January	Death of Sir Francis Drake.
June	Anglo-Dutch fleet attacks Cadiz.

1598

September	Death of King Philip II of Spain.

1603

March	Death of Queen Elizabeth I of England.

1604

August	Peace Treaty signed in London between England and Spain.

✤ The Invincible Armada

Introduction

To the rest of Europe, it seemed that in 1588, Philip II's Spanish Empire was an unstoppable force. Spanish troops were widely regarded as the finest and best-equipped soldiers on the continent, and the victors of a string of battles against the French, the Dutch and the Moors. The maritime resources available to the Spanish crown were also impressive. It maintained a powerful standing fleet, which included some of the largest and most powerful warships in the world. It was augmented by the smaller but equally robust galleons of the Indies *flota* (fleet), designed to transport the plunder of the New World to Spain.

Then there was the enormous fleet of galleys and galleasses which the Spanish and their allies maintained in the Mediterranean Sea, as a bulwark against the Ottoman Turks and the Barbary Corsairs. Like the Spanish army, these vessels and their commanders had enjoyed a string of victories, the most notable of which was the battle of Lepanto in 1571, one of the most decisive naval engagements in history. Finally the Spanish crown could draw on a substantial fleet of armed merchant vessels, which could hurriedly be converted into makeshift warships in time of need. In the 16th century the difference between warship and armed merchantman was not as marked as it became later, and so both the Spanish and the English augmented their fighting ships with merchantmen during the campaign.

Above all the Spanish crown had the resources it needed to fund Philip II's 'Great Enterprise' against England. Every year two *flotas* returned from the New World, carrying silver from the mines of Peru and Mexico, gold from Colombia, emeralds from Venezuela, and spices shipped across the Pacific to Mexico. A sizeable portion of this great wealth was earmarked for the royal coffers, and was used to pay for Spain's military and naval endeavours in Europe. In a way this income made Spain's rise to greatness possible. While her armies and fleets were the envy of Europe, the men still had to be paid, and so these annual *flotas* became the cornerstones of Spanish military and naval achievement.

Above all, the great Armada assembling in Lisbon and in secondary ports around the Iberian coast was about to embark on a great crusade. Its ships and men carried the blessing of the pope, and many were decorated with symbols of the Catholic faith – crosses on the sails, images of the Virgin Mary on the poop, and priests on the quarterdeck. This would be a holy war, fought against the leading 'heretical' power in Europe. The army in Flanders waiting to embark would be accompanied by Jesuits, inquisitors and all the paraphernalia of the war against the faithless. At the time the Armada was preparing to sail the Counter-Reformation was in full flood, and so this fleet would become the floating embodiment of this fleet. Its objective would be nothing less than the crushing of Protestant 'heresy' in England, and the re-establishment of the Catholic faith throughout the British Isles.

King Philip II of Spain (1527–98, reigned 1556–98), a 17th-century oil painting by a painter of the Spanish School. The Spanish monarch is shown wearing tournament armour rather than his usual attire of plain dark clothing. Philip was the true architect of the 'Great Enterprise' against Elizabethan England (National Maritime Museum, Greenwich, London).

The Fleet

The fleet gathered in Lisbon for Philip II's 'Great Enterprise' consisted of ships from all corners of Spain's European territories and those of her allies. It even included neutral ships which were impounded and commandeered, such as the Scottish vessel *St Andrew*, which became the *San Andres*. Probably the most formidable vessels in the Armada were the great Portuguese galleons captured in Lisbon harbour eight years before, most of which had already seen action during the battle of São Miguel in 1582. They formed the fighting core of the fleet, supported by other substantial warships from the Indies *flotas*, or large armed merchantmen pressed into Spanish service. Many of these vessels had a displacement of more than 750 tons, which made them some of the largest warships in the world. It was inevitable that these great ships would be in the thick of the fighting.

For administrative purposes the Armada was divided into squadrons with territorial designations: Andalusia, Biscay, Castille, Guipúzcoa, the Levant and Portugal. In addition there was a squadron each of hulks, galleys and galleasses. These squadron-sized formations were not primarily designed to be tactical units, like the squadrons or divisions of later sailing ships of war. Instead, ships of a similar type or origin were grouped together, allowing the fleet commander to issue orders to sections of his fleet rather than to the whole entity. This also meant that ships of similar speeds and with similar sailing qualities would operate together, which at least in theory would simplify the control of the fleet.

The Ships

Many of the terms given in these accounts are a little confusing, as the way ships were described changed in the years before and after the Armada campaign. The same type of ship could even be called different things by English and Spanish commentators. For example, the term galleon was used to describe everything from a small 250-ton ship from the Indies *flotas* to one of the towering warships of the Portuguese Squadron. The English used the term when speaking about large purpose-built warships. It was later used to cover all the ships in the

Opposite

A carrack before the wind, an oil painting by Peter Brueghel. While it depicts a typical carrack of the mid-16th century, the vessel is similar to many of the lumbering merchant vessels pressed into service by the Spanish during the campaign. Its hull was never designed to stand the firing of larger broadsides of artillery, or to withstand the pounding of enemy shot (National Maritime Museum, Greenwich, London).

Lisbon served as the embarkation port for the Spanish Armada. During the spring and summer of 1588 this harbour was filled with ships, and the docks were teeming with men, munitions and supplies. This was the greatest logistical operation of the 16th century. Copy of an engraving by Theodore de Bry (Stratford Archive).

Armada, regardless of what the ships looked like, or how they were built. In fact the vessels of the Armada contained a mixture of ship types and building styles.

As most of these ships were gathered from the ports of the Iberian Peninsula or the Mediterranean, these origins were reflected in the appearance of the vessels, which were often markedly different from the ships seen in more northerly waters. However, the fleet also contained vessels that betrayed signs of Northern European construction, or which – like the galleon itself – represented an amalgam of European shipbuilding traditions. Therefore it might be useful to list the main ship types that were found in the Armada, and to explain how they differed from the rest of the fleet.

Galleon

Originally designed to transport the treasures of the New World home to Spain, the Spanish galleon was an amalgamation of a merchant vessel and a warship, with a large cargo capacity and a powerful armament. Its distinctive features were its size, with some larger galleons displacing over 1,000 tons, and a high sterncastle structure. The galleons of the squadrons of Castille and Portugal formed the fighting core of the Spanish Armada in 1588. As an example, the Portuguese *San Martín* of 1,000 tons was the flagship of the Duke of Medina Sidonia, and was purpose-built as a warship, the 'battleship' of its day. The galleons used to guard or accompany the annual Spanish treasure fleets were usually smaller, with an average displacement of around 500–800 tons. They were lower than the larger galleons, and reportedly were more weatherly. The lines of an Atlantic galleon of this type were given in the *Instrución Nautica of Garcia de Palacio* (1588), and evidence from treasure galleons excavated by both archaeologists and treasure hunters in American waters confirms the general principles of construction laid down in the treatise. While the smaller galleons carried around 20 bronze guns, the larger galleons in the Armada campaign could support twice that number. These archetypal Spanish warships will be examined in more detail later.

Galley

The principal type of warship used in the Mediterranean during the late 16th-century, galleys were unsuited for operations in the Atlantic or the Caribbean. The four galleys which accompanied the Armada from Lisbon in 1588 were forced to turn back before the fleet reached the English Channel, but in several other actions (Cartagena in 1586, and Cadiz in 1596, for example), they proved moderately useful to the local Spanish commanders. They were principally oar-powered, but retained a lateen sail or two as a form of auxiliary power. Although they carried a small forward-facing battery in their bow, they were exclusively a close-quarters vessel. The English fleet in 1588 contained a handful of galiots, a smaller version of the true galley, but (at least with English vessels) fitted with additional square-sailed masts.

The Spanish Armada included a squadron of four galleys, but these were detached before the fleet reached the English coast. These vessels would have been invaluable during any landing operation, as they were able to move close inshore, and fire their guns in support of the landing forces (Stratford Archive).

45

Galleass

A hybrid combination of a galley and a square-rigged sailing vessel, the galleass carried guns in a round forecastle and on the quarterdeck, with a small broadside battery mounted over the rowing decks. These vessels were rarely used outside the Mediterranean, and the four 600-ton galleasses commanded by Hugo de Moncada during the Armada campaign were all from the kingdom of Naples (these vessels were named the *San Lorenzo*, *Girona*, *Zúñiga* and *Napolitana*). Although their displacement made them slow and difficult to manoeuvre under oars and clumsy under sail, they proved useful during the calm winds which featured prominently during the fighting off Portland Bill.

Nao

Called a 'carrack' by the English, this three-masted square-rigged ship was the standard merchant vessel of the era. Both the Spanish and the English cut gunports in their carracks and included them in their fleets. Compared to the more streamlined galleons, they had wider and more rounded hulls, giving them a 'chubby' appearance. Although slow they could absorb a significant amount of hull damage, as shown by the Spanish vessels during the Armada campaign, and the French fighting carracks during the Azores campaign of 1582. Carrack features included high forecastle and sterncastle structures which were well-suited for fighting boarding actions. Engravings by artists such as Pieter Bruegel the Elder have provided a range of contemporary depictions of carracks, shown both as merchant vessels and as warships, while a growing body of archaeological evidence from Spanish naos provides useful clues as to hull construction and armament.

Hulk (or 'urca')

These vessels were used by the Spaniards as transports during the Armada campaign, carrying the military stores needed for the invasion of England or acting as supply ships for the Armada itself. They were simple, three-masted vessels with little of the ornamentation and fighting structures found on the larger Spanish ships. The wreck of *La Trinidad Valencera* (1588) wrecked off Donegal and *El Gran Grifón* (1588) located off Fair Isle have both provided information about these vessels and the stores they carried during the campaign. One vital point which emerged from the archaeological evidence is the vulnerability of the hull structure. Designed to contain the pressures created by a cargo such as grain (which expands when wet), they were ill-prepared for stresses imposed in the opposite direction, namely English roundshot striking their outer hull. The 650-ton *El Gran Grifón* was one of the larger hulks in the Armada, and the North German vessel has been described by one historian as having 'bluff bows and a broad beam'.

Patache (or zabra)

This was a small two or three-masted craft, with a displacement of less than 100 tons. They appear to have been lateen rigged, but were capable of using oars if needed. The Spanish used these fast vessels as scout ships, and to relay orders between other ships in the fleet. During the Armada campaign, pataches were grouped together into a communication squadron commanded by Agustín de Ojeda, who, like the commanders of destroyer squadrons of the First World War, sailed in a larger command vessel. A Mediterranean variant of the patache was the felucca or falúa, which was a small sailing or rowing vessel used as a coastal trader. The larger feluccas resembled galleys, with lateen sails on one or two masts, although three-masted versions were also used. These vessels could operate under oar and sail at the same time.

Carvel

Although rarely used as a warship, carvels formed part of the Spanish communication squadron during the Armada campaign. They were the same type of vessel which accompanied Columbus' flagship the *Santa Maria* in 1492, and were the archetypal vessels of the age of discovery. Carvels were still regularly used as coastal or short-haul sailing vessels in the Mediterranean, along the African coast or in the Spanish Main, and are mentioned in several contemporary sources such as accounts of Hawkins' slaving voyages off West Africa and Drake's raid on St Augustine in 1586. The typical carvel was a vessel of less than 200 tons and under 100ft long, with three masts fitted with a combination of lateen and square sails. As these were essentially coastal traders, their armament was usually minimal.

Contrary to popular myth, the majority of the ships in the Spanish Armada were armed merchant ships rather than elegant galleons. Most would have been similar to this carrack, shown in a mid-16th century engraving by Pieter Breugel the Elder (Stratford Archive).

Organization

Although the original intention was to operate these squadrons as distinct units, after the first battle off Plymouth (31 July), the scheme was abandoned and individual ships were grouped by size and firepower rather than by administrative sub-division. In the past, historians have placed too great an emphasis on these units and consequently have encountered problems with the command exercised by the fleet commanders.

The Spanish Armada's battle formation was outlined in a letter written to the Duke of Tuscany by his ambassador in Lisbon in May 1588. This detailed plan was surprisingly accurate, and reflects the Armada's dispositions as it engaged the English fleet off Plymouth on 31 July 1588 (Archivo di Stato, Florence).

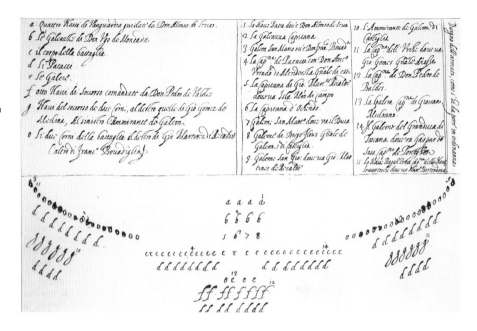

For example, Martín de Bertendona, who commanded the Levant Squadron, was given command of a 'van', during the battle off Portland (2 August), which consisted of the most powerful ships from several squadrons.

Juan Martinez de Recalde was the commander of the Biscay Squadron but sailed in the vice-flag of the Portugal Squadron as deputy fleet commander. The squadron structure also tended to group similar vessels together. The Portugal Squadron consisted of powerful and well-armed ocean-going galleons captured from the Portuguese in 1580. These ships became the core of the Armada and participated in the forefront of most of the battles in the Channel. The Castille Squadron was composed of galleons earmarked for the annual treasure fleets. They were robust and low-hulled, designed for transatlantic sailing, where performance was more important than armament.

The Levant Squadron was made up of large Mediterranean grain vessels, converted into warships for the campaign. The squadrons of Biscay and Guipúzcoa relied on Spanish merchant vessels from the northern Atlantic seaboard, and these Basque-built ships were regarded as excellent. The Andalusia Squadron used similar vessels from Spain's southern coast. They were less robust ships, but made up for their deficiency by being particularly well armed. The four galleasses came from Naples, and represented a hybrid form of vessel, combining the oar-powered mobility of a galley with the firepower and sails of a galleon. They were clumsy vessels, but proved useful in the light breezes and calms encountered during the Armada's progress down the Channel. The Squadron of Hulks was comprised of bulk merchant ships pressed into service from all over Europe. Ideal for carrying grain, they were not well suited to conversion as warships and so were used to transport stores, troops and supplies for the rest of the fleet.

Apart from the four galleys which returned to Spain before the start of the campaign, the rest of the fleet was made up of 34 smaller craft – carvels, pataches, falúas and zabras. These vessels served as dispatch boats, scouting vessels and for communication between the ships of the fleet. In effect the fleet consisted of three tactical groups of ships, each drawn from a number of different squadrons. This included the main fighting ships – the 'fire brigade' of the Armada, who would

The Spanish musketeer (centre) wears a plumed morion, a peascod doublet, trunk hose and canions and a scarf. He is armed with a heavy musket and rest and carries his priming powder in a small flask. His main charges of gunpowder are in wooden bottles or boxes worn on a bandolier. Originally worn over either shoulder, the custom eventually became to have it over the right shoulder, following the publication of illustrated drill books, notably that of De Gheyn in 1607. While he follows that rule, the musketeer breaks the policy of holding the burning match in a separate hand to his musket – despite the pan cover, a stray spark could easily set off the priming, causing the weapon to fire prematurely. Scruffily-dressed in broad-brimmed hat, wing-shouldered doublet and baggy breeches tied at the knee, the caliverman (right) probably gives a realistic image of the common soldier in the Army of Flanders, forced to resort to theft and pillage to survive. The Spanish heavy pikeman (left) come from the 'tercio of the dandies' and decorates his armour with ribbons and feathers. He wears an expensively decorated 'classical' peaked burgonet helmet and appears to have profited well from the sack of the captured Dutch towns (Richard Hook).

move where the fighting was thickest. For the bulk of the fleet, numbers and the maintenance of a tight formation offered some form of collective protection, and combined offensive capability. Finally there were the vessels which had little or no fighting potential – the hulks, the storeships and the transports. These had to be protected by the rest of the fleet.

A popular misconception is that the Armada consisted of large, well-armed galleons. The reality is that it was made up of a hastily gathered force of shipping from all over Europe and that the handful of real warships was supplemented by converted merchant vessels. Although it represented the largest concentration of 16th-century shipping ever assembled, it was far from being a homogenous force. It was also an experimental one, at least in terms of its fighting potential. Nobody had ever commanded a force of sailing ships this big before, and nobody had the definitive answer as to how the Armada should be handled in battle. The Spanish had developed their own distinctive naval doctrine, based on their experience of naval warfare in the Mediterranean, augmented by the experiences of the battle off the Azores in 1582. The campaign of 1588 would be the ultimate test for this polyglot but impressive fleet, and for the men who commanded it in battle.

The Spanish Way of War

The Duke of Medina Sidonia and his senior commanders were faced with a major problem. The English were largely an unknown force. While a Spanish fleet had successfully fought and beaten a French fleet just six years before, no

A gun foundry in the Spanish Netherlands, from a contemporary engraving. While the Spanish Armada was armed with ordnance form all over Europe, Flemish gun foundries such as the one shown here were regarded as being the best in Europe. Archaeological evidence shows that many of the Italian, Spanish or Portuguese guns carried in the fleet were of a much poorer quality than the Flemish pieces (Stratford Archive).

Spanish commander had fought a naval battle against the Tudor Navy. The defeat of Hawkins two decades before was the only engagement of any size, and it was fought in port rather than at sea. It also resulted in a Spanish victory. The best Medina Sidonia could hope for was that his commanders would be able to fight the type of naval engagement they were used to, transplanting the tactics which worked in the Azores to the waters of the English Channel.

The problem was, the Spanish relied almost exclusively on a doctrine based on close combat. Although their ships were well armed, they preferred to fire on the enemy in a single devastating volley at point-blank range, and then overwhelm their opponent with boarding parties. This was reflected in the composition of the crew, where the seamen were supported by two or three times their number of soldiers. For example, the fleet flagship *San Martín* (a 1,000-ton galleon) carried 161 sailors and 308 soldiers. The *Santiago* (a 520-ton galleon in the same squadron) was crewed by 307 soldiers and only 80 sailors. Spanish naval experience had for the most part been gained through fighting the French, Portuguese and Ottoman Turks, who all relied on similar boarding tactics. If any English ship had been grappled by a large Spanish warship, then this predominance in trained and experienced soldiers would have guaranteed victory. The problem was that throughout the campaign the English refused to let themselves be boarded.

Throughout the age of the galleon, the Spanish never realized the full potential of their naval artillery. For most of the 16th century, shipborne ordnance was regarded as a supporting weapon, used to soften up the enemy prior to the decisive boarding action. After the experience of the Spanish Armada campaign of 1588, Spanish naval commanders came to view their artillery as a more versatile weapon, and trained their crews to conduct stand-off artillery duels as well as boarding actions. Indeed, this practice had begun as early as the 1520s, but it was never fully adopted by the Spanish apart from when engaging targets on shore. During the 16th and early 17th centuries, Spanish naval ordnance was invariably mounted on single-trailed, two-wheeled carriages, more akin to those found on land than associated with use at sea.

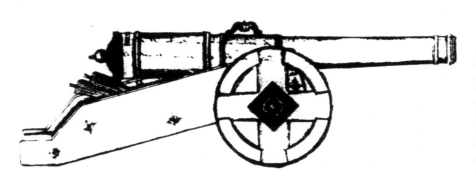

A Spanish artillery piece, mounted on a Spanish-style sea carriage of the Armada period. During the campaign the Spanish mounted their guns on two-wheeled carriages, which were less well suited to use on board warships than the four-wheeled carriages used by their English adversaries (Archivo General de Simancas, Valladolid).

This changed during the first half of the 17th century, as the Spanish gradually adopted the form of carriage which by this stage was widely used by all other maritime powers. Therefore, by 1630 at the latest, the heavy ordnance carried on board galleons was exclusively mounted on practical four-wheeled carriages using trucks rather than large wheels; in effect primitive versions of the carriages used by all Atlantic naval powers throughout the 18th century. In addition, the obsolete wrought-iron breech-loading guns, which were carried for much of the 16th century, were gradually phased out and replaced by more reliable bronze muzzle-loading pieces. Of course, these changes came too late to help the Duke of Medina Sidonia.

The wrought-iron pieces carried by many ships in his Armada were adequate when used as point-blank weapons, but lacked the range to participate in longer-range bombardments or artillery duels. Although some of these old guns were still carried on the larger ships of the Armada, for the most part they had been relegated to the protection of hulks and supply ships, not the galleons which made up the main striking force of the Spanish fleet. In effect they were obsolete guns, pressed into service to augment the firepower of the armed merchantmen that made up the bulk of the Armada.

By the time of the Armada, Spanish galleons carried modern bronze ordnance (albeit mounted on inefficient two-wheeled carriages), but their commanders had still not worked out the best way to use them. A detailed analysis of ammunition expenditure during the campaign (published in Martin & Parker, 1988) shows that even as late as 1588 the Spanish still clung to the notion of fighting boarding actions at sea rather than artillery engagements. The larger guns of the fleet were rarely fired, while the expenditure of shot by smaller *versos* was prodigious.

This is explained by the Spanish method of using naval ordnance during this period. Each Spanish gun was placed under the command of a ship's gunner, assisted by a crew of sailors and soldiers. Once the piece was loaded, the crew dispersed to their other action stations, leaving the gunner alone, clutching his burning matchcord, waiting for the order to give fire. Spanish naval doctrine emphasized the collective firing of the ship's broadside guns immediately before boarding an enemy vessel. The superbly trained Spanish infantry would then board the enemy vessel 'in the smoke'. Given this tactic, there was simply no need to reload the gun until the action was over.

In other words, the Spanish viewed their ordnance as weapons designed to support their infantry rather than the primary offensive weapon of the ship. Throughout the era of the galleons, it was the ship-borne Spanish infantry who formed the most potent weapon in the Spanish naval arsenal. Other maritime powers were unable to match these Spanish infantry in close combat at sea, which meant that if a Spanish galleon managed to grapple and board an enemy ship, the enemy vessel was as good as lost. During the battle fought off the Azores in 1582 the effectiveness of this doctrine was demonstrated when Spanish boarding parties

Opposite

This unarmoured pikeman (left) comes from the 'tercio of the sextons', famous for their sombre dress. The light pikemen were more manoeuvrable than the heavy pikes, though obviously this advantage came at the expense of defensive armour. Eventually, this policy was adopted by pikemen across Europe, though it took nearly a century for it to be accepted.

Traditionally, the army was a respectable career for the younger sons of Spanish nobility, where the prospects of fame and plunder on the battlefield offered means to move beyond their station. The Armada drew many such officers in, as the wealthy English estates and promises of Philip II's rewards were a strong temptation. The officer (right) wears what was the height of fashion for an ambitious officer of the 1580s. His morion and peascod breastplate are lavishly engraved, inlaid with gold and well-kept, his truck hose are delicately 'pinked' (in patterns of small cuts and slashes) and his 'canions' are fastened below the knee like breeches.

The Spanish ensign (centre) wears a decorated over-doublet open to display the expensive under-doublet beneath. He has exchanged his battlefield helmet for a comfortable hat, and bears the ragged red cross of St. Andrew and Burgundy on his banner, the distinguishing mark of the Spanish forces (Richard Hook).

captured the core of the opposing French fleet in a brief but hard-fought action. In 1588 the Spanish simply planned to use the same tactic.

The 1588 campaign demonstrated that, in terms of tactical thinking, the Spanish had been overtaken by their rival maritime powers. During the campaign the English commanders consistently refused to let the Spanish board their ships, preferring to remain outside 'caliver range' and fight an artillery duel. This forced the Spanish to re-evaluate their tactics, and come up with a way to use their ordnance in a more versatile fashion. The first remedy was to detach the soldiers from artillery duty, leaving it up to the sailors to handle the guns. After all, they were more skilled in the mechanical tasks involved. Next, a review of carriages was made and, although it took four decades, the Spanish introduced more suitable carriages. Finally they turned their back on large and prestigious (and therefore cumbersome) warships, favouring smaller galleons, such as those built for the Indies trade rather than service in the fleet in European waters. All this took time. To be fair, other maritime powers were also trying to work out how to use warships as floating batteries, and it was not until the mid-17th century that the English and Dutch developed the concept of the line-of-battle.

The Spanish Armada of 1588 had also managed to fulfil its task of maintaining a tight formation as it progressed up the English Channel. Only two ships were lost during this period from a fleet of 120 vessels, and those losses occurred through accidental damage rather than from enemy fire. The Spanish may have re-evaluated their tactical doctrines, but little change was made to the way a fleet was handled. If anything the 1588 campaign vindicated Spanish fleet handling.

After the débâcle of 1588, the Spanish authorities printed instructions, governing how ships should be used in battle. The speed with which this was accomplished suggests that at least some of these doctrines were first developed during the years before the Armada sailed, but those relating to gunnery were never fully put into practice. However, those concerning the way ship-borne troops were used almost certainly reflect the doctrine practised by the Spanish during the 1588 campaign.

Detailed instructions were provided concerning the use of naval artillery. In theory guns were kept ready for use at all times, although the time needed to prepare a ship for action was increased on galleons of the Indies *flotas*, as the gun deck was usually filled with stores and cargo as well as the crew and their belongings. Also, most galleons were armed with guns of several calibres. Shot of each calibre was stored separately, and, to avoid errors during a battle, the calibre of each gun was painted on a notice pinned on the beam over each gun. Normally, one gunner supervised each gun, and the remainder of his crew (normally six to eight men) were formed from the ranks of the remaining *gente de mar* (mariners), with each piece being allocated a certain number of able seamen, apprentices and pages.

The pages were used to maintain the supply of ammunition, running between the *pañol de pólvora* (powder magazine) and the guns with bags of powder carried in leather containers. Occasionally, soldiers would be drafted to assist in the operation of the guns. The master gunner took his orders from the infantry commander during an action rather than the ship's master, and he controlled the operation of all heavy guns and *versos*. In effect, this meant that the infantry commander took charge of the ship during an action, regardless of whether he was a soldier or naval commander.

During a battle the infantry were stationed throughout the ship. According to operational orders, a squadron containing the most experienced men should be stationed in the forecastle, under the command of its squadron chief, or *cabo*. Other squadrons were grouped in the waist, on the quarterdeck and on the poop deck. Ideally, if sufficient men were available, a reserve would be kept below decks, for use as a boarding party, or to repel any attack. As approximately half of the soldiers on board were armed with small-arms, infantry firepower played a major part in any close-range battle. Each squadron (whether in the forecastle, waist, quarterdeck or poop) relied on its musketeers and arquebusiers to open the battle, firing in two makeshift ranks, allowing one to fire from the gunwale while the other retired to the centreline to reload.

Soldiers armed with close-combat weapons mustered on the opposite side of the deck, keeping out of the way until called into action. If an attack was ordered, the boarding party would usually muster in the forecastle. According to the guidelines issued to the *Armada de la Guardia* (The Guard Fleet of the Spanish Main) in the late 16th century, these boarders should consist of men with sword and buckler, *chuzos* (half-pikes) and arquebus in equal proportions. Any assault would be accompanied by the throwing of incendiaries and grenades, while the men in the waist remained ready to extinguish similar projectiles thrown by the enemy. Similar instructions issued in 1630 prove that a similar mixture of troops was used during the early 17th century.

Opposite

Firearms were more common amongst the ranks of the Spanish cavalry than they were in the English army, and 'shot on horseback' was an established and accepted branch of the army. The hargulatier (right) combined the roles of light horseman and petronel, and were used as patrols and skirmishers by the Army of Flanders. Warfare in the Low Countries was, however, dominated by sieges, so the hargulatiers had little chance to practise fighting in large formations.

Spanish lancers (left) appear in Dutch engravings opposing the charges of English and Dutch demilancers, but they were not numerous, as the Spanish suffered from the same problems as their enemies – the need to supply many strong horses as mounts. The cassack is a common feature of the costumes in the illustrations, and may have been standard battlefield wear, worn over the armour.

The infamous German mercenary Ritter (mounted), clad in his distinctive black armour, was a common sight in the armies of the English, Dutch, French and Spanish alike – their loyalty dictated only by their pay. The Spaniard Bernardino de Mendoza in his *Theorique and Practise of Warre* (English translation 1597) says: 'some soldiers of late years would prefer pistoliers ... with apparent reasons that pistols were of most advantage for the souldiors, who were easily carried away with the beliefe therof, in that they found the launce a weapon of much trouble and charge, and the pistol not so much'. Sir Roger Williams agreed with this theory, stating that, when used by a well-trained and determined soldier, the pistol was far superior to the lance, but that many inexperienced pistoliers fired their volley too soon, and lacked the range to damage their target before being charged by enemy lancers as they wheeled away to reload and regroup (Richard Hook).

The Commanders

The Spanish command structure was complex and somewhat contradictory, but at its pinnacle was King Philip II, based in the monastic palace of El Escorial, north of Madrid. He was involved in virtually every aspect of the planning and preparation of the Armada, taking a passionate interest in the whole enterprise. He was advised by an inner circle, the most notable members of which were Don Juan de Zúñiga and his Captain-General of the Ordnance, Don Juan de Acuña Vele. Strategy was dictated by the king, although he also involved his two principal commanders the Marquis of Santa Cruz and the Duke of Parma in the business of planning the operation. These four men sat on his council of war, a body which included several experienced military and naval advisors, while members of his council of state and of his treasury (the *Contadurías*) were able to advise the monarch on the non-military aspects of the operation.

The Armada itself was under the direct command of the Duke of Medina Sidonia, who assumed control of the fleet following the death of the Marquis of Santa Cruz. The Duke held the rank of Admiral of the Ocean Sea, which effectively meant that he was in overall command of the operation. However, as he lacked much military and naval experience, he relied on the counsel of his leading commanders. His second in command, Juan Martinez de Recalde, was a competent and highly experienced naval commander, who also — at least on paper — commanded the Biscayan Squadron. However, his real function was to command the ad-hoc 'fire brigade' of warships charged with protecting the fleet as it made its way up the English Channel.

There were eight other squadron commanders in the fleet, each with administrative responsibility for the ships and men under their command. In theory these commands were administrative rather than actual, and during the campaign the organization of the fleet was altered when the more powerful vessels were grouped together. The Duke of Medina Sidonia then divided naval control of the rest of the fleet between these subordinate commanders. They all held the rank of *cabo* (chief of a squadron). In addition the duke maintained his own staff on board

A fragment of a pennant, which was reputedly salvaged from the 750-ton Spanish galleon *San Mateo*. The galleon was badly damaged during the battle off Gravelines, and was captured by the Dutch the following day. This painted linen banner hung in a church in Leiden for three centuries after the battle (Stedelijk Museum, Leiden).

his flagship, which included his own secretary (Jeronimo de Arceo), and various military or naval aides. The most senior of these staff officers were Diego Flores de Valdés, who advised the duke on naval matters, and Don Francisco de Bobadilla, who commanded the embarked infantry.

On each ship the command structure was equally complex. The fleet carried five *tercios* (regiments) of veteran Spanish infantry, and these were divided throughout the fleet. Each had its own command structure, under the command of the *maestre de campo* (regimental commander), supported by around 25 more junior officers.

This seaborne army was independent of the Duke of Parma's Army of Flanders, and in theory at least it was commanded by the Duke of Medina Sidonia. He was assisted by various military staff, who would look after the welfare of these soldiers once they disembarked. These included the *veedor general* (inspector general), Don Lópe Manrique, supported by the *proveedor* (commissary general), Bernabe de Pedroso, and the *pagador* (paymaster), Juan de Huerta. In addition to the *tercios* were a number of independent companies of soldiers, as well as an artillery train, under the command of the lieutenant-general of ordnance, Alonso de Cespedes. There was also a medical team, which was divided up among the various squadrons of the fleet, but which was controlled by the duke's chief of staff and administrator, Don Martín de Alarcón.

Finally each of the 176 infantry companies in the fleet had its own officers. In theory these were self-contained units, with around 25 companies in each *tercio*. These retained their own command structure on board ship, as they remained together, while the *tercios* did not. They would only be reorganized into cohesive fighting formations once they were landed on English soil. For practical purposes they would be attached to the Duke of Parma's command, but the exact details were vague. Naturally the Duke of Parma retained control of his own army, and the coastal vessels he was gathering in Flemish ports to use as invasion transports.

Finally there was the question of overall command once the Armada had made contact with the Army of Flanders. Philip II gave the Duke of Medina Sidonia complete control of operations until the fleet managed to effect a rendezvous with the Duke of Parma. From that point on command would be shared between the two dukes, even though Parma was both the most experienced commander and the holder of a higher aristocratic rank. Although Parma lobbied the king for complete control of the enterprise, Philip ordered him to comply with his instructions, and to accede to a shared command. After all, the fleet needed its own senior commander, whose role was every bit as important as that of the army commander during the invasion and its immediate aftermath.

At this point it is worthwhile to look at these leading commanders in a little more detail:

King Philip II of Spain (1527–98, reigned 1556–98) was the man who selected the plan, choosing a compromise between the recommendations of his principal military and naval commanders. The fact that this compromise led to a flawed plan of campaign is largely his responsibility, and that of his principal advisor, Don Juan de Zúñiga. In 1583, when the notion of an invasion of England was first proposed to him, Philip declared that the scheme had merit, and requested the Marquis of Santa Cruz to develop a plan. He then made the mistake of asking for a similar proposal from the Duke of Parma. This compromise was largely the result of financial concerns, although they greatly increased the risk of failure.

Worse still, the political consequences of defeat during the campaign would far outweigh the penny-pinching benefits of modifying the virtually foolproof original plan.

The invasion of England was by necessity a naval operation first, and a military one second. After all, before his veteran soldiers could engage the enemy, they first had to be successfully transported to England, and safely set ashore, along with all the supplies they needed. This was the job of the Spanish fleet, and therefore the king should have listened more attentively to his highly experienced naval commander. Once the preparations for the 'Great Enterprise' got underway, Philip began to 'micro-manage' the operation, bombarding both Santa Cruz and Parma with often contradictory orders and demands, many of which did little to improve the potential for success in the operation. Therefore the failure of the enterprise was largely the fault of the king himself, rather than that of the men he appointed to carry out the operation.

Don Alvaro de Bazán, 1st Marquis of Santa Cruz (1526–88) was the original architect of the Spanish Armada. He was already an experienced naval commander, having fought at Lepanto (1571) and the Azores (1582), as well as in several smaller engagements. It was his fervent belief that Protestant England represented a grave threat to Spain's overseas empire, and he was an ardent supporter of the 'Great Enterprise'. In fact, after his victory over the French at São Miguel he wrote to King Philip, suggesting that this success should be exploited by launching an invasion of England. This was the first mention of the enterprise, and as originally planned by Santa Cruz, the operation stood every chance of success.

A skilled administrator, he drew together the forces needed for the enterprise, although he remained opposed to the king's scaling down of the expedition, which incorporated a rendezvous with the Spanish Army in Flanders rather than shipping the troops from Lisbon. He drew up estimates and inventories, ordered the gathering of ships, men and supplies, and supervised the transformation of a motley collection of armed merchantmen into warships capable of defending the honour of Spain. At 62, the marquis was really too old for such an important command, but his drive was apparent in the efforts he made to ready the fleet, fighting corruption, malaise and royal interference in equal measure.

If he had actually led the Armada into battle, he would probably have succeeded in delivering the fleet intact to the Flemish rendezvous, and he might even have been able to keep it there while the army embarked. Despite his age he still had the strategic and tactical skills needed to make the enterprise a success. In the end his health deteriorated as a result of all this work, and through the lack of support offered him by his king. Consequently, when the marquis died in Lisbon in early February 1588, the ultimate success of the Armada was placed in jeopardy.

Don Alonso Pérez de Guzmán el Bueno, 7th Duke of Medina Sidonia (1550–1619) was appointed as the new commander of the Armada within days of the death of the Marquis of Santa Cruz. He was appointed by the king himself, more because he was a leading nobleman and royal favourite than for any military or naval qualifications he might have had. Medina Sidonia was also more likely than his predecessor to follow the king's instruction to the letter, rather than make his own decisions. The head of one of the richest and most powerful aristocratic houses in Spain, he has been described as honest, pious and magnanimous. He was a short, heavy-set nobleman of 38, possessed of great diplomatic skills, and was a member of the Order of the Golden Fleece, the most prestigious chivalric order in Spain.

Don Alonso Pérez de Guzmán, 7th Duke of Medina Sidonia (1550-1619). Although he lacked naval experience, the commander of the Spanish Armada displayed great personal courage and tactical skill, making the most of the motley collection of vessels under his command (Fundación Archivo, Casa de Medina Sidonia).

He was also a highly intelligent man, although relatively inexperienced in naval warfare. When he was appointed, he wrote to the king pleading ill health and lack of financial resources, and although he eventually accepted the command, this reluctance has cast a doubt over his suitability for the task. He knew he was a landsman, and would have to rely on his experienced subordinates to ensure the operation went smoothly. The Duke of Medina Sidonia displayed great personal courage during the campaign, and kept the Armada intact as it sailed up the English Channel, but he was not really up to the challenges that the command thrust upon him.

He lacked the initiative or self confidence to exploit English mistakes, such as the separation of their fleet off Portland. He also seemed to have greatly underestimated the importance of maintaining communications with the Duke of Parma and his army. This failure alone was enough to place the whole enterprise in jeopardy. However, it was created by the king, not the duke. He simply lacked the courage to make his own decisions, and to make a faulty plan better. The duke flew his flag in the galleon *San Martín* (1,000 tons).

Juan Martinez de Recalde (1526–88) was born in Bilbao, northern Spain. He served as a royal official for 20 years, overseeing shipping between Bilbao and the Spanish Netherlands. During this period he gained extensive maritime experience commanding royal vessels, and in 1572 King Philip II placed him in command of

Juan Martinez de Recalde (1526-88), an oil painting by an unknown artist. The most experienced of all the Spanish naval commanders, the second-in-command of the Spanish Armada favoured a more aggressive strategy than Medina Sidonia. During the campaign he remained in the thickest of the fighting (Disputación Floral de Vizcaya, Bilbao).

the fleet bound for Flanders. He remained in Flanders for the next eight years to command Spanish naval forces and fight Dutch 'Sea Beggars'. In 1580 de Recalde escorted the Spanish amphibious expedition to Smerwick in Ireland, and in 1582–83 he commanded a squadron in the Azores campaign. By 1588 he was seen as one of Spain's most experienced naval commanders, and a Knight of Santiago. He was also an old man of 62, and suffered badly from sciatica.

De Recalde was described as being 'tall and slender, of a light complexion, with smooth flaxen hair, a mild and temperate manner, and strong, deliberate speech.' It was claimed he was revered by his men. During the campaign he consistently proved himself as the best tactical commander in the Armada, and was usually found in the thick of the fighting. Although he survived the campaign, he died two weeks after his return to Bilbao, a sick and broken man. If he had commanded the fleet during the campaign, the outcome might well have been different. His flagship was the *San Juan de Portugal* (1,050 tons).

Don Alonso Martinez de Leiva (*c.*1540–88) was a favourite of the King of Spain, and regarded as the epitome of the Spanish chivalric ideal. Don Alonso had extensive military experience as a soldier, having campaigned in Italy and North Africa. In 1576 he campaigned with Don Juan de Austria against the Dutch rebels, then returned to Italy and was appointed Captain-General of the Sicilian galleys. As a naval commander he took part in the conquest of Portugal (1580), before being given command of the Milanese cavalry. In 1587 he was given command of the amphibious troops embarked in the Armada. Although he held no formal naval command, Medina Sidonia put Don Alonso in charge of the vanguard squadrons. He also carried a secret document which named him as successor if the duke were to die (therefore bypassing Recalde). Don Alonso drowned in the galleass *Girona* when it was wrecked off Antrim in October 1588. During the campaign his flagship was *La Rata Santa María Encoronada* (820 tons).

Alessandro Farnese, Duke of Parma (1545–92) was a grandson of King Charles V of Spain, making him a nephew of Philip II. Although born in Parma in Italy, he had been educated in the Spanish court. In 1571 he took part in the Lepanto campaign as an aide-de-camp, and in 1578 he was appointed Governor of the Netherlands. This placed the 38-year-old general in charge of Spain's veteran Army of Flanders, and he displayed considerable martial abilities against the Dutch rebels, recapturing most of Flanders, including the key city of Antwerp.

His version of the invasion plan involved a landing in Ireland by way of a diversion, then a dash across the English Channel from Flanders when the English commanders were distracted. The Duke of Parma was a military commander of considerable experience. However, his limited knowledge of naval matters meant that his version of the plan was fatally flawed. It failed to take into account the problems of wind and tide, the lack of suitable embarkation and landing sites, the activities of the Dutch fleet, and the possibility that the English might still retain a powerful naval force in the eastern end of the English Channel – the Downs Squadron.

By 1588, when orders came to form part of the 'Great Enterprise' against England, he was engaged in the piece-by-piece conquest of Holland. The invasion was a diversion from his main objective, and it appears he was reluctant to be distracted by what he viewed as a risky venture. However, as a skilled soldier and diplomat, he possessed the ability to outwit his English adversaries if he were able to land. He had a ruthless ability to grasp the military situation, and to deploy his troops accordingly. Given the elite troops at his disposal, the success of his army once it managed to land in England would have been all but guaranteed.

The Men

In all the fleet consisted of 130 ships, containing 29,453 men, including almost 17,000 soldiers. By the time the two fleets first sighted each other the Spanish had been at sea for a week since leaving La Coruña. They had actually been cooped up on board their ships for the best part of two months, and the vessels were hopelessly overcrowded. Within these ships every available space was taken up with stores for the ship or for the army, makeshift cabins for the numerous officers, adventurers, priests and hangers-on, and of course the unwashed bodies of hundreds of soldiers and sailors. There was no privacy, and little or no sense of hygiene. Then all these men had to be fed, required a place to sleep, and needed to be able to work the ship, or to defend it from the enemy. Fortunately nobody expected the Armada to remain at sea more than two or three weeks. Conditions would only become a problem if the disembarkation was delayed.

Shipboard Organization

Before the Armada sailed, each ship was allocated a set number of soldiers and sailors, according to strict guidelines. At least that was the theory. These were based on the experiences of organizing and provisioning the Indies *flotas*, which sailed between Spain and the New World. The basic rule was that one man was allocated to a galleon for every *tonelada* (Spanish ton) of burden, although for the Armada this was increased to approximately two and a half men per ton, due to the need to embark the five *tercios* of infantry. Of these, approximately four soldiers were carried for every *gente de mar* (mariner). In practice, the manning of these galleons varied considerably, and financial considerations played a major part in reducing the size of the crew on some of the larger ships in the fleet, often to less than half the 'one man per *tonelada*' ratio.

Administrative returns from the time show that, on average, the ships carried crews of approximately 90–100 men per vessel, excluding soldiers. While the proportions of seamen to untrained landsmen or specialist gunners or pages and servants might vary slightly, a broad notion of crew numbers can be obtained. A

A sea battle, as depicted in a late 16th-century engraving. This is an engagement fought in the Spanish manner – an initial exchange of broadsides, while the crews prepare to fight it out hand-to-hand. The English preferred to keep their distance, and to rely on their ordnance to win the battle for them (Stratford Archive).

typical 500-*tonelada* galleon carried approximately 15 officers, 26 seamen, 19 apprentice seamen, 10 pages and 21 gunners: 91 men, or one man per 5 ½ ton, not counting the soldiers. Using the formula given above, the same galleon would have a company of approximately 125 soldiers on board, giving a total complement of 216 men, not counting any supernumeraries, passengers or embarked troops in transit.

These figures reflect the individual records of Spanish galleon crews during this period, although it appears that the number of soldiers embarked on a ship of this size could vary by as much as 25 per cent, depending on need. However you look at it, the number of soldiers carried on board these Spanish ships was strikingly high, and far in excess of those embarked on English ships. Typically, each Spanish ship carried five or six veteran infantrymen for every one carried on board an English ship.

Again, at least in theory, organization within a squadron, or in individual ships, was clearly defined. First, the Armada as a whole was commanded by a *capitán-general*, appointed by the king. In this case it was the Duke of Medina Sidonia. In his *Itinerario* (1575), Juan Escalante describes the perfect *capitán-general* as: 'a very good man, of good family and well born, a native of Seville, a good Christian and experienced on the sea ... of a proper age, neither old, nor young.' The duke fell well short of this ideal, especially when it came to experience.

Fortunately, most of his squadron commanders came close to the ideal. Men such as Don Pedro de Valdés, Miguel de Oquendo, Martín de Bertendona or Don Hugo de Moncada were all products of the Spanish aristocracy, the chivalric military orders and the Spanish military machine. Skilled courtiers, diplomats, soldiers and mariners, these commanders held great responsibilities, but usually rose to the challenge. They embarked on the flagship of their squadron (known as the *capitana*), along with a small staff, which usually included royal officials as well as their own entourage. The squadron second-in-command was the *almirante* (admiral), an officer appointed by the *capitán-general*. He was responsible for the seaworthiness of the squadron, the maintenance of its sailing and battle formations, and all aspects of its maintenance, readiness and efficiency. By necessity the *almirante* was usually more of a seaman than a soldier. Traditionally, his flagship (known as the *almiranta*) took up position at the rear of the squadron, or on the opposite side of a formation from the *capitana*.

On board individual galleons, the senior officer was the *capitán* (captain). During the period there were two different types of ship commander. The *capitán de mar* (naval captain) was usually a professional seaman, but had no jurisdiction over the troops embarked on his ship, even though he might be the senior officer on board. These men were rare, and normally the *capitán* was a soldier (*capitán de guerra*), not a sailor, who relied on the master (whose role is described below) to operate the ship on his behalf. While other maritime powers favoured a sole commander on their vessels, the Spanish continued to rely on joint command even after the failure of the Armada exposed the weakness of their command system.

Usually, a *capitán de mar y guerra* was appointed to command, who in theory had jurisdiction over everyone on board his galleon, but usually had little or no experience in maritime affairs. While officers with suitable experience on both land and sea existed, the majority tended to be primarily infantry commanders, and their involvement in the maritime operation of their own ships was limited to bureaucratic rather than practical matters.

The *maestre* (master) was effectively the principal seaman on board, and while the duties of the *capitán* were largely administrative, his were practical. In effect, he commanded the ship, while his superior the *capitán* commanded the infantry. Juan Escalante described the ideal *maestre* as being: 'a skillful mariner ... [worthy] of credit and confidence.' He went on to liken the *maestre* to a queen bee in its hive. Unlike other officers, who were appointed for the duration of a voyage, the *maestre* usually remained with a particular ship for the duration of its active service. He was responsible for sailing his galleon, the supervision of its provisioning, and the maintenance of its timbers. As his role was often administrative, many of his operational duties were taken over by an *alférez de mar* (naval first lieutenant). Next in the chain of command was the *piloto* (pilot), responsible for the safe navigation of the galleon. In a squadron, the *piloto mayor* (chief pilot) determined the course the squadron would set, while the individuals on each ship followed his lead. These men should not be confused with harbour or bar pilots, who were embarked in coastal or riverine waters, such as when transiting the harbours of Lisbon or La Coruña.

After the *piloto*, the next maritime officer in rank was the *contramaestre* (roughly equivalent to boatswain). As the principal assistant to the *maestre*, his duties involved the loading of the ship, operation and maintenance of the sails and rigging, and the smooth running of the ship. He was assisted by a *guardián* (boatswain's mate), who had the extra duty of supervising fire safety on board, such as the use of galley fires, candles or lanterns. Another assistant was the *despensero* (which roughly equates to chief steward). His responsibilities were the preservation and dispensing of the ship's provisions – food, wine and water – and their rationing in time of shortage. For the latter, a seaman was appointed as the *alguacil de agua* (water dispenser) to assist the *despensero* in his duties. The duties of the *codestable* (master gunner) are described below. The remaining supernumeraries on a galleon were the *capellán* (chaplain), appointed by the *capitán-general*, and the *cirjano* (ship's surgeon), appointed by individual ship captains.

As for the crew, apart from a handful of specialists, the *gente de mar* (mariners) were divided into four groups: *marineros* (able seamen), *grumetes* (apprentice seamen or 'landsmen'), *pajes* (pages, or ship's boys) and *artilleros* (gunners). The specialists comprised the non-commissioned officers on board; they were collectively known as the *maestranza* (artificers), and usually included the ship's carpenter, a diver, a cooper, a caulker and one or more trumpeters. The *artilleros* regarded themselves as superior to other *gente de mar*, and under the watchful eye of the *codestable* they maintained the guns and operated the pieces in battle, each supervising a crew comprising non-specialist *gente de mar*. *Marineros* were usually skilled seamen as opposed to the *grumetes*, who were usually teenage apprentice seamen, who learned their craft while at sea. The same division of skills can be found in most ships during the age of sail.

At the bottom of the maritime hierarchy were the pages or *pajes*, sometimes the relatives of serving officers or their friends, but more usually orphans or runaways. Aged 12–16, these youths performed all the menial duties, such as scrubbing decks, preparing meals or helping the seamen. The *gente de mar* were divided into two or sometimes three 'watches', set by the *maestre*, ensuring the ship could be sailed throughout the night. Mariners who were not on duty could be called upon to assist the watch on deck.

Finally, there were the soldiers, who formed their own organization within the ship. All embarked troops in the squadron were commanded by the *capitán-general*, although he was assisted by a *gobernador* (military governor), who was usually a *capitán* of one of the non-flagship galleons (which was duly called the *gobierno*). On each galleon, the infantry were commanded either by their own *capitán* or by the ship's *capitán de mar y guerra*. In effect, each galleon carried a company of troops on board, and its organization reflected contemporary Spanish practice on land. The *capitán* was assisted by an *alférez de guerra* (military lieutenant), who supervised discipline amongst the troops, and saw to their accommodation on board. As in almost any army, the lieutenant relied on the *sargento* (sergeant) to supervise the day-to-day activities of the men. The embarked company was divided into 'squadrons' of 25 men, equating to a modern infantry platoon.

Each was commanded by a non-commissioned *cabo de escuadra* (squadron chief, or platoon commander). Like the seamen, the soldiers were divided according to experience, with *soldados aventanjados* (experienced soldiers) receiving greater pay. These included the *abanderado* (standard bearer), two *tambores* (drummers) and one *pífano* (fifer). In addition, *mosqueteros* (musketeers) and *arcubuceros* (arquebusiers) were paid more than other *soldados*. An examination of contemporary rolls has shown that 50 per cent of a typical company were *soldados* (armed with half-pikes or halberds), while the remainder were divided equally between *mosqueteros* and *arcubuceros*.

Conditions on Board

Space was extremely limited on board a Spanish galleon. A typical vessel in the Armada, such as the 530-ton *San Pedro* in the Squadron of Castille, had a crew of around 200 men, excluding soldiers, who numbered roughly the same again. They had to fit inside a hull whose main deck measured just 53 by 17 *codos* (99ft by 31½ ft), or just over 15 square feet per man. Of course, for the *capitán* and his officers, conditions were relatively more comfortable. The captain's cabin was at the after end of the upper deck, a space shared with the *capitán de guerra* if one was carried. The pilot lodged in the *camarote*, the space aft of the poop deck, while the master lodged on the deck below, near the helmsman's position. The chaplain also lodged in the cabin space of the upper deck. While the *capitán* and his other senior officers had some degree of privacy (particularly the *capitán*, whose accommodation was the most spacious compartment on board), junior officers or passengers often had to make do with temporary sleeping spaces, screened from the rest of the ship by curtains or wooden screens. In daylight, most of these temporary screens were removed.

As for the rest of the soldiers and crew, in theory they slept on the lower deck, but many preferred the fresh air of the upper deck when at sea. The master gunner and his men lodged together, at the stern of the lower deck, amongst any stern chase guns which might be carried. Immediately forward of this space the surgeon lodged amid his chests, saws and potions. Further forward, the able seamen berthed in the space between the main-mast and the mizzen, or on the forward part of the quarterdeck. Apprentice seamen berthed on the lower deck between the fore and main masts, while the pages slept in whatever spaces were left.

The soldiers had their own system, with any embarked company sleeping on the starboard side of the lower deck (or upper deck in good weather), along with their sergeant. If an *almirante* or *capitán-gene*ral was embarked, the *capitán* gave up his accommodation, unless the vessel was commodious enough to have two large stern cabins. Everyone then moved down one in the accommodation pecking order. If extra troops were embarked, they invariably slept on the main deck, or even on a network of ropes resembling a large fishing net, slung over the waist, and stretched between the forecastle and sterncastle.

With all this humanity crammed into a small space, sanitation was considered a major problem. A lack of proper toilet facilities meant that, while on some ships men used *jardines* (gardens) hung over the stern quarters, or heads in the prow, many others employed buckets, or the bilges, which soon stank of human excrement. (The bilge was the space below the hold where seawater and waste collected, and in warm waters anyone opening the hatches into the bilges was liable to be knocked unconscious by the noxious fumes.) Eugenio de Salazar, a passenger writing of his experiences on board a galleon in 1573, recorded that in the waist the pump which 'sucked up the foul waters from the bilge' was always 'steaming like hell, and stinking like the devil'.

This attracted rats, which were not only a health risk; they also ate stores, polluted fresh water supplies and damaged sails and cordage. Galleons frequently carried animals for slaughter as provisions, most commonly chickens, pigs, goats and sometimes cattle. Horses were also transported in some of the hulks, in specially contrived slings. They were to be used by cavalry scouts, officers, artillery teams and messengers once the Armada had landed its embarked troops on the English coast. Most ships also carried cattle, pigs and goats. This obviously added to the sanitary problems on board. Another problem was the smaller kinds of vermin: cockroaches, scorpions, mice, and of course lice and fleas. Even when cabins and lower decks were regularly fumigated, there was almost no escape from fleas or lice on board a galleon during this period, whatever the social rank of the sailor, soldier or officer.

When a ship of the Armada was at sea, the daily routine was according to a system of watches, and the passing of time was noted by the turning of a sandglass located beside the helmsman's position. A three-watch system was used, with each third of the ship's company standing a four-hour watch twice a day. The first watch from midnight to 8am was supervised by the pilot, the forenoon and afternoon watch by the master, and the evening watch by the captain. The crew changed watches in the middle of each eight-hour watch period. By 1588 it is likely that the afternoon watch was split into two 'dog watches', to permit a rotation of the watch rota. Daybreak was marked by the chanting of prayers by the pages, followed by a 'Pater Noster' and an 'Ave Maria'. Religious chanting also marked the change of each watch, and even the turning of the 30-minute 'hourglass'. Meals were taken around the times of the daylight watch changes.

While officers and gentlemen adventurers provided their own stores of food, the fare of the seamen and soldiers was extremely limited. Ship's biscuit made from wheat flour (1½lb per man per day) and a portion of *menestra* (a mix of chickpeas, lentils, rice and broad beans) were the basic staples. The men were also given a daily ration of ½ *azumbre* (2 pints) of rough red wine each. Traditionally, this was augmented by boiled salted beef on four days of the week, while boiled salted fish or sardines were eaten on Wednesdays, Fridays and Saturdays. Beer or cider was often used instead of wine.

Records from *La Trinidad Valencera*, part of the Levant Squadron, tell us that the following foodstuffs were carried: 1,858 quintals of biscuit, 992lb of fresh mutton, 96 quintals of rice, 8 quintals of octopus, plus wine from Candia, carried in barrels. Cheese was sometimes served instead of meat when bad weather or impending battle made it impossible to light the galley fires. Olive oil, vinegar, and usually onions, olives and garlic helped improve the flavour of the food. Cooking was performed at prescribed times either individually, or in ad hoc groups. Incidentally, because of this largely Mediterranean diet, Spanish seamen suffered less from scurvy than the seamen of other maritime nations. In fact, it was so uncommon that the Spaniards called it the 'Dutch Disease'. While not particularly appetizing, it was at least a sustaining and reasonably healthy diet.

Although the diet might have been satisfactory, conditions on board were often appalling, and galleons provided a rich breeding ground for disease. Mortality rates were high throughout 16th- or 17th-century Europe, but on board these Spanish ships the situation was much worse due to the overcrowding, a problem which only increased after the debacle off Gravelines. In the Indies *flotas*, mortality rates of 15–20 per cent of the ship's company were commonplace for a return trip from Spain to the Indies, and by the time the Armada ships limped home to Spain, many of the ships were so short of men that they could hardly be sailed at all. In other words, life on board a Spanish warship during the Armada campaign was similar to that in the plague-infested and overcrowded cities at home, with the added risk of death through naval battle or shipwreck. If the soldiers managed to disembark, then they would face a whole new range of problems and threats during their march on London.

Ship Profile:

The Spanish Galleon

It is worth taking a closer look at a typical Spanish ship, to see how it was built, how it operated, and how it was armed. While the fleet contained a wide range of vessels, the majority of the most effective warships were galleons, either from the former Portuguese fleet, or from vessels drafted into service from the Indies *flotas*. The Spanish galleon is one of the most romantic ship types in history. Long associated with sunken treasure, pirates, conquistadores and of course the Spanish Armada, these ships have come to epitomize Spanish maritime power during the 16th and 17th centuries. Hollywood has much to answer for, and although these galleons were spectacular vessels they were nothing like the grandiose ships of the Spanish crown portrayed on the silver screen. Rather they were the workhorses of Spain's maritime empire, protecting her interests in European waters, and ensuring that the Spanish crown benefited from the extraordinary wealth produced in her American colonies.

We are fortunate in that the Spanish during this period were meticulous record keepers, giving us a wealth of information to help us define exactly what a galleon was. During the early 17th century, the Spanish government issued a series of detailed instructions, specifying exactly what they meant by a *galeon* (or 'galleon'; for simplicity's sake we shall use the more commonly accepted modern English spelling). We know the proportions of these craft, how they were fitted out and provisioned, what guns were carried aboard them, and how many men crewed them. We also have an abundance of pictorial evidence to support this rich source of documentary evidence, allowing us to understand fully how these ships were built, sailed and fought during the period. Unfortunately due to the popularity of galleon shipwrecks with treasure hunters (as opposed to archaeologists), there is a less impressive caucus of underwater archaeological evidence to supplement these other sources. This said, a number of highly publicized discoveries have

been made, and these have revealed a tremendous amount of information on the objects carried on board these vessels, even though little hard archaeological data was recovered.

The principal role of the galleon is almost as important as its physical description. Although its origins are obscure, it eventually became closely associated with the Indies, the Spanish term for their American colonies. Silver from Peru and Mexico, plus gold, emeralds and pearls from the northern coast of South America (known more romantically as the 'Spanish Main') became essential to the maintenance of Spain's position as a world power. The galleons made sure this treasure reached the royal coffers. Galleons also formed the spearhead of Spain's *armadas* which were sent to fight her kings' enemies in European waters. This latter role is the one given to these ships during the summer of 1588. Instead of carrying specie, their holds were filled with the supplies, munitions and weapons of war, and their decks crammed with soldiers, ready to play their part in the fighting on land or at sea.

There were 22 galleons in the Armada, of which ten of the largest were grouped together into the Squadron of Portugal. These included the fleet flagship *San Martín*, the equally impressive *almiranta San Juan*, and five large galleons captured from the Portuguese eight years before. Eleven more galleons constituted the Squadron of Castille, which for the most part was made up of galleons taken from the Indies *flotas*. Finally there was the *San Juan Bautista* of the Squadron of Andalusia, which was another 810-ton leviathan. While these ships all shared the characteristics of the galleon, more than half were far larger than the typical galleons of their day, and were therefore some of the most formidable fighting vessels in Europe. They would be pitched into battle against the largely untested English galleons, which followed similar lines, but which were altered to suit the English way of war. This would be a battle between two schools of galleon design as much as a fight between two nations, two fleets, two monarchs or two religions.

The Design of the Galleon

The origins of the galleon are somewhat obscure, but certainly the term first appeared during the early 16th century. It has been argued that the first Spanish vessel to merit the term was built in 1517 to fight Barbary pirates in the Mediterranean. This was probably a vessel that combined oars and sails, like the Venetian *galleoni* of the late 15th century. The Portuguese used similar small vessels, which they called *galleones*, in the Indian Ocean during the 1520s, where they functioned as patrol vessels; 21 such craft were listed in an inventory dated 1525. A Spanish document dated the following year records royal *galleones* in the Spanish fleet, but no further details are given.

The term was evidently recognized by the 1530s, when French sources refer to *galeons* as being Spanish warships, while the first visual depictions of the ship type also begin to appear. By this period galleons were no longer considered oared vessels, although Spanish galleons were being built to accommodate secondary sweeps (oars) as well as sails as late as the 1560s. These galleons were sailing ships, with a distinctive appearance that set them apart from contemporary carracks. The early 16th century was a time of maritime innovation. Designers were experimenting with the best way to employ artillery on board ships, and new sailing rigs were being introduced. In the Mediterranean, the carvel was a small, light, lateen-rigged trading vessel. Two such vessels accompanied the larger carrack *Santa Maria*, Columbus' flagship, on its transatlantic voyage of discovery in 1492; the carvel soon became the most commonly used vessel of exploration.

In northern Europe, immense armed carracks were being built as symbols of national power; the *Henry Grâce à Dieu* in England or the *Great Michael* of Scotland are prime examples. Larger and more cumbersome, the carrack (known as a nao in the Mediterranean and Iberian peninsula) was more closely related to the cog of medieval northern Europe, but it used a Mediterranean-style lateen-rigged sail on its mainmast, and a northern-style square-rigged sail on its foremast. The other difference between the nao and other ship types was that the former tended to be 'carvel built', with planks laid alongside each other on the outer hull, while the northern European carracks used 'clinker-built' construction, where the planks overlapped. Until the arrival of the galleon the nao and carrack remained the most common ship types in Spanish waters.

It has been argued that the first galleons were developed from the carvel, as both ships share similar features, such as a low forecastle (at least when compared to the nao or carrack), and the first galleons appear to have been relatively small vessels. In fact pictorial evidence shows that galleons and naos of the mid-16th century also shared similar features, such as strength of construction and their sailing rig. It is probably better to see the galleon as a product of an amalgam of Mediterranean shipbuilding styles and traditions; a vessel created to fill a gap in the range of available ship types.

By the late 1530s the galleon had come into its own. During the battle of Prevesa (1538), a Venetian vessel described as a galleon fought off several Turkish galleys, demonstrating that vessels of this type were well armed, and obviously able to defend themselves. This was clearly a stronger vessel than other Mediterranean sailing craft, as naos were not designed to withstand a heavy pounding from enemy fire. Rather they were commodious merchant vessels, though they could be armed with ordnance and filled with troops in time of war. Clearly galleons took this a step further, and were built as warships from the keel up. In a period when specialized warships were rare, the galleon was in a class of its own.

By the time of the accession of King Philip II of Spain in 1556, the Spanish government had been running a convoy system between Spain and the New World for three decades. Initially these convoys were escorted by a single armed nao, but in 1536 the term galleon appears and from that point on small galleons were the escort vessel of choice. They also appeared in increasing numbers, as the growth of European interlopers in Spanish American waters led to an increase in the protection afforded to these Indies convoys. Ordinances of 1536 and 1543 stipulate how these ships should be armed, and what their roles were. Investigations of the wreck of the galleon *San Estebán*, lost off the coast of modern-day Texas in 1554, have provided us with hard evidence concerning ship construction and provision, while the survival of a growing number of pictorial references attests to the development of this new ship type.

During the decade before Philip II's reign, galleons were generally smaller than naos; some listed galleons had an average burden of just 120 *toneladas*. This ties in with the near-contemporary description of them being capable of operating under oar power as well as sail. Larger vessels would have been extremely difficult to move

using 'sweeps'. Naturally the use of oars was confined to coastal waters, the Mediterranean, or completely calm ocean conditions. By 1556 galleons listed in royal inventories had an average burden of 334 *toneladas*, or almost three times that of galleons of a decade before. Similarly, galleons sent to Flanders in 1558 had an average burden of 367 *toneladas*. The size of the typical galleon was clearly increasing. One confusing element is the Spanish bureaucratic tendency to refer to any armed vessel of this period as a galleon, but with some effort the armed naos can be isolated from the growing number of galleons.

The term was also being adopted by other maritime powers. In 1545 Henry VIII of England's navy boasted a 'gallyon' (a small patrol craft fitted with sweeps), and Portuguese, French and Flemish galleons are also noted in documents of the mid-16th century. Clearly the term was used generically to define a warship in Spain, and described a specific type of warship in Portugal and a vessel of similar proportions and appearance to these Iberian vessels elsewhere in Europe.

Through a combination of pictorial evidence, ship models, archaeological data and historical records, we can determine exactly what a galleon of the mid-16th century looked like. Typically it was a high-sided vessel with a very tall sterncastle structure (usually split into two or more levels), a lower forecastle, a flat stern, a protruding beak at the bow (like the spur on a galley), and usually a single unbroken gundeck. The hull had a pronounced tumble-home (hull sides sloping inward from bottom to top), and this tapering continued into the sterncastle. A galleon's lines were graceful, and particularly fine at the stern, in contrast to its somewhat bluff bow. We know that galleons of this period were sleeker than naos, having a length-to-beam ratio of 4:1, as opposed to the average nao ratio of 3:1. We have already determined that the average galleon of *c*.1550 had a burden of over 300 *toneladas*. Its hull shape made it a stable platform for artillery, while the high sterncastle proved a bonus in close-range fighting, as it served as a bastion for the embarked soldiers. Beneath the gundeck there was a decently proportioned hold, while the high superstructure provided room for the carrying of passengers or extra troops.

The typical galleon had a bowsprit, a foremast, a mainmast and a mizzen mast, and favoured a largely square-rigged sail plan. The largest galleons (of over 800 *toneladas* burden) often carried a second mizzen mast aft of the first, called a bonaventure mizzen. The bowsprit carried a square spritsail, while the foremast and mainmast both carried three square sails (main, topsail and royal). The mizzen carried a lateen sail, as did the bonaventure if one was fitted. The biggest change over time was in size. By 1570 galleons of 500 tons were commonplace, and by the time of the Spanish Armada in 1588, the crown was able to commandeer three 'great' Portuguese galleons of around 1,000 *toneladas* burden, as well as eight of approximately 800 *toneladas*. Although styles changed, these basic characteristics continued to define the Spanish galleon at the time of the Spanish Armada campaign.

Opposite
The *San Juan Bautista*, 1588
One of 22 galleons to take part in the Spanish Armada campaign of 1588, the *San Juan Bautista* (one of two participating galleons bearing the same name) was the *almiranta* of the Squadron of Castile. She was a modern vessel with a burden of 750 *toneladas*, a crew of 296 men (including soldiers), and an armament of just 24 guns, excluding the smaller *versos*. For much of the progress of the Armada up the English Channel she was detached from her squadron, and instead formed part of an ad hoc formation of the most powerful vessels in the Spanish fleet. This 'fire brigade' protected the rest of the Armada formation, and consequently the *San Juan Bautista* participated in all of the principal engagements of the campaign. During the fighting off Gravelines (8–9 August) she was one of the four galleons which supported the fleet flagship *San Martín* during her legendary fight against the bulk of the English fleet, and was badly battered in the day-long engagement, her decks reportedly awash with blood. She not only survived the battle, but she subsequently managed to limp home to Spain. The *San Juan Bautista* was built for service in the Indies *flotas*, and was well built, with a relatively low profile compared to other galleons. This also accounts for her poor armament as, traditionally, Indies galleons were less well armed than those which saw regular service in the Armada del Mar Océano. Before she sailed from Lisbon in 1588, her regular armament was augmented by the embarkation of a dozen *versos* of various sizes (Tony Bryan).

Shipbuilding

In the 16th century the Spanish had two main shipbuilding areas: the Basque coast of northern Spain from La Coruña to Santander, and the southern Andalusian coastline, with its busy ports of Cadiz and Seville. For various reasons the Mediterranean coast from Barcelona to Cartagena was not considered suitable for the construction of galleons, although the region was the primary source of galley production in the country. From 1580 onwards, the Spanish were able to build ships in Portugal, mainly in the mouth of the River Tagus near Lisbon. To a lesser extent the Spanish could draw upon the resources of other European ports, in Italy, Sicily and even Flanders, but these were rarely if ever used to produce warships, unless they were vessels that were purchased after completion by the Spanish crown.

Of all these shipbuilding regions, the most highly regarded area was in northern Spain, in and around the port of Bilbao. Bilbao oak was considered superior to the oak of central and northern Germany, while the Basque region also boasted a thriving iron industry, and was a centre of artillery production. Another bonus was its strong maritime tradition, and its extensive trading links with northern Europe, ensuring a steady influx of long timbers such as pine for masts, and materials such as pitch, cordage and canvas. Galleons were usually produced by private shipbuilders, who worked under contract for the Spanish government. By undertaking the work, the shipbuilders or their financial backers could expect preferment for themselves and their family. Alternatively, government officials could simply force private shipbuilders to work in partnership with royal shipwrights, but this policy often resulted in poor workmanship, lengthy production times and escalating costs. Most Spanish shipyards of the period were primitive, and construction was usually undertaken in the open air. In this period, the availability of skilled labour and materials was more important than elaborate facilities.

Regulations governed almost every aspect of design, materials and construction, from the angle of slope of the sternpost to the way the dry provision store was planked. Apart from that, the process of shipbuilding was fairly straightforward. First, suitable timber was selected, usually from trees that had been cut during the winter. The *quilla* (keel) of the galleon was laid out on the ground (an area known as the *astillero*), its length determined by the size of the finished ship. Then the *roda* (stem) and *codaste* (stern) were added, each curving upwards from the keel at the prescribed angle in the government ordinances. Until the late 16th century, shipbuilding was usually a matter of good eye and judgement, but after 1580 designs had to follow a set of mathematical principles, and shipwrights had to measure everything.

The key measurement in this was the *manga* (beam), as all other measurements were given in proportion to it. Next a series of *cuaderna* (ribs) were constructed, starting with the *cuaderna maestre* (major ribs) to create the basic shape of the galleon

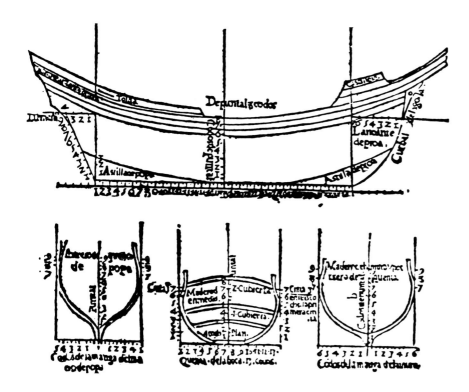

The graceful lines of a Spanish treasure galleon, dating from the 1580s. These drawings emphasize the importance of cargo space on these vessels, which after all were primarily designed to carry the wealth of the Americas to Spain. From Diego Garcia de Palacio; Instrucción Nautica (1587) (Stratford Archive).

below the *cintas* (gunwale). The shape of these varied considerably, from a 'U' shape amidships to a 'Y' at the stern, conforming to the elegant *garbo* (sheer) of the finished vessel. With the *cintas* in place, the shape of the hull was set. For a ship with a keel of 42 *codos*, 33 pairs of ribs would be used.

The vessel would then have its internal decks laid out, and these would be supported by knees. The *bodega* (hold) was usually kept free of internal decking between the *primera cubierta* (lower deck) and the decking built on top of the keel, although temporary mezzanine deck spaces could be inserted as required when the ship was in service. The mast steps were laid in place, then incorporated into the structure by creating supports around which the masts sat. Next came the planking of decks and the outer skins of the hull, using both wooden trenails and iron spikes. The use of iron spikes was faster, but less reliable, and the best hulls had a combination of both, giving both flexibility and linear rigidity to the timbers.

The thickness of the wooden planking increased towards the keel. The hull planks were then caulked using hemp fibres to make the hull as water-tight as possible. A layer of tar was then added to the seams to protect the caulking. Teredo worms and other timber-eating marine organisms are particularly virulent in the Caribbean. In order to protect the hull of ships bound for the Indies, the portion of the hull below the waterline was covered in a thin layer of lead sheeting, separated from the outer planking by a layer of tarred sailcloth. As a final precaution, the lower part of the hull was then coated with a mixture of tar and vegetable or animal fat. The masts were lowered in place, and once secured the riggers would set about laying the miles of supporting stays which kept them in place.

Virtually the last element was the installation of the rudder, hung from pintles on the sternpost. Unlike later sailing ships, all galleons were steered using a *caña* (tiller), which moved the rudder by means of a *pinzote* (whipstaff), allowing the ship to be directed from the helmsman's position in the forward portion of the upper deck known as the *puente* (bridge). Then, apart from the finishing off of the rigging, the placement of internal bulkheads, ladders and capstans, and the hoisting up of spars, the galleon was complete. From start to finish the whole process would usually take two years.

Shipbuilders received payment for their work in three or four stages, usually made on signature of contract, on completion of the frame, and on completion. The number of lawsuits in the archives suggests that payment was rarely straightforward, as royal officials supervised virtually every stage of construction, and wanted to check that every element of the process met the government guidelines. Clearly there was extensive scope for corruption, and periodically monarchs or leading bureaucrats launched their own investigations and audits to make sure the government was not being cheated. During construction the shipbuilder had to pay for materials, for the high labour costs involved in hiring specialist workers, and for the lodging of government inspectors, and wait for reimbursement later. Clearly the whole process was worth it, as contracts were often issued to previous recipients, this was part of the preferment mentioned above.

The crown then received the ship, and was responsible for the outfitting of all other items not covered in the shipbuilding contract. This included the embarkation of ordnance, navigational instruments, lanterns, the ship's boat (which was usually towed astern, or else hoisted into the waist) and myriad other essentials. Then came the decoration of the vessel. It was usual to paint a portrait of the galleon's namesake on the flat face of the stern; this was usually a saint, the Virgin Mary or some other religiously inspired figure. Gilding was added to the poop cabins, the beak, the figurehead, and elsewhere when funds were available. Otherwise the interior of the ship was left unpainted, while the upper portions of the outer hull and superstructure were often painted in bands; these were predominantly black or ochre, but also bright yellow, red, blue and sometimes white. Flags were supplied for each mast, usually bearing the royal coat of arms, while additional flags were brought on board when the vessel was serving in a particular fleet, or to signify that a fleet commander was embarked. The last step was to provision the ship, a process which could take weeks, or even months. The galleon was then ready for use.

The nomenclature of the decks developed from the design of medieval castles rather than ships. The *bodega* (hold) and the *primera cubierta* (lower deck or gun deck) were shared with other Spanish ships such as naos and carvels. Behind the mainmast the sterncastle rose up in tiers. Collectively it was called the *tolda*, meaning 'awning', a reference to the makeshift protection of earlier ships. More commonly, the space was called the *alcázar* (fortress). At the top of the *alcázar*, the little cabin at the end of the poop deck was known as the *toldilla*, again signifying a temporary shelter from the elements. The space beneath it as far as the waist was known as the *camarote*; this space provided the living quarters of the highest-ranking people on board. Further forward the forecastle was known as the *castillo* (castle).

The terms *alcázar* and *castillo* are indicative of the way the Spanish viewed tactics, relying on their infantry to dominate the battle rather than their ordnance. Furthermore these high structures had a detrimental effect on the sailing qualities of the ship, making it hard to handle in certain winds, and prone to creep to leeward. This said, galleons were not the lumbering vessels they have often been portrayed as, and compared to most contemporary ships such as naos or carracks they were nimble sailing ships. With their elegant lines, it could even be said that they were graceful vessels, and if their high stern structures did little else, it made them appear imposing, like floating bastions filled with the finest-trained musketeers of the day.

Arming the Armada

The furnishing of ordnance for the galleons was the responsibility of the crown, which meant that royal administrators maintained meticulous records of guns, ammunition and artillery equipment. Even the captains of surviving ships from the Armada of 1588 were expected to produce detailed returns explaining just how much powder and shot they used during the campaign, and why. Legislation also laid down the regulation number and size of guns to be carried on royal galleons, and from 1552 this also specified the manning ratios of ordnance, and their standard allocation of powder and shot. Fortunately for us the Spanish took their bureaucracy very seriously, and each ship of the Armada had its own file, detailing the guns carried, their allocation of shot – and – if they returned home again – the number of shot they fired at the English.

The crown furnished its galleons with guns produced in royal foundries, and in most cases with powder and shot produced in royal workshops. Guns were allocated to a specific ship for the duration of the campaign, with most being issued from the Lisbon arsenal. If the ship returned safely, these guns and their related stores would be unloaded and returned to the royal warehouses. It was a cumbersome procedure, but it managed to make the best possible use of resources, and it usually resulted in the galleons having the guns they needed for a particular mission. Although there was a shortage of suitable ordnance in the 1580s, the Spanish managed to procure guns from abroad, most notably from the foundries of northern Italy, Flanders and central Germany.

A Spanish technical specification showing three *media culebrinas* (demi-culverins), c.1587. The ordnance experts who drew the diagram argued in the document that the middle gun is ideally suited for use on board a ship, being short and easy to handle. Despite this, many of the guns recovered from Spanish Armada wrecks more closely resembled the longer, older guns shown in this diagram (Archivo General de Simancas, Valladolid).

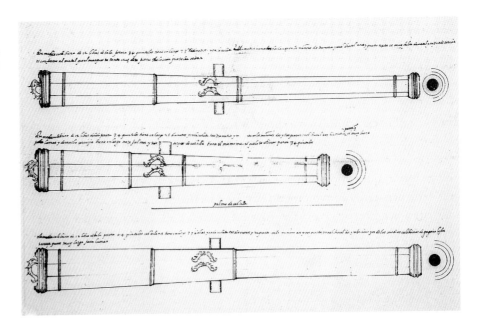

The Spanish used several families of guns: *canões* (cannons), *culebrinas* (culverins), *pedreros* (stone-shotted guns), *bombardettas* (wrought-iron guns) and *versos* (swivel guns). Of these, the *canões* were large, stubby, heavy pieces, with a higher ratio of calibre to length than the more commonly used *culebrinas*. This latter group was subdivided into *culebrinas* and *media culebrinas*, both of which were longer and lighter than *canões* or the even larger *canões de batir*. *Pedreros* were becoming increasingly rare during the later 16th century, as the cost of producing specially shaped stone shot was becoming increasingly high. Short-range weapons, these *pedreros* were short-barrelled pieces, with a smaller powder chamber than bore. They were primarily seen as close-range anti-personnel weapons and though still carried on galleons until the 1620s they were no longer considered modern weapons.

Bombardettas were the wrought-iron, breech-loading pieces which had first appeared on board Spanish vessels around 1400. Their range was considerably less than a similar-sized bronze gun, largely due to the leakage of gas from the breech (and therefore a loss of muzzle pressure) when the weapon was fired. They remained in use until the final years of the 16th century, but they last saw service on Spanish royal galleons in the 1570s. Most inventories of the 1580s and later referred to them as 'obsolete weapons', although they were issued extensively to the armed merchantmen which made up the bulk of the Squadron of Hulks and the Levant Squadron in the Armada.

The final group, the *versos*, were short-range anti-personnel guns, fired from swivel mounts attached to the ship's rail. These came in a range of types and sizes, but in general terms the *verso* fired a 1lb ball, the longer and larger *verso doble* a 1½lb shot, and the largest of the group, the *esmeril*, fired a 2½lb projectile. All weapons of the *verso* family were breech-loading, meaning they could be reloaded extremely quickly when required. They could also fire either solid shot or anti-personnel grapeshot.

The following table shows the most common artillery pieces carried on board Spanish galleons during the campaign, with the approximate corresponding English ordnance name in parenthesis. It must be noted that these figures represent the average in a wide range of weights, calibres and gun sizes, as there was little attempt at standardization during the period. Each piece of ordnance was somewhat unique, and was even listed in the Spanish archives by its weight, as it was extremely rare for two pieces to weigh exactly the same. To avoid confusion, while gun weight is given in *libras* (Spanish pounds), all other figures are presented in their English form.

Average gun sizes, 1570–1640

Gun type	Shot weight	Calibre (bore)	Gun Weight (bronze)	Gun length
Canón (Demi-cannon)	24 libras	6in.	5,400 libras	11ft
Culebrina (Culverin)	16 libras	5½in.	4,300 libras	12ft
Medio culebrina (Demi-culverin)	11 libras	4½in	3,000 libras	10ft
Sacre (Saker)	7 libras	3½in.	2,000 libras	8ft
Medio sacre (Minion)	3½ libras	2½in.	1,400 libras	7ft

In most accounts of the Armada, the 22 galleons which participated in the enterprise are described as varying considerably in size and armament. Eight were between 500 and 600 *toneladas* and carried around 24 guns, eight more were larger 700–850-*tonelada* galleons carrying 30–40 guns, and three were enormous 1,000-*tonelada* vessels armed with approximately 50 guns apiece. In addition three smaller galleons of 250–350 *toneladas* were armed with 20–24 guns each. Like all vessels of the period, the total armament included all ordnance, from the largest *canónes* to the *verso dobles*. However, it appears that, in most cases, *versos* were not counted, as they usually fired a ball smaller than a falcon (or *falconeta*), the equivalent of an English 'falconet', the smallest listed artillery piece of its day, firing a 1lb or 1¼lb shot.

Discounting approximately a quarter of the pieces as being large swivel guns, this meant that a typical Spanish Armada galleon of 500 *toneladas* carried approximately 18 heavy guns, while a larger 750-*tonelada* galleon would have carried 24–30 large pieces. As they usually had to carry specie, passengers and a company of soldiers, most Spanish galleons of the late 16th century were adequately rather than generously provided with artillery. However, it was expected that the guns would be used to fire a single broadside before the Spanish and English ships collided, at which point the Spanish soldiers would swing into action and win the day. It was all part of a scheme of armament based on a tactic that made the best possible use of the Spanish infantry on board. All the galleon commanders had to do was to manoeuvre their ships alongside the enemy.

✢ Elizabeth's Navy

Introduction

Queen Elizabeth I of England was unable to match her Spanish rival when it came to resources. However, by 1588 the Navy Royal had been built up into a respectable force of 34 royal warships, while another 192 privately owned armed merchantmen of various sizes were available, and could be pressed into service to make up numbers. Of course, these totals hid the fact that many of these ships were too small to take an active part in the fighting. Instead they were used to ferry troops, to carry messages and supplies, and to give the appearance of parity in numbers with the Spanish fleet.

Just as significantly, the English had no large standing army, capable of standing up to the Spanish if they managed to establish themselves on the coast of England. The Duke of Parma's veterans would be faced by a small band of professional soldiers supported by a substantial but largely untrained and inexperienced militia. That meant that if the Spanish succeeded in landing, then nothing short of a miracle could prevent them marching on London. Still, Elizabeth and her advisors made the best use of their limited resources that they could. First, they enlisted the help of their Dutch allies, whose ships were able to pin the Duke of Parma's army and landing ships in the Flemish ports. Only the arrival of the Spanish Armada would drive them off, and allow the duke to begin his Channel crossing.

The key to the assembly of the Tudor fleet was the royal dockyards in Deptford, Portsmouth, Chatham and Woolwich, as well as the private facilities in ports such as Plymouth, Southampton and Bristol. This was where the armed merchantmen were fitted with extra ordnance, and where the royal warships were prepared for battle. Queen Elizabeth and her advisors were well aware that the survival of the realm depended on the fleet, and so all available resources were used to prepare and arm the ships, ready for the coming fight. While the militias watched the coast, and signal beacons were prepared, this fleet of warships gathered in Plymouth and the Downs, and its commanders decided how best to handle their charges.

Above all, Elizabeth relied on her experienced naval commanders to divert the Spanish Armada from its course. After all, men such as Drake, Hawkins and Frobisher had a lot of experience in naval combat with the Spanish, and while their opponents might have been unaware of the full naval potential of Elizabeth's fleet, these men knew what to expect when the Spanish appeared. They knew their enemy, and how best to defeat, or at least to divert them. The whole campaign now hinged on the activities of this small band of 'sea dogs'. Unable to match the Spanish in numbers, they hoped to use the English advantage in naval gunnery to win the day. This was the great English 'trump card'. Unable to match the Spanish in a boarding action, the English had little option but to place their faith in gunpowder, and the Protestant religion.

Queen Elizabeth I of England (1533–1603), an oil painting by John Better the Younger. Elizabeth actively encouraged the 'cold war' with Spain, but her open support of the Protestant rebels in the Netherlands made a full-blown war all but inevitable (National Maritime Museum, Greenwich, London).

85

The Fleet

The mainstay of the Elizabethan fleet during the Spanish Armada campaign were the 34 warships of the Navy Royal. Of these, only 13 were large, well-armed warships of modern design – race-built galleons of 500 tons or more. The remainder were substantially smaller. By comparison, the Spanish Armada consisted of 130 ships, over half of which were 500 tons or more, and seven of these exceeded 1,000 tons. In short, for the most part the English ships were not as large as their Spanish adversaries. They also possessed smaller crews, and only a relatively small number of soldiers were embarked. This placed the English ships at a grave disadvantage if the Spanish managed to board them.

Queen Elizabeth's royal warships comprised only 18 per cent of the total English fleet. In addition to the 34 royal ships, the English fleet also consisted of 34 armed merchant ships from Plymouth, 33 from Portsmouth and 30 from London (with an average tonnage of around 150 tons), plus 43 armed coasters (with an average displacement of around 100 tons). In all, the fleet consisted of 197 ships and 15,925 men. While this meant it was more numerous than the Spanish in terms of ships, many of these vessels were too small to do anything other than make up the numbers.

The Ships

Like that of their Spanish opponents, only a small portion of the English fleet consisted of royal warships. Queen Elizabeth I maintained 21 warships of 200 tons or more, and of these, only four had been built in the decade preceding the Armada. These four – the *Revenge*, the *Vanguard*, the *Rainbow* and the fleet flagship *Ark Royal* – were designed from the keel up as 'race-built' galleons, under the supervision of John Hawkins. Compared to Spanish galleons, the English ships had far less superstructure and carried a more homogenous and powerful armament. They were also faster than Spanish vessels of a similar size, and the sail plan of one of them (presumably the *Revenge*) shows a graceful ship which combined power with speed.

The genius of Hawkins as a naval administrator lay in the work he conducted on the rest of the royal fleet. Most of the remaining vessels were carracks: the equivalent

Opposite
Francis Drake, pictured during his raids on the Spanish Main in the 1570s. More than anyone else, he was responsible for the escalation of tensions between England and Spain during this period. To the English he was a national hero – to the Spanish he was nothing more than a pirate.

FRANCISCVS DRAECK · NOBILISSIMVS
EQVES ANGLIAE · IS EST QVI TOTO T
TERRARVM   ORBE CRCMDVGO

jd circumducto pernosco
in longitudine, in latitudi
ne est impossibile, etc

This small 250-ton galleon was built during 1573 by Peter Pett, the Royal Master Shipwright at Deptford, and the father of several shipwrights, including Phineas Pett, who built the *Sovereign of the Seas* (1637). The *Swiftsure* was one of the first of the English race-built galleons designed by Sir John Hawkins, and until the launch of the Revenge four years later, she and her sister the *Dreadnought* were considered the fastest warships in the fleet, despite criticisms in some quarters that they were too lightly built. This criticism might well have led to the rebuilding of both vessels in 1592, making them the only Hawkins galleons to be rebuilt during their designer's lifetime. The *Swiftsure* formed part of the usual Guard Fleets in home waters during the 'Cold War' with Spain, and participated in the Siege of Smerwick in 1580. During the Armada campaign of 1588, she formed part of Drake's squadron, under the command of Captain Edward Fenner (Tony Bryan).

of the Spanish nao, although designed as warships rather than as merchantmen. The bulk were built during the 1560s, when English naval doctrine was similar to the Spanish, placing an emphasis on the ship as a bastion – a platform from which to fight a boarding action or to repel one. Hawkins instituted an extensive programme of refurbishment and refitting from 1578, and by the time of the Armada campaign they had been transformed into vessels more akin to the latest race-built galleons. Even though they were old and broader in the beam than the latest vessels, they were still faster and more weatherly than any Spanish opponent.

In 1587 the royal shipwrights Peter Pett and Matthew Baker surveyed the entire royal fleet of 34 vessels and proclaimed that several of the older royal warships, such as the *Mary Rose*, built in 1557, were in 'dangerous' condition. However, the *Mary Rose* still took an active part in the campaign. These royal ships were the best warships afloat, and more than a match for the powerful galleons of the Spanish fleet. The bulk of the English fleet consisted of merchant vessels bought into the queen's service for the

Specifications

Displacement:	350 tons
Keel length:	74ft (22.6m) approx.
Beam:	30ft (9.1m)
Armament:	34 guns
Crew:	130 sailors, 20 gunners, 30 soldiers

Service notes:
Built 1573. Rebuilt 1592. Renamed *Speedwell*, 1607. Foundered off Dutch coast, 1624.

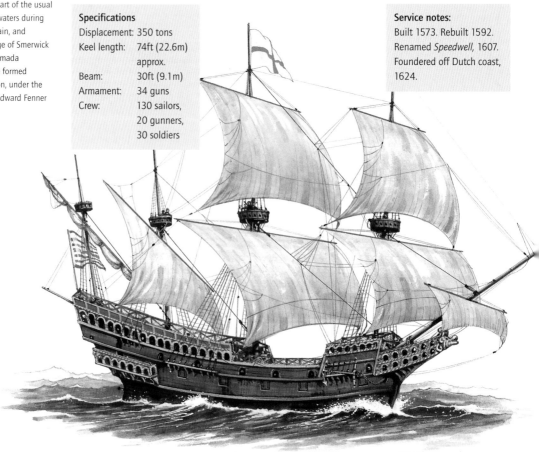

duration of the campaign. Records concerning the hiring and equipping of these ships are fragmentary, but enough survive to provide an outline of this auxiliary force. One part was a 'volunteer reserve' of armed merchant ships which had volunteered to form part of the fleet; others were simply pressed into service, along with their crews.

Some 30 or so of these armed merchant ships displaced over 200 tons, and carried up to 40 guns, making them the equivalent of many of the armed merchant vessels in the Spanish fleet. Some were veterans of Drake's privateering expedition to the Spanish Main three years earlier, and others had taken part in the raid on Cadiz in 1587. Many were owned by the senior English commanders or by families connected to them by marital or mercantile bonds. Lord Charles Howard owned seven privateers or armed merchant vessels which took part in the campaign, while Hawkins owned two and Drake three. One problem was that of the 163 private ships which took part in the campaign, 108 displaced less than 100 tons. In the words of Sir William Winter, the Master of Ordnance for the Tudor navy: 'If you had seen what I have seen of the

Tiger, 1580
The *Tiger* was first built as a 160-ton galleass, a reaction to Henry VIII's witnessing the French galley fleet in action off Portsmouth in 1545. She was launched in 1546, but within three years she was re-designated as a ship. The original probably involved little more than the removal of her sweeps. Her galley-like hull shape set her and her sister ship the *Bull* apart from the rest of the fleet, and made the two converted vessels ideal candidates for a second conversion. This time the hulls were modified considerably, in accordance with the design ideas proposed by Sir John Hawkins. The rebuilding was a success, and so from 1570 onwards the *Tiger* was re-designated as a 200-ton galleon. The illustration shows the *Tiger* as she looked during the siege of Smerwick in 1580, based on her depiction in a contemporary illustration of the action (Tony Bryan).

Specifications
Displacement: 464 tons
Keel length: 70ft (21.3m)
               approx.
Beam: 28ft (8.5m)
               approx.
Armament: 43 guns
Crew: Approx. 100 men

Service notes:
Built 1546. Rebuilt 1570.
Converted into floating
battery at Chatham,
1600. Condemned, 1605

simple service that hath been done by the merchant and coast ships, you would have said that we had been little helped by them, otherwise than that they did make a show.' They were of little practical use in the campaign, but the English were facing an unprecedented threat and any vessel was better than none at all.

This collection of ships included carracks, hoys, pinnaces and cromsters, terms which needs some explanation. Certainly we need to understand how these vessels differed from the more prestigious race-built galleons and older converted royal carracks which made up the striking force of the Navy Royal.

The race-built galleon

From 1575 onwards, English shipwrights developed a variant of the galleon, encouraged by revolutionary administrators such as John Hawkins and master shipwrights such as Matthew Baker. The 500-ton *Revenge* completed in 1577 was the first of the type, and boasted a hull with smooth, graceful lines, designed for speed as well as the capacity to hold a powerful armament. Compared to Spanish galleons, these vessels were lower, having much less superstructure, with the towering galleon sterncastle replaced by a gently sloping quarterdeck. These English ships had a larger hull length to beam ratio, giving them the racy profile the designers wanted, powered by a sail plan which allowed for more canvas to be carried than on larger Spanish vessels. Above all, these vessels were designed from the hull up to fight in a gunnery action, not to serve as a platform from which to board the enemy. Hawkins also rebuilt the older galleons and carracks of the Elizabethan navy to resemble the smoother lines of his race-built design.

The royal carrack

The *Jesus of Lubeck*, the royal warship lent to John Hawkins in 1568, typifies this vessel type. The 700-ton German carrack was bought into English service by Henry VIII in 1545, and 20 years later was considered unseaworthy. The elderly vessel was converted by cutting down the towering forecastle and sterncastle structures, and its hull was patched before it could be used by Hawkins, although it retained the advantage of being a good artillery platform and had a spacious hold. Several of these royal carracks (sometimes referred to as galleons) including the *Triumph*, *Victory*, *White Bear* and *Elizabeth Bonaventure* were refitted during the Hawkins administration between 1578 and 1589. The aim was to turn them into race-built galleons, but, given their broad hulls and bluff bows, this was only partially successful, the refitting concentrating on reducing superstructure and improving the sail configuration. They were rarely used before or after the Armada campaign, but comprised some of the most powerful and best-armed vessels of the English fleet. Slower than pure race-built galleons, they were significantly more manoeuvrable than their Spanish counterparts, and were superior to the larger Spanish galleons in terms of sailing qualities.

Pinnaces, shallops and hoys

The small auxiliary vessels went by a variety of names, the distinctions between them remaining obscure. A pinnace in an illustration depicting the English fleet's attack on the Spanish fortified beachhead at Smerwick in Ireland (1580) shows a three-masted vessel with a 50ft keel and a beam of around 17ft, and displacing approximately 60 tons. This is one of the larger vessels of the pinnace type, as others have been recorded as displacing 20–40 tons. The typical pinnace could be powered by oar or sail, and most probably resembled the patache used by the Spanish, although it frequently served as the towed auxiliary boat for a larger warship rather than as an independent vessel. A larger version of the pinnace was the bark, which was a three-masted vessel of between 100 and 250 tons, capable of transatlantic voyages. A common type of English merchant vessel during the late 16th century, barks were frequently used by Elizabethan commanders as small warships.

Cromsters

The cromster was a Dutch vessel which became increasingly popular as an English trading vessel during the late 16th century. They were small, beamy and shallow-draughted vessels, initially designed for trade in Dutch waters, but capable of being converted into miniature warships. They carried fore-and-aft rigged sails and spritsails, and their sturdy construction allowed them to carry a heavy armament. With a small draught, cromsters were ideal for operations in the estuaries of the Netherlands, and they became the mainstay of the coastal fleets of the Sea Beggars.

Many of these ships were tiny – often displacing less than 100 tons. Still, small ships of this kind had already been used extensively by the Elizabethan 'sea dogs' during their raids against the Spanish Main, and the majority of these small royal ships or armed merchantmen were capable of adding their firepower to the rest of the fleet.

The fleet therefore contained a cross-section of the vessels used by the English during the period, from large royal carracks to armed merchantmen, privateering vessels and small barks and pinnaces. The latter were towed during the transatlantic voyage, but were included to act as scouting craft.

A reconstruction of the 100-ton *Golden Hind* was built in 1974, providing a practical tool with which to understand the performance of these smaller vessels. The original *Golden Hind* was the vessel used by Sir Francis Drake during his voyage of circumnavigation (1577–80). Originally called the *Pelican*, the vessel carried a powerful armament of 18 demi-culverins on truck carriages. Approximately 70ft long, it had a beam of around 20ft (although as its displacement and dimensions were not recorded, historians are still arguing about its size). The small main deck was pierced by a hold, and gave access to compartments under the sterncastle which

For the individual required to supply a weapon for militia service, a bow was far cheaper than a firearm. The archer of the York levy (centre left) is a farmer performing his own service as he cannot afford a paid substitute. Though he has supplied all the required equipment, its state of repair leaves much to be desired. His armour is a 'jack' coat of iron plates sewn onto canvas – a popular, though increasingly outdated alternative. In his quiver, eight of the 24 arrows would have had thinner feathers to increase their range, though this came at the expense of accuracy. The militia's cheapest available weapon was the bill. Often improvised from an agricultural or forestry tool, many soldiers regarded the bill as next to useless, and efforts were ongoing to re-arm billmen (centre right) with pikes. In 1590 Sir George Carew wrote from Ireland that the best use he had for 'brown bills' was to sell them to farmers of the Dublin pale. This billman would have inherited his equipment and the brigandine – a doublet reinforced by metal studs and plates – he wears, dates from Henry VIII's campaigns. Replacing the hackbut as the standard firearm during the middle of the 16th century, the caliver was popular due to its standard bore, which made training and ammunition supply much easier, and for the economy of its use. Sir Roger Williams claimed that a caliver would fire 20-30 shots for each pound of powder, while a musket would only manage 8-12. He was not complete in his praise, however, as he also recognised that the musket's heavier bullet would do much more damage. Despite this flaw, calivermen (left) were the most common firearms troops in the English armies. With thousands of men available to be enrolled in the militia but few arms to equip them with, the government decided upon the formation of pioneer units (right), which were put to work fortifying possible landing beaches and select places of retreat. They were armed with sword, dagger and the shovels, mattocks and axes of their trade (Richard Hook).

formed a cabin, a whipstaff (steering) position and a chartroom all in one, and a forecastle space used to house two bowchasers and a boatswain's store. Above the cabin was a small poop deck and Drake's small cabin.

The main gundeck ran the full length of the ship and housed the armament and the crew quarters, while below it the orlop deck was used to hold stores. The vessel seems impossibly small today, but in 1577 it sailed with a complement of 80 men and boys crammed into its hull. Drake enjoyed his comforts, and his small cabin contained oak furniture and silver plate, while musicians were embarked to provide amusement. The seamen were not so fortunate, and even the officers shared a space

smaller than most prison cells today. The foremast and mainmast carried two square sails each, while a spritsail was bent onto the bowsprit, and the mizzen mast carried a triangular lateen sail. The replica vessel carries over 4,000 square feet of canvas, and on occasion has exceeded eight knots. The hull length–beam ratio of roughly 2:1 is typical of armed merchantmen of the period, but the race-built galleons envisaged by John Hawkins and built by shipwrights such as Matthew Baker had a 3:1 ratio, and consequently were faster through the water. Vessels of this type formed the true backbone of the fleets which sailed under the leading 'sea dogs' of the Elizabethan period.

The figures in this plate represent the English veterans who were recalled from service in the Low Countries to resist the Armada and are based upon De Gheyn's 1587 series of drawings of Dutch soldiers. The musketeer (centre) wears an early example of the low-crowned, broad-brimmed hat which was to become almost the standard headgear for musketeers in the next century. He wears a padded doublet under a short cassack with nagging sleeves, and carries a musket rest. The caliver (left) continued in Dutch military service until 1609, but it is not clear how it and the musket were arranged in battle. In the battle plan drawn up for the English army at Tilbury the musketeers were used to screen the advance of the pikes, but formed a small percentage of the total of the shot. This pikeman (right) wears the full equipment of the 'corslet', comprising a combed morion, gorget, peascod breast and back plate, tassets to protect the thigh, pauldrons and vambraces to protect the arms, and metal-faced gauntlets (Richard Hook).

Organization

We have already noted that warships of the Navy Royal only made up a relatively small portion of the Tudor fleet in 1588. The English fleet that sailed out of Plymouth in late July 1588 consisted of just 19 warships of the Navy Royal, accompanied by no fewer than 54 armed merchant vessels. A further 21 armed merchantmen temporarily joined the fleet during the fighting off the Devon coast. A secondary force stationed off the Downs in Kent was more equally balanced, with seven royal warships and seven armed merchantman in the squadron. However, this force was reinforced by 17 additional armed merchantmen mid-way through the campaign, making the proportion of royal ships to hired ships in the squadron similar to that in the main fleet.

If we discount the 15 volunteer merchantmen that displaced less than 90 tons, we find that the main fleet consisted of 19 royal ships and 79 merchantmen, the royal ships being approximately 24 per cent of the total. Similarly, if we include the additions to the Downs Squadron, we reach a tally of seven royal ships to 31 merchantmen, or 23 per cent of the total. This means that for every royal ship that sailed out to fight the Spanish that year, three armed merchantmen sailed alongside her. While Hawkins' race-built galleons might have formed the fighting core of the fleet, the majority of the force — some 44 ships, or 40 per cent of the English fleet — consisted of privately owned vessels displacing between 150 and 250 tons. Although the records of the time described the vessels as armed merchantmen, this was something of a misnomer. Many of these were the ships used by men such as Drake and Hawkins during their expeditions, or else were fitted out and operated as 'privateers', or private warships. Some were even race-built galleons, and so were the equals in manoeuvrability and firepower to equivalent-sized warships in the Navy Royal.

Initially, the organization of the fleet was extremely loose, with the fleet operating as a large body and commands allocated without a clear rationale, though we shall see that the lessons learned during the early battles led Lord Charles Howard to adopt a more sensible structure after 3 August 1588.

Of course, the whole English Navy Royal had always been organized along fairly footloose lines. In times of peace warships were often leased out to private shipowners, or lent as the royal 'stake' in a large privateering venture. Although the process of hiring out warships for commercial gain had been practised by her father Henry VIII, Elizabeth turned this procedure into a form of strategic policy, one that greatly reduced the cost of maintaining her fleet and offered the chance of substantial profit. Above all, it turned the business of England's naval defence into a commercial venture, where men such as Drake, Hawkins, Frobisher and Raleigh all stood to gain from their achievements. This unusual policy worked, creating a breed of commanders willing to take extraordinary risks in the service of their queen — and for their own profit. The question remained whether such a haphazard system would still work during the largest and most important naval campaign in English history.

The English Way of War

The major advantage the English had over the Spaniards was in gunnery. The Spanish relied on an older design of two-wheeled gun carriage for their armament and usually lashed these guns and carriages to the sides of their ships to absorb the recoil when they were fired. By contrast, the English had developed a four-wheeled truck carriage that allowed the gun to be run up closer to the gun port, making the piece easier to aim or to traverse. Also, the gun's weight was distributed between four points, each of them a small truck wheel. The Spanish relied on two-wheeled carriages which resembled land guns, but with solid or almost solid wheels. On some vessels, these wheels could be as much as three feet high, making the piece unwieldy, and also distributing the weight onto three points (two wheels and a trail). Another significant innovation was that the English developed a simple system of blocks, ropes and tackles which allowed the guns to be pulled inboard by their own recoil, reloaded and then run out again with the minimum amount of effort. The same system was refined until it became the standard form of mounting and firing naval guns in the 17th century. First seen on the *Mary Rose* (1545), this system remained in use with very little variation until well into the 19th century.

An English race-built galleon, showing the way Tudor warships of this period were painted and decorated. Also of note are the bronze guns mounted on four-wheeled carriages in the waist of the ship. From Matthew Baker's *Fragments of Ancient English Shipwrightry* (c.1582) (By permission of the Master and Fellows, Magdalene College, Cambridge).

This simple advantage, combined with a dearth of 'sea soldiers', dictated English tactics: to avoid boarding and to bombard the Armada using artillery. It was only in the closing battle of the campaign that the English commanders used this to best effect, moving within close range so that every shot would count. The English could effectively outmanoeuvre and outshoot their Spanish opponents, dictating when, where and how the engagement was fought.

Gun crews were smaller than in later periods. Sir Walter Raleigh stated that late 16th-century gun crews usually consisted of four men, while early 17th-century sources list crews numbering between two and five men, depending on the size of the gun. The Anthony Roll of 1546 gives the organization of late Tudor crews, with the *Mary Rose* (as an example) carrying 30 heavy guns, 30 gunners, 185 soldiers and 200 mariners. This procedure continued throughout the Elizabethan period, although the number of soldiers was gradually decreased during the last half of the 16th century. It is clear that one gunner was allocated to each gun, but if a full gun crew was supplied from the ranks of the soldiers and mariners, firing and reloading would involve most of the ship's complement, apart from archers, arquebusiers, swivel gun crews and a handful of sailors to handle the ship.

English bronze and even cast-iron guns were considered of high quality, and English sailors using four-wheeled truck carriages could rely on their equipment and skill to maintain a constant fire, limited only by the available supplies of powder and shot. The fact that the English were running out of ammunition in the middle of the Armada campaign and the Spanish were not is clear evidence of the different gunnery methods the opponents relied on to win the battle.

By the mid-16th century, artillery had established itself as a necessary tool in naval warfare. It was still not the dominant weapon type, but instead formed part of an integrated range of weaponry. Evidence from the warship *Mary Rose* which sank in Portsmouth harbour in 1545 emphasizes this integrated approach. It

These soldiers are based on the *Image of Ireland* by John Derricke, 1581, which depicts the English army on campaign against the Irish rebels. They may be taken to represent militiamen from the maritime counties whose dress and equipment was up to the required standard but not of the most up-to-date style and fashion.

The caliverman (centre) wears a combed morion, a canvas 'jack' tightly laced across the chest, 'Venetian' breeches, stockings and low shoes. He carries a left-handed caliver, as do all the shot in Derricke's plates. One picture shows these being fired from the left shoulder.

The pikeman (right) wears full armour, but with no tassets. His breeches are of the 'trunk hose with canions' style more often worn by officers, probably indicating that he is somewhat more wealthy than the average soldier.

At this time, and for a century to come, officers (left) did not wear uniform coats even where these had been issued. This officer wears a highly decorated burgonet-style helmet and an impressive but impractical ruff. His breast and back plates are worn over a leather jerkin (Richard Hook).

Again based on the *Image of Ireland* by John Derricke, 1581, this ensign (centre) wears a feathered flat cap that was fashionable under Henry VIII but outdated by the time of the Armada. His lack of armour save for a gorget and decorated clothes could mark him as a young or newly-appointed officer. The standard he bears depicts the cross of St. George and four Tudor roses.
The drummer (left) wears a flat-topped, narrow-brimmed hat and a peascod with small shoulder wings, a small stand-up collar and very small skirts below the waist. His breeches are trunk hose with canions, worn with a codpiece.
Recruited from amongst the ranks of the reivers of the Anglo-Scottish border, the border horseman (right) served in the northern English counties to defend against possible Scottish invasions. they were armed with their own equipment, and wore long mailcoats, spears and small bucklers, here bearing St. George's cross (Richard Hook).

carried a mixture of ordnance, including large bronze pieces as well as wrought-iron breech-loading guns mounted on wooden beds. Swivel guns mounted on the ship's rail provided close-range firepower, augmented by hackbutts and arquebuses. On board, archers outnumbered firearm-carrying infantry, while bills and other staff weapons were provided for use during a boarding action. To complete the array, firepots and other incendiary weapons were carried in limited numbers. The *Mary Rose* was designed primarily as a platform for close-range weaponry, and its ability to engage in a protracted artillery duel was minimal.

Naval tactics had developed by the middle of the century to take advantage of the revolution created by ship-borne artillery. Two theories had emerged, the more traditional based around using the ship as an integrated weapon and favouring boarding actions; the other, more revolutionary notion advocated using the artillery carried on board as the primary offensive weapon. The English, and to a lesser

The battle off 'Dunne Nose' – St Catherine's Point on the Isle of Wight – from *The Armada's progress from Plymouth to Gravelines*, a series of contemporary engravings by Claes Jansz Visscher. Although tactically inaccurate, the artist gives a good impression of the ships involved, and the way in which they fought (Stratford Archive).

extent the Dutch and the French, took full advantage of the introduction of reliable artillery to rethink their approach to naval warfare. Although circumstance largely dictated which approach was used, these nations tended to develop a doctrine based on the use of artillery as an offensive weapon. In short, the Spanish relied on boarding to win a sea battle, while their enemies preferred to keep their distance and rely on gunnery to win the fight.

The Spanish were also deficient in the way their gun crews were organized. During the Armada campaign, gun crews consisted of a gunner and six soldiers. Once the gun was loaded the soldiers picked up their weapons and prepared to fight a boarding action. From all this it is evident that if more than one salvo was fired, reloading would involve a significant drop in the vessel's ability to fight a boarding action. In other words, it was one or the other, boarding or broadsides, but not both. It has been suggested that before a ship engaged in combat the captain would decide what sort of engagement he planned to fight, and would organize his crews accordingly.

An analysis of the artillery shot recovered from Spanish Armada wrecks provides an invaluable insight into Spanish gunnery during the campaign of 1588. Archival research recorded what quantities were issued when the various ships sailed. While almost no swivel gun or wrought-iron breech-loading ammunition was recovered, most of the shot issued for the larger guns was still carried on board when each ship went down. This indicated that the larger the gun, the less often it was fired during the Armada battles. It is imagined that much of the close-range firing was performed during the battle off Gravelines, the last engagement of the campaign. The problems of reloading large demi-culverins on two-wheeled carriages were so acute that the pieces were rarely fired, in some cases only one or two shots being fired each day from the biggest guns.

The short-range breech-loaders and swivels were easier to reload, and consequently were used more. Another factor was the reliability of guns. From a sample of around two dozen Spanish Armada bronze guns, two show significant structural defects, and one of these apparently blew a chunk out of its barrel when it was being fired. The Spanish usually elected to fight a boarding action, and their guns were designed to fire once prior to boarding. If reloading them would disrupt the ship's preparedness for fighting a boarding action, and if some of the guns were considered unreliable, then the lack of Spanish enthusiasm for fighting a gunnery action is understandable.

English bronze and even cast-iron guns were considered of high quality, and English sailors using four-wheeled truck carriages could rely on their equipment and skill to maintain a constant fire, limited only by the available supplies of powder and shot. The fact that the English were running out of ammunition in the middle of the Armada campaign and the Spanish were not is clear evidence of the different gunnery methods the opponents relied on to win the battle.

Once these guns were fired, they had to be reloaded. The physical problems have already been discussed, but reloading had tactical implications as well. In a number of contemporary accounts of gunnery actions, vessels are said to have fired a broadside, then turned, presenting their bow or stern guns to the enemy and fired the other broadside after continuing to turn. This derived from the notion that in order to reload in safety, a ship would have to retire to a safe distance from the enemy, or alternatively, reload on the disengaged side while firing the rest of its armament at the enemy. The tactic used was similar to the carracole, a contemporary cavalry evolution, where a column of riders took turns to fire at the enemy, retiring to the rear rank to reload. It was not uncommon for a warship to fight an enemy by sailing in a 'figure of eight', alternately firing each part of its heavy armament at the enemy while reloading on the disengaged side. These tactics were a far cry from the 'line of battle' actions fought from the late 17th century onwards.

The Spanish Armada campaign was the ultimate test for English theories about naval gunnery. Unfortunately, despite the ability of the English to bombard the enemy at long range while keeping out of trouble themselves, gunfire alone was never powerful enough to weaken the Spanish Armada seriously. The exception was the close range engagement fought off Gravelines, a loose mêlée when the English ships came close enough to their opponents to inflict serious damage. For the entire campaign, the Spanish maintained a dense formation, where each ship was supported by several others. In a number of occasions during the progress up the English Channel the Spanish broke the formation to rescue ships which had fallen behind, or to attack isolated groups of English ships.

The English were unable to make any impression on the dense Armada formation. Gunnery alone seemed unable to break up an enemy fleet. It was only when the formation was broken that the English were able to gain a tactical advantage over their adversaries, and with their faster vessels and efficient artillery were able to concentrate on individual Spanish ships. Throughout the campaign the Spanish relied on their 'boarding action' tactic, but the English simply stayed out of the way, although often the two fleets came close enough to fire arquebuses at each other. The successes of many of the Elizabethan 'sea dogs' arose from their ability to understand the tactical problems facing both themselves and their opponents, and their skill in adapting these limitations to their advantage.

Lord Thomas Howard, Sir Walter
Raleigh and the capture of Cadiz,
1596.
In 1596 a massive Anglo-Dutch
expedition was launched to attack
Cadiz, consisting of 30 warships,
a fleet of transports and 8,000
English and Dutch soldiers.
A Spanish fleet lay in Cadiz roads,
protected by shore fortifications. At
a council of war held on the evening
of 20 August on board the *Ark Royal*,
it was decided to attack the fleet first,
then assault the town. The following
morning Sir Walter Raleigh led the
attack which forced its way into the
inner harbour, and in a hotly
contested engagement he defeated
or forced aground the entire Spanish
fleet. The city then lay at the mercy of
the allies, who stormed and captured
Cadiz, holding it for several weeks.
In this reconstruction of the council
of war, the fleet commander Lord
Thomas Howard (left) is arguing with
his second-in-command Sir Walter
Raleigh (right) over the best way to
attack the Spanish fleet. Robert
Devereaux, the Earl of Essex (centre)
commanding the land force
is shown gesticulating towards Cadiz,
futilely advocating that the land
assault should take precedence.
Personal feuds between Howard,
Raleigh and Devereaux created
tensions during the operation, and
were typical of several of the larger
Elizabethan maritime ventures,
when personality clashes proved
a detriment to the operation. This
animosity is evident in the scene,
and the lesser naval commanders,
including Sir Francis Vere (back right)
and Sir William Monson (foreground),
are evidently supporters of either
Howard or Raleigh. Note the richness
of dress of the participants, who are
dressed for a formal gathering rather
than battle (Angus McBride).

The Commanders

While the English command structure might have lacked the rigid hierarchy of the Spanish system, it did share several important characteristics. For a start, the commander-in-chief was the monarch – Queen Elizabeth I. Her commands were expected to be obeyed, whatever the personal cost to the officers involved. Her father, King Henry VIII, had not been averse to using the threat of draconian punishment to keep his noblemen in line, and Elizabeth assumed the same apparatus of state, and its implied expectation of duty. Unlike Philip II, she did not involve herself in the minutiae of naval or military preparations – instead she delegated that responsibility to able subordinates. Also, just like her Spanish counterpart, she relied on one man to command her fleet, and once it sailed from port he was in complete operational control. In effect, responsibility for the future of England now rested on the shoulders of Elizabeth's Lord Admiral, Charles Howard.

During the preparations for the campaign, Elizabeth was advised by a naval council of war, whose ranks included Lord Howard, as well as most of his senior commanders, including his vice-admirals Sir Francis Drake and Lord Henry Seymour, Sir John Hawkins, Lord Sheffield, Lord Thomas Howard, Sir Henry Palmer, the Earl of Cumberland, Thomas Fenner, Sir Martin Frobisher and Sir William Winter. The majority of these men were highly experienced seafarers, and their ranks included all of the leading 'sea dogs' of the era. All of these men also held naval commands, while Drake, Hawkins, Seymour and Frobisher were later given command of their own squadrons within the English fleet. Hawkins and Frobisher actually received their knighthoods in an attempt to deflect criticism from the noblemen on the council of war. However, when it came to appointing commanders, both Queen Elizabeth and Lord Howard clearly favoured experience over social standing.

At the start of the campaign, the fleet was organized with no clear structure, and commands were allocated on an ad hoc basis. For instance, when Drake sailed to Plymouth that May, he held no formal rank, but was still given command of a group of English ships, including royal warships. By June he and the other leading

commanders were given flag rank – Drake for instance was named as a vice-admiral. The extremely fluid command structure – or rather the lack of any structure – was due to Lord Howard, who preferred to organize the fleet as he saw fit, once he had seen the enemy, and established what the Spanish dispositions would be. This seemingly chaotic structure continued until 3 August, by which stage the Spanish Armada was halfway up the English Channel.

Contrary to popular belief, the English fleet failed to break up the Spanish battle formation as it progressed up the English Channel, and it was the lessons learned during the early fights that led to an important revision of fleet tactics and operations. From 3 August, following the battle fought off the Isle of Wight (which we shall examine in more detail later), Lord Howard divided his fleet into four more manageable squadrons, commanded by himself, Sir John Hawkins, Sir Francis Drake and Sir Martin Frobisher. Seymour commanded the fleet stationed off the Downs, where it was able to react to any move made by the Duke of Parma. This fifth squadron joined the rest of the fleet off Calais, just before the battle fought off Gravelines. This was a far more sensible organization, though it was foisted on Lord Howard more by circumstances than by design.

Once battle began Lord Howard had little chance to consult with his subordinate commanders, or to exercise tactical control over their commands. There was no plan for signalling between the ships, other than for calling all his senior commanders together for a council of war – the hoisting of a 'flag of council'. His only other signalling option was to light the stern lanterns on his flagship the *Ark Royal*, and hope that the rest of the fleet would follow him. The sole way other messages could be sent to constituent squadrons of the fleet was by small boat. This made communications nigh-on impossible, and explains why Lord Howard failed to make better use of tactical opportunities as they presented themselves off Portland and the Isle of Wight.

As we shall see later, Howard more than once made use of the Council of War option, most notably on 7 August off Calais, when he ordered the sending in of fireships, and again on 13 August, to justify his order to call off the English pursuit of the Spanish. In effect he used the council of war as a means of finding consensus amongst his commanders, and for protecting himself from royal criticism. The decision of 13 August was made in the cabin of the *Ark Royal*, and before his subordinates left, Lord Howard had them all sign a document which ensured that the decision was seen as a unanimous one. The Lord Admiral knew full well that while he was given a free rein at sea he was also accountable for his actions, and the Tudors had a nasty habit of rewarding failure with imprisonment or worse.

Lord Howard's other problem was that he knew that he could not always rely on his leading subordinates to follow orders. Hawkins, Frobisher and especially Drake were all men who had more experience as privateers than as naval commanders. They were used to fighting for plunder and glory rather than for the national good.

After the campaign, all of these men became embroiled in bitter rounds of accusations and counter-accusations, all of which centred on the division of prize money. Drake, for example, absented himself from the fleet without permission off Start Point, in order to pick off a potentially lucrative Spanish straggler. In that instance it was clear that despite his later protestations, his main incentive was financial rather than tactical.

Indeed the issue was wider than that – these men were also prickly, aggressive commanders, who were used to having things their own way. All of them were ready to bridle if they received orders that they saw either as not in their personal interest, or as favouring their maritime rivals. For instance, Lord Seymour complained when after the battle off Gravelines he was ordered back to the Downs, where he could maintain his watch on the activities of the Duke of Parma. He viewed that as a personal affront – an attempt to deny him the glory which he thought was still to be had in a final battle with the Spanish Armada. Ultimately the successful handling of these characters, and the maintenance of control over the English fleet during the campaign, was a triumph for Lord Howard. Indeed his leadership did much to ensure the ultimate failure of Philip II's 'Great Enterprise', and the salvation of Elizabethan England.

We should now take a closer look at Lord Howard, and his senior commanders:

Charles Howard, 1st Earl of Nottingham (1536-1624), an oil painting by Daniel Mytens the Elder. Lord Howard proved an effective commander, but he was unable to break up the Spanish formation as it progressed up the English Channel. However, he did approve the use of fireships off Calais, a tactic which proved devastatingly effective (National Maritime Museum, Greenwich, London).

Charles Howard, Lord Effingham (1536–1624) was appointed Lord High Admiral in 1585 and in December 1587 he took command of the naval force gathered to counter the Armada. His command style was by necessity based on collaboration, achieved through a regular council of war. He showed little ability to maintain close tactical control over his fleet once it was in action, but instead led by example. Following the campaign he was awarded the earldom of Nottingham. His flagship was the *Ark Royal* (540 tons).

Lord Henry Seymour (1540–c.1600) was appointed as the Admiral of the Narrow Seas Squadron in 1588, becoming Howard's second-in-command. He was an experienced naval leader,

Sir Francis Drake (c.1540-96), an oil painting by Marcus Gheeraerts the Younger. Despite his status as a national hero, and second-in-command of the fleet, Drake was a pirate or privateer at heart rather than a naval commander. His lucrative pursuit of the damaged galleon *Rosario* off Plymouth even threatened to jeopardize Lord Howard's strategy (National Maritime Museum, Greenwich, London).

having commanded royal squadrons in home waters since the early 1570s. His principal duty was to prevent any landing on the south-east coast by the Duke of Parma's army. His relationship with his cousin Charles Howard was strained, and after the campaign he complained that Howard tried to deprive him of the honour due to him. His participation was restricted to the battle off the Flemish Banks, but he proved himself a skilled commander. His flagship was the *Rainbow* (384 tons).

Sir Francis Drake (c.1540–96) is the best remembered of all the English naval commanders, known mainly for his career as a privateer. Drake participated in the débâcle at San Juan de Ulúa (1569), then spent the next three years raiding the 'Spanish Main', returning to England a wealthy man. His circumnavigation of the globe earned him even greater wealth (plundered from the Spanish), and he was knighted by a grateful Queen Elizabeth, who called him 'my pirate'. This open support for a man who had illegally attacked the Spanish made war inevitable. Further privateering in the Caribbean (1585/6) was curtailed when Drake was appointed to lead an attack on Cadiz (1587). At the start of the campaign Drake's stock was high and he was regarded as an unofficial second-in-command. His true privateering tendencies were revealed when he chased after the *Rosario* off the Devon coast, in direct contradiction of his orders from Howard. Although he performed well, he was criticized for his lack of discipline. His flagship was the *Revenge* (441 tons).

Sir John Hawkins (1532–95) was a Plymouth merchant who was one of the first interlopers in the Spanish Main. In 1568 his trading squadron was forced to shelter in the Mexican anchorage of San Juan de Ulúa. Before he could leave, the annual Spanish treasure fleet arrived and the Spanish launched a surprise attack. Hawkins barely managed to escape, leaving behind most of his ships and men. In 1578 he was made Treasurer of the Navy and he performed miracles, refitting and modernizing the fleet, improving its efficiency and ultimately laying the groundwork for the English victory in the Armada campaign. He was also accused of financial irregularities. During the campaign he helped prepare the fleet for action, then assumed command of a squadron. Although he failed to distinguish himself, he proved a capable, brave and energetic commander. His flagship was the *Victory* (565 tons).

Sir Martin Frobisher (*c.*1537–94) was another of the 'sea dogs', whose expertise lay in exploration rather than in privateering. Born in Yorkshire, he had been brought up in London, and participated in slaving expeditions to West Africa. In the 1560s he operated as a privateer before becoming involved in exploration. During the period 1574–77 he undertook three voyages in search of the Northwest Passage, and in 1585/6 he accompanied Drake on his Caribbean adventures. In 1588 he was appointed one of Howard's squadron commanders, and although he was criticized for his performance off Portland, he showed great spirit. He was knighted by the Lord Admiral during the campaign, but his animosity towards Drake led to a subsequent war of words between the two commanders. His flagship was the *Triumph* (760 tons).

Robert Dudley, Earl of Leicester (*c.*1532–88), was one of Queen Elizabeth's favourites and

a leading courtier, but he lacked any military experience. Nevertheless, he was appointed Governor-General of the English army in the Netherlands in 1586. He returned to England in 1588, and the queen immediately gave him the command of the army gathered at Tilbury. He died just after the Armada campaign, and Elizabeth was reportedly distraught for weeks after hearing the news. A mediocre commander, he would have been hard pressed to offer much of a challenge to the Duke of Parma.

Sir John Hawkins (1532–95), an oil painting c.1581, by a painter of the English School. While he was another of the Elizabethan 'sea dogs' and a privateer, he more than anyone else contributed to the English victory through his work as a naval designer and administrator in the years preceding the Armada campaign (National Maritime Museum, Greenwich, London).

The 'Sea Dogs'

One of the phrases which is often bandied about in history books of this period is 'sea dogs' – a collective term which summons up images of swashbucklers, plunder on the high seas and England's sailors standing up against the overwhelming might of Spain. It is worth looking at the phrase a little more closely, as these men were the principal leaders of the Tudor fleet during the Spanish Armada campaign, and their contribution to the English victory was significant.

The era when mariners sailed as privateers, explorers, merchants or in the service of Queen Elizabeth is one of the most colourful in English history, and has been

A facsimile of an English pocket map dating from the late 16th century, which once reputedly belonged to Sir Francis Drake. It shows the Iberian Peninsula, the Bay of Biscay and the waters surrounding England. Cartography was in its infancy, and errors caused problems for both sides during the campaign (Hensley Collection, Ashville, NC).

the subject of numerous books and films. Although the basic history of the defeat of the Spanish Armada and the raids of Sir Francis Drake on the Spanish Main is well known, a combination of nationalism and a lack of knowledge about the available source material has resulted in a very stilted view of the period. The 'sea dogs' – adventurers such as Drake, Hawkins, Raleigh and Frobisher – were not always as successful as the writers of Victorian histories would have us believe, and their actions were often influenced by profit rather than by any feeling of patriotic duty.

The emphasis on English naval heroes has almost obscured the fact that the Dutch and the French were also actively engaged in the often undeclared war against the Spanish empire, and many of the greatest successes of the Elizabethan heroes were brought about through co-operation with these Protestant allies.

To the Spanish, men like Drake and Hawkins were pirates, and if caught would be treated as such. To the English, the legal status of these 'sea dogs' was often vague and, technically at least, many of their actions strayed from privateering into the realms of piracy. The circumstances which permitted them to get away with piracy were unique, and in the eyes of much of English society their actions were perfectly acceptable. Many late 16th-century English seamen regarded trade and plunder as inseparable, performed by all kinds of men, from smugglers and cut-throats to the

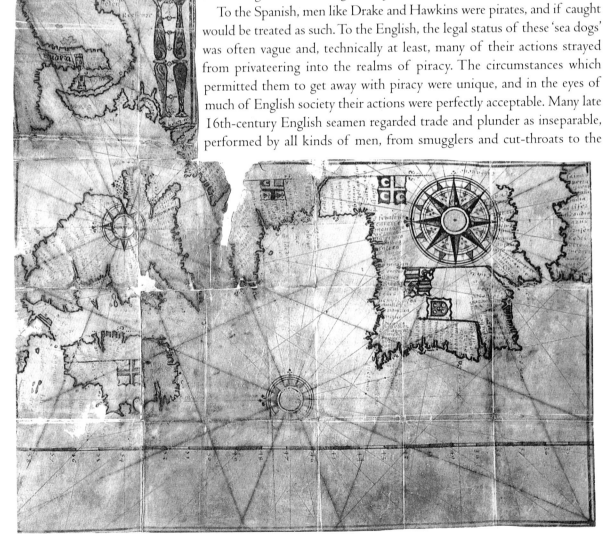

nobility, taking forms which varied from legitimate privateering to unrestricted piracy. During this period, Elizabethan sea-plunder became increasingly identified with patriotic motives, and with the struggle to maintain the Protestant religion.

The difference between a pirate and a privateer is that a privateer attacks the enemies of his country under licence from the government, while a pirate attacks anybody, irrespective of nationality. In theory, attacks on Spanish ships by men who did not hold a privateering licence were acts of piracy, but as the authorities usually turned a blind eye or even condoned these attacks, the state was effectively giving its illicit support to piracy. In western England piracy was partly legitimized by support from the gentry and local authorities. Piracy still existed, but increasingly the crown ceased to condemn the pirates, provided they attacked foreign ships, preferably Spanish ones. Small-scale piracy continued to thrive throughout the Elizabethan era with the government only half-heartedly attempting to suppress it. If provoked, the queen would restrain the pirates. When her envoy carrying a christening gift to the French court was attacked in the English Channel in 1573, she sent her fleet and troops into the West Country to round up hundreds of pirates. Most, however, were eventually released.

In the West Country gentry with maritime connections were often the first to flout the law and engage in 'discriminating piracy' (as privateering was sometimes called). For them patriotism, plunder and Protestantism amalgamated to produce the motivation which fuelled the fires of piracy and privateering. Often the same men, or their neighbours, held positions of local authority and were responsible for policing piracy in the west of England, the Bristol Channel, or along the south coast. In Southampton the mayor regularly released captured pirates, while the mayor of Dartmouth was fined when his open piratical connections were discovered by the queen. Francis Drake came from a background of rural gentility in Devonshire, and was related to his mentor, John Hawkins. Hawkins himself was the son of a prominent Plymouth gentleman merchant and shipowner, with powerful local connections. Martin Frobisher was a Yorkshireman, but was raised in London in the house of his uncle, a knight who invested heavily in maritime ventures, including 'discriminating piracy'. Walter Raleigh was born into the Devonshire nobility, but became involved in privateering through investment and speculation.

In other words, these 'sea dogs' emerged from a society which saw plundering on the high seas as an acceptable pursuit for gentlemen merchant adventurers and where their actions were supported by their peers. As the officials who should have curtailed piracy often invested in piratical ventures themselves, or were related to the pirates, these activities were effectively legitimized. It was this large-scale participation of the southern gentry in 'discriminating piracy' which transformed the petty piracy in the English Channel of the mid-16th century into the transatlantic plundering of the Elizabethan 'sea dogs' from the 1570s.

Sir Martin Frobisher (c.1537–94), an oil painting by Cornelius Ketel. An explorer as much as a 'sea dog' and privateer, Frobisher played a prominent role in the Spanish Armada campaign, and was knighted for his efforts after the enemy's defeat (Bodleian Library, University of Oxford).

Unless operating directly under the orders of the queen, most expeditions conducted by the Elizabethan 'sea dogs' were speculative ventures, backed by investors or even companies and shareholders. The profit motive was paramount, particularly when the voyage or expedition combined trade with plunder. For example, when, in 1560, Thomas White was returning to England from the Barbary Coast of North Africa, he came upon two Spanish ships carrying quicksilver.

Although he was on a trading voyage, he attacked the ships, captured them, and took them back to London. The authorities in London ignored what was clearly an act of piracy, his investors reaped an immense profit and his crew were awarded prize money. Everyone benefited from White's action apart from the Spanish.

The main point here is that these men – the 'sea dogs' – were all answerable for their actions to the queen, but bridled at the restraints imposed on them by Lord Howard. For them, naval warfare was a way of making money, and the Spanish Armada campaign was as much an opportunity to profit through the capturing of prizes as it was about repelling the Spanish invaders.

Richard Drake (1535-1603), an oil painting by George Gower. Richard was the cousin of Sir Francis Drake, and a courtier of some repute. He also served as the prize agent to his cousin, and during 1588 he took command of the Spanish prisoners landed in Devon (National Maritime Museum, Greenwich, London).

The Men

According to the history books, in 1588 England was saved from disaster by three things: her fleet, her leading 'sea dogs'— and her doughty seamen. Almost 16,000 men were employed for sea service in 1588, a total which included soldiers and gunners as well as seamen, carried in 197 vessels ranging in size from large 1,000-ton race-built galleons to small 30-ton pinnaces. Much has been written about the talents of the Elizabethan seamen, but they were probably no more skilled than other competent mariners from France or Spain. What really set them apart from their continental rivals was their religion, and their desire for plunder in the form of prize money. While national pride, professionalism and loyalty to their ships, shipmates or captains were all involved, the majority of the best seamen in the fleet had cut their teeth as privateersmen. Consequently they saw the campaign as much as a chance to make money as a necessary duty. This said, the men who took to sea against the Spanish Armada were for the most part highly experienced, competent seamen, and could be relied upon to play their part in the coming battle.

Service as a seaman in an English privateer might have been miserable, but it was still considered preferable to manning one of the queen's ships in time of war, when pay and provisions were generally less forthcoming. As the veteran naval commander Sir William Monson wrote, it is strange 'what misery such men will choose to endure in small ships of reprisal, though they be hopeless of gain, rather than serve Her Majesty, where their pay is certain, their diet plentiful and their labour not so great'. The prospect of a larger share of plunder was clearly a greater incentive than patriotism.

Shipboard Organization

Each of the ships in the royal fleet (the Navy Royal) was commanded by a captain who owed his position either to royal appointment or to selection by private backers. He might also be a captain-owner, as was the case with many of the smaller privateers, armed merchantmen and ancillary vessels which made up the bulk of the fleet. The appointment of all of these commanders had been approved by the crown,

HONI SOIT QVI MAL Y PENSE

THE MARINERS MIRROVR

Wherin may playnly be seen the courses, heights, distances, depths, soundings, flouds and ebs, risings of lands, rocks, sands and shoalds, with the marks for th'entrings of the Harbouroughs, Havens and Ports of the greatest part of Europe: their seueral traficks and commodities: Together w.th the Rules and instrumets of NAVIGATION.

First made & set fourth in diuers exact Sea Charts, by that famous Nauigator LVKE WAGENAR of Enchuisen And now fitted with necessarie additions for the use of Englishmen by
ANTHONY ASHLEY.

Heerin also may be understood the exploits lately atchiued by the right Honorable the L. Admiral of England with her Ma.ᵗⁱᵉˢ Nauie and some former seruises don by that worthy Knight
Sᵗ. FRAⁿᶜ DRAKE.

An English seaman of the Elizabethan period, from a detail taken from a contemporary navigation guide. His baggy clothes were practical garments, and were often coated in a light tar-based solution – a little like the coating of a waxed jacket, which provided some degree of waterproofing. Engraving by an unknown artist, c.1580 (Stratford Archive).

or at least by the Lord Admiral, Lord Howard. In warships of the Navy Royal, the captain was assisted by several other officers, the most senior of which was the master. While the captain might have little or no maritime experience, having been selected due to his rank, the master was a highly experienced seamen, who effectively ran the day to day operation of the ship.

In 1588 England had no body of professional naval officers to draw on, in the way we would expect today. Instead, ships were officered by men who were hired into service for a set period, or for a particular mission. The same was true of the crew, who were hired or pressed as circumstances demanded. They were also discharged when the crown had no further need of their services. Before the Armada, the majority of English seamen in the Navy Royal earned their living in merchant vessels or privateers. Warships were kept in reserve, and crewed by a skeleton crew in an attempt to keep running costs low. The ships were brought up to their full working complement only when they were being prepared for sea – in this case during the early summer of 1588. Consequently everyone on board, from the captain to the lowliest landsman or ship's boy, served 'for the duration' of the campaign, and its immediate aftermath.

Other senior officers on board included the master gunner, in charge of the guns, gunners and ordnance stores, the boatswain, in charge of all matters related to the operation and maintenance of the ship, the quartermaster, who looked after stores, provision and administration, and the captain of infantry, who commanded the contingent of soldiers carried on board. The master, the quartermaster, the master gunner and the boatswain all had mates, as did the ship's carpenter. Other named ranks on board included the surgeon (carried only on the larger royal warships), the pilot, who was answerable to the captain and the master as their navigating officer, and the purser, who assisted the quartermaster but was responsible for all aspects dealing with the pay of the crew.

Finally each of the larger ships in the fleet included a named cook, a yeoman of the tacks and jeers (in charge of the rigging), a coxswain (who ran the ship's boats), a trumpeter and a steward (who attended the needs of the captain). In addition captains on the larger vessels were assisted by a number of gentlemen officers, the majority of whom were volunteers – often relatives of the captain or other officers, or of the owner if the vessel was privately owned.

The master gunner was one of the most important men on board. He commanded the gunners, approximately one of whom was placed in charge of each of the major guns on board. For instance, the *Triumph* (Sir Martin Frobisher's flagship) carried 40 guns of 'saker' size or larger (i.e. 6-pdrs or above), excluding the obsolete wrought-iron 'port pieces' which did not really need specialists to operate. It carried a complement of 40 gunners – exactly one for each gun. They were assisted by men drawn from the ranks of the mariners on board, who – for the most part – were skilled in the handling of naval ordnance.

Compared with the queen's ships, discipline on Elizabethan privateers seems to have been extremely lax. Even hard taskmasters such as Drake found it difficult to control the crews. The execution of one of his captains, Thomas Doughty, in 1578 (charged with treason, mutiny and necromancy) may have been an attempt to enforce his will over a crew who were reluctant to sail through the Straits of Magellan into the Pacific, fearing that they would never be able to return home. With disorderly crews and frequent instances of drunkenness and fighting, it is surprising the Elizabethan commanders accomplished what they did. The last recorded words of Sir George Carew who commanded the *Mary Rose* just before it sank in July 1545 were that he led 'the sort of knaves whom he could not rule'. This sounds similar to Thomas Cavendish's last words, when he called his sailors an 'insolent, mutinous company' in 1591, although the explorer and privateer was showing signs of extreme paranoia by the time he died. To experienced commanders such as Drake, the lack of discipline was a problem which could be overcome by dynamic leadership, but even he encountered problems when prize money was not forthcoming, or his sailors thought a venture was too dangerous.

Lord Henry Seymour, Admiral of the Narrow Seas, in an oil painting attributed to the circle of Federico Zucchero, c.1588. Seymour's reserve fleet had a dual mission – blocking any landing attempt by the Duke of Parma, and to reinforce the main fleet when called upon to fight the Spanish Armada (Parham Park, Storrington, West Sussex).

Conditions on Board

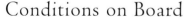

From contemporary sources it is apparent that active privateering ships in the 1570s and 1580s carried around one man for every two tons of displacement. The same held true of the royal warships and armed merchantmen which constituted the English fleet in 1588. To the royal or private backers and their commanders, large crews meant strong and efficient gun crews, and also allowed them to provide extra crews to man captured vessels. Almost exclusively, seamen on Elizabethan privateers received no wages, but instead were given a portion of the plunder or cargo taken from their victims. However, during the campaign all the ships and their men were deemed as serving at the request of the crown, and so they were paid a wage from the royal treasury.

Conditions on these ships were harsh, and death from starvation or disease was commonplace, especially on a long voyage. The handful of men who returned with John Hawkins after the failure of his 1568 expedition were almost dead from starvation and thirst, while numerous instances are recorded of crews being decimated by disease, particularly when operating in the Spanish Main. Both Drake and Hawkins died from fever, probably brought on by the 'bloody flux', or dysentery, which flourished in the unsanitary conditions found on late 16th-century ships. A lack of basic hygiene simply provided a breeding ground for disease.

The ships were also cramped, although conditions were never as notoriously bad as they were on the over-manned warships of the Spanish Armada. For instance, on the 500-ton royal galleon *Elizabeth Jonas* commanded by Sir Robert Southwell, some 500 men – 300 sailors, 150 soldiers, 40 gunners and 10 servants – shared a space which was just 143ft long and 38ft across. The ship was also fully provisioned, and carried its full quota of ordnance and stores. In other words, it was unpleasantly crowded on board, even for the ship's officers, who must have envied Sir Robert his few square feet of private cabin at the stern of the poop deck.

The typical diet of an Elizabethan seaman was bread or ship's biscuit, salted beef, pork or fish, peasemeal, butter and cheese. Beer was readily available, and wine was issued to the crew when a Spanish vessel was captured. The lack of fresh fruit and vegetables led to scurvy, known as 'the plague of the sea' and food and beer rotted very quickly. Food poisoning caused by rotting food was a major cause of death during the campaign, a problem compounded by vermin. One source even suggests the planning in of officers' cabins, 'for avoydinge of myse and ratts'.

Work was hard and dangerous, which meant that seamen over the age of 40 were a rarity in Tudor times. Pay was low – an average of 10 shillings per month for the average sailor in the royal fleet – and this was exacerbated by the crown's failure to pay the men promptly. This in turn caused discontent amongst the crew, and warranted letters of complaint from the Lord Admiral to the royal exchequer.

Pay for officers varied from the 6 shillings 8 pence a day issued to senior captains, to 2 shillings 6 pence to junior ones, who commanded the smaller ships in the fleet. The social niceties were also observed – the captain was allowed two servants for every 50 men of his crew and four men if he held the rank of a knight of the realm. The way this was handled was that captains tended to draw pay for their servants, whether they employed their full quota or not. In effect it became an extra perk. In 1588 lieutenants (the rank held by masters, captains of infantry and quartermasters) drew between 1 and 2 shillings a day depending on experience, while lesser officers were paid 17 shillings a month or less. Strangely enough the surgeon and the trumpeter were placed on the same pay level (15 shillings a month).

Little is known about the dress of the seamen who manned the privateers and warships of the Elizabethan era. Certain common features can be determined from contemporary depictions. Clothing worn by a seaman was usually simple. A tunic of leather or a worsted material was worn on its own, or with the addition of hose and a seaman's jacket. One-piece hose were worn on the *Mary Rose* (1545) and by Spanish seamen in the 1580s, so clearly remained popular throughout the period. Baggy woollen breeches similar to those worn on land appear to have been common, although Sir William Monson mentions seamen in petticoats or baggy canvas breeches.

The petticoat or sailor's smock was a canvas or white duck skirt which reached below the knees, and was a common form of maritime wear from at least the 15th until the early 19th century. These could be worn as a simple skirt, or split into separate legs, in the style of modern culottes. Coarse shirts, frequently called 'undershirts' or 'stomachers', appear often to have been collarless, the neck closed by a simple drawstring. Seamen's jackets in the late 16th century were wool, and seldom reached below the waist. These tight-fitting garments ended in simple rolled collars and were fitted with tubular sleeves without cuffs. A rolled tube of wool at the shoulder is shown on the jacket of one of the seamen from the *Mariner's Mirrour* (1588), and reflects civilian fashion.

Both of the seamen in this illustration wear typical brown baggy woollen breeches and hose, but beyond that their clothing must be considered unusual, as one wears a decorated and padded coat, while both are shown wearing civilian collar ruffs. If worn, these embellishments may have been reserved for shore-going clothing by the more affluent gentlemen mariners, and there is no evidence that this was ever worn at sea. Archaeological evidence from the *Mary Rose* suggests that leather jerkins were also common. Another depiction of Elizabethan seamen shows a seaman in breeches, shirt, seaman's jacket and fur hat. Other forms of headgear in contemporary illustrations included berets, high or low-crowned felt hats, headscarves, woollen knitted caps and soft felt 'Phrygian' caps. Footwear recovered from the *Mary Rose* included leather shoes with a slash decoration, although most seamen would have gone barefoot on the high seas.

Given the general overcrowding, the poor rations, the general squalor, the harsh conditions and of course the risk of death in battle, it is remarkable that these English sailors managed to achieve what they did. When the time came they succeeded in out-sailing and out-shooting their Spanish opponents, and the majority even lived to tell the tale. A lucky few even managed to earn the prize money coveted by so many, although few men apart from Drake made much of a profit from the 'Great Enterprise'. For most, the ability to return safely to port must have seemed reward enough.

Ship Profile:
The English Race-Built Galleon

We have already said that in 1588 the Tudor fleet consisted of 197 ships, including 34 royal warships, both great and small. Many of the private ships in the fleet were effective warships, especially those which had been designed and operated as privateers in the years before the campaign. However, the real fighting potential of the fleet consisted of a relatively small group of warships – the 16 largest and most prestigious vessels in the fleet. These included Lord Howard's flagship the *Ark Royal*, plus a number of ships which had been recently converted, or which had joined the fleet within the past decade. All of these – whether specially built or converted – were described as 'race-built galleons'. They were based on a radical design by Sir John Hawkins, but ironically enough they owed their origins to the Spanish galleons which were first seen in English ports during the reign of Elizabeth's older sister, Queen Mary.

The Development of a Masterpiece

The fleet inherited by Henry VIII's daughters Mary and Elizabeth was essentially a modern one, where the main fighting force – in effect the 'battleships' – was the 'great ships' or carracks that were similar to the ill-fated *Mary Rose*, which sank off Portsmouth in 1545. However, the last great ship to be built in England was the 450-ton carrack the *Pauncy*, which entered service in 1543. As a Catholic, Mary allied herself with Spain, and consequently English warship designers and shipwrights were able to study Spanish ship design at first hand. While in general the Spanish royal warships resembled those of other northern European maritime powers, a new ship type – the galleon – was beginning to appear amid the Spanish royal fleet. By 1554, when the Anglo-Spanish alliance was cemented by the marriage of Mary of England and Prince Philip (later Philip II) of Spain, Spanish galleons formed part of the main

Specifications
Displacement: 741 tons
Keel length: 100ft (30.5m)
Beam: 40ft (12.2m)
Armament: 46 guns
Crew: 340 sailors,
40 gunners,
120 soldiers
Service notes:
Built 1561. Rebuilt 1596.
Condemned, 1618

Specifications
Displacement: 550 tons
Keel length: 100ft (30.5m)
Beam: 37ft (11.3m)
Armament: 38 guns
Crew: 268 sailors,
32 gunners,
100 soldiers
Service notes:
Built 1587. Rebuilt 1608.
Wrecked off Tilbury, 1636

A small Elizabethan galleon – a detail from a contemporary chart. Unlike larger merchant vessels, these small ships – built according to the principles espoused by John Hawkins – were able to sail close to the wind, and consequently were far more manoeuvrable than most other vessels of the period. In effect they could stay out of reach of the enemy, while firing at them with their ordnance (Stratford Archive).

Spanish royal fleet. It was inevitable that English shipwrights would learn what they could from these Catholic visitors.

During her five-year reign, Mary ordered the construction of three English-built galleons, the first real departures from the great ship or carrack designs constructed under the orders of her father. These ships, the 550-ton *Philip & Mary* (1554), the 600-ton *Mary Rose* (II) (1556) and the 500-ton *Golden Lion* (1557), represented a new phase in English warship construction. The importance of these vessels has long been overlooked by historians, largely due to a combination of Elizabethan propaganda and English national pride. The truth is, the English race-built galleons associated with Drake, Frobisher and Hawkins were all developed from prototypes that followed the designs of warships built for the Spanish.

It has been suggested that the three galleons built during Mary's reign drew upon English as well as Spanish influences. After all, the *Great Bark* that was rebuilt in 1543 was later referred to as the *Great Galleon*, which suggests that the galleon influence pre-dated the building of the *Philip & Mary*. However, no evidence has been found to support this theory, save the name. It might be safer to assume that the *Great Bark*, which was a rebuilt galleass (confusingly called the *Great Galley*), simply had a length to breadth ratio more akin to these new galleons than to the rest of the contemporary Tudor fleet. In other words, these three ships were markedly different from everything that had come before. In fact, the conversion of the *Great Bark* might well have inspired the ordering of a similar refit for six of the smaller galleasses in the Navy Royal, as in 1558 the galleasses *Hart*, *Antelope* and *Swallow*, as well as the smaller vessels *New Bark*, *Jennet* and *Greyhound*, were all rebuilt as small galleons, following the Spanish model.

Much has also been made of the difference between the armament of English and Spanish ships during the Elizabethan period. Yet the groundwork for the English operational advantage in gunnery had been laid already during the reign of Henry VIII, as proved by several of the guns and carriages recovered from the *Mary Rose*. It has to be supposed that even as early as 1557, English commanders would have regarded their own gunnery system to be superior to that of their new-found Spanish allies, and consequently would have armed their ships following the accepted English pattern. What these new ships did was to raise the possibility of using the ships and their armament in a different way.

Just how successful the three large English galleons were is reflected in their longevity. The *Golden Lion* remained in service without undergoing any alteration to

The English warship *White Bear*, from a contemporary engraving by Claes Jansz Visscher. This old 1,000-ton royal carrack was rebuilt as part of Hawkins' programme, and during the Spanish Armada campaign it was ably commanded by Lord Sheffield (Stratford Archive).

119

its original design until 1582, while the *Philip & Mary* survived without a major refit until 1584 (when it was renamed the *Nonpareil*). The *Mary Rose* was only refitted in 1589, the year after the Spanish Armada episode. This refitting was part of the general programme in which the fleet was rebuilt along the lines of the race-built galleon conceived by Sir John Hawkins. Clearly until this refit, and for some three decades after they were first built, all three galleons were considered the equals of more modern additions to the fleet. Even more surprisingly, all three ships remained in service until well into the 17th century.

At the accession of Elizabeth I in 1558, the Navy Royal therefore consisted of three large galleons, as well as the *Great Bark*, which can be grouped into the same category. In addition there was also the group of six small galleons that were still in the process of being converted from galleasses when Mary I died. At that point the fleet also contained four great ships or carracks (*Matthew, Jesus of Lubeck, Pauncy* and *Mary Hamborough*), five ships that were essentially smaller carracks (*Trinity Henry, Sweepstake, Saker, Mary Willoughby, Falcon*), a 450-ton galleass (*Anne Gallant*) four small galleasses (*Salamander, George, Tiger* and *Bull*), all of which had been converted into ships, and two galleys (the *Galley Subtile* and *Mermaid*), as well as several smaller craft such as pinnaces and rowing barges.

As was often the case when a new regime took charge, the ships of the English Navy Royal were surveyed, and several were condemned as unfit for use, or else were sold out of service. In the six months following Elizabeth's accession, her fleet would be trimmed considerably, as the 600-ton *Matthew*, the 400-ton *Mary Hamborough* and the 450-ton *Pauncy* were all decommissioned. This meant that by 1559 only the *Jesus of Lubeck* remained of Henry VIII's fleet of great carracks. Many of the smaller carracks suffered the same fate, leaving only the *Mary Willoughby*, the *Falcon*, the *Saker* and the *Phoenix* on the Elizabethan establishment. Of the smaller craft, the galleasses had already been reconfigured as ships by replacing their oar decks with gunports, and of the four, only the *Tiger* and the *Bull* survived the survey, as did the two galleys.

In effect, the Elizabethan navy began its life pared down to a meagre collection of five large warships and ten smaller ones, plus two galleys and a collection of tiny support vessels. It was therefore hardly in a position to take on the maritime might of Spain.

The fleet soon became even smaller. In 1558 the 700-ton *Jesus of Lubeck* was chartered out for private use, and would soon be associated with the expeditions to the Spanish Main commanded by Sir John Hawkins. Oared warships were surveyed annually, compared to roughly five-year surveys for the rest of the fleet. Consequently, the 200-ton French-built *Galley Subtile* was condemned in 1560, just two years after the survey conducted at Elizabeth's accession. The galley *Mermaid* suffered the same fate three years later.

All these cuts meant that in the late 1550s, while Elizabethan England was embarking on a 'cold war' with Spain that would last for almost three decades, the

Jesus of Lubeck, 1558

Despite her name, this 700-ton carrack was purchased in Hamburg in 1544. She was one of the few great ships of Henry VIII's navy to be retained by Elizabeth I, although by the late 1560s she was no longer considered seaworthy. However, in 1564 she was leased to Sir John Hawkins, who spent a considerable sum refitting her and partially rebuilding her hull by cutting down her superstructure. She still remained an awkward vessel, and even before she sailed from Plymouth in September 1567 her officers complained that she was difficult to sail. The poor sailing performance would cost her dear in late 1568, when she was unable to escape when Hawkins' flotilla was attacked as it lay off San Juan de Ulúa, in the Mexican port of Vera Cruz (Tony Bryan).

Specifications

Displacement: 700 tons
Beam: 30ft (9.1m)
Crew: Approx. 240 men
Keel length: 115ft (35m) approx.
Armament: 26 guns
Service notes: Built c.1540. Bought into service 1544. Rebuilt c.1566. Captured by Spanish, 1568.

Navy Board was considering how best to build up the Navy Royal along modern lines. The two key figures on the board were its Treasurer Benjamin Godson and William Winter, its Surveyor and Master of Ordnance. Together they embarked on a programme of rebuilding that would begin piecing together a fleet capable of confronting the Spanish.

During the 1560s, they ordered the construction of three new large galleons, all improved versions of those built at the order of Elizabeth's older sister. The first of these was the galleon *Elizabeth Jonas* of 750 tons, built in 1559. As it was used as an example of shipbuilding in the 'old way' by the innovative ship designer Matthew Baker when he wrote a shipbuilding treatise in 1582, we know something about its dimensions. It had a 100ft keel, a 40ft beam, and a draft of 18ft. These dimensions are largely comparable to those after its rebuild in 1598, although its original displacement was reduced by a little over 50 tons, suggesting that its superstructure was lowered. It also suggests that it began life as a fairly sleek vessel, and its length to beam ratio of about 2.5:1 is comparable with other later Elizabethan galleons.

Even after they were rebuilt, the three original large galleons built in the mid-1550s had narrower beams, giving an average ratio of about 3:1. The extra beam of the *Elizabeth Jonas* has been attributed to the desire to provide a more stable platform for ordnance, although this theory has never been proved. Another smaller vessel, the *Hope* (420 tons), was built in Deptford in 1559. Little is known about it apart from its armament and its dimensions. Its keel was 94ft long, it had a 33ft beam and the depth of the hold was given as 17ft. As it remained in near-constant service, however, and survived without being rebuilt until after the death of Queen Elizabeth, then it can be assumed that it was considered a sound and useful addition to the fleet.

Two other larger galleons were added to the fleet during this period. The *Triumph* (740 tons) was built in 1561, and was followed two years later by the *White Bear* of 730 tons. Although we know little of these ships before their rebuilding in the late 1590s, it is fairly safe to assume they were similar to the *Elizabeth Jonas*, as all three ships shared very similar specifications after the rebuild. Figures for the late 1590s suggest that while the *Triumph* was generally similar to the earlier galleon, the *White Bear* was beamier, with a length to beam ratio of 3:1. Contemporary or near-contemporary depictions of these ships show vessels that followed the general lines associated with Spanish galleons, merging this Iberian ship design with the English emphasis on viewing the ship as a floating gun platform. All three galleons saw service during the Spanish Armada campaign, the *Triumph* in particular distinguishing itself in its role as the flagship of Sir Martin Frobisher. Another important addition to the fleet during this period was the *Aid* (240 tons), built in Deptford in London between 1559 and 1562.

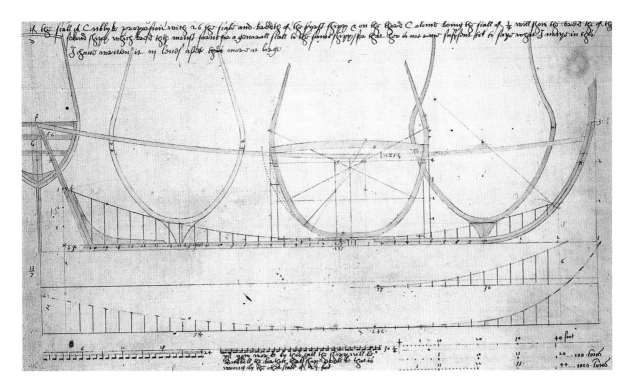

Although the five ships were all major additions to the fleet, new warships were costly, and took time to build. The Board therefore decided to augment the building programme by purchasing armed merchantmen that were suitable for conversion into warships. The first, and also the largest, of these was the *Victory*, which began life as the *Great Christopher* (800 tons) before being bought from London merchants in 1560. It was expensive to man and operate, however, and only went to sea three times during its service life – in 1563, 1588 and 1589. The Board also bought the *Primrose* (800 tons) in the same year, before selling it out of service in 1575, and then the *Elizabeth Bonaventure* (600 tons) from the London merchant Walter Jobson in 1567. Another smaller purchase was the 300-ton ship *Minion*, bought in 1558.

The loss of the *Jesus of Lubeck* in battle with the Spanish in 1568 highlighted the problems inherent in leasing out ships of the Navy Royal for private use. The venerable carrack had been hastily converted into something akin to a galleon by Sir John Hawkins as he prepared it for a trading voyage to the Spanish Main in 1566–67. It may have exuded prestige through its sheer size, but by all accounts it remained unwieldy and of limited value. The smaller *Minion* was also hired out to Hawkins, but along with Francis Drake's own ship the *Judith* it managed to escape the disaster at San Juan de Ulúa. Although this meant the Navy Royal had lost two valuable ships, it did mean that Hawkins returned to England, where his next business venture proved more beneficial.

A plan showing the cross-sections of the hull of a typical English race-built galleon, which illustrates just how sharply the hull narrowed towards the stern, thereby reducing water resistance. From Matthew Baker's *Fragments of Ancient English Shipwrighty* (c.1582) (By permission of the Master and Fellows, Magdalene College, Cambridge).

Hawkins' Design

In 1570 Hawkins entered into partnership with Richard Chapman, at that time a private master shipwright, who would later enter the service of the crown. Together they tendered to build or rebuild ships for the Navy Royal using the facilities at the Deptford shipyard. As his father-in-law Benjamin Godson was the Treasurer of the Navy at the time, the tender was approved. The two business partners had their own ideas about ship design, and they put them to the test in their first design, the small 300-ton galleon *Foresight*. The new design involved a length to beam ratio of 3:1, a hull form below the waterline that resembled the fleet's earlier small galleasses, but with a deeper draught than before, and a stepped but continuous gundeck.

The superstructure was kept low, sweeping upwards from waist to stern, while a long beakhead and rakish stem were designed to improve its handling in rough seas. Finally, the foremast was placed further forward than normal, and was raked forward a little, which slightly improved the vessel's handling. It had a 78ft (23.8m) keel, with a 27ft (8.2m) stem rake, a 27ft beam, and a depth of hold of 14ft (4.2m). Even more importantly, it carried a powerful armament for its size of 28 guns.

Foresight proved to be a great success, prompting the former galleasses *Bull* and *Tiger* to be rebuilt along the same lines later that year. In effect, the *Foresight* was the start of a new breed of vessel, which correctly or not has been classified by historians as the Elizabethan 'race-built galleon'.

Leaner, faster and more deadly than earlier galleons, these vessels would form the fighting core of the Elizabethan fleet in 1588. Two more galleons were soon commissioned following Hawkins' principles, the *Dreadnought* (360 tons) and the *Swiftsure* (350 tons), both of which were built at Deptford in 1573, followed that same year by the smaller 100-ton ships *Achates* and *Handmaid*, both of which were essentially smaller versions of the *Foresight*. The *Swiftsure* and *Achates* were built by Peter Pett, while Matthew Baker supervised the construction of the other two warships.

Hawkins would further refine his design based on the performance of these ships in the fleet. The practical experiences of serving officers tended to suggest that Hawkins had got it right. William Borough, Comptroller of the Navy, grouped his fleet into three categories. The first were vessels of: 'The shortest, broadest, and deepest sort – to have the length by the keel double the breadth amidships and the depth of the hold half its breadth ... this order is used in some merchant ships for most profit.' In other words, they were slow, tubby armed merchantmen, unable to keep up with the most powerful warships of the fleet. However, they were considered suitable for patrolling, for the escort of fishing fleets or for the carrying of supplies.

Borough's second group were: 'The mean and best proportion for shipping for merchandise, likewise very serviceable for all purposes.' He described these ships as having a 'length of keel two or two and a quarter that of the beam. Depth of hold eleven-twenty-fourths that of the beam.' These were the armed merchantmen that could be bought into service like the *Elizabeth Bonaventure* or the *Victory*, or else hired from merchants in time of crisis. The core of Borough's fleet were: 'The largest order for galleons or ships for the wars made for the most advantage of sailing.' These ships had a 'length of keel three times the beam … a depth of hold two-fifths of beam.' On this basis, his perfect warships were the ones designed by Hawkins.

Other innovations introduced by Hawkins were less visible. First, his hulls were deeper than on previous vessels, and they acted much like a centreboard on a sailing dinghy, functioning as a counterbalance to the force of the wind on the sails to reduce the effect of heeling. This design made his ships more stable gun platforms than previous vessels. Another innovation was the sheathing of the lower hull with a double layer of planks, with a hair and tar mixture laid between them, in an attempt to reduce hull corrosion caused by the toredo worm. This measure pre-dated the introduction of copper-sheathed ship bottoms by almost a century, and was almost certainly the result of Hawkins' own experiences of operating in the worm-infested waters of the Caribbean Sea.

Hawkins' ships were also more streamlined than those that had come before, the result of his moving the largest frame of the ships further forward than normal, resulting in a more significant tapering off towards the stern of his vessels. The drawback of this design was that it reduced buoyancy towards the stern, which limited the weight of ordnance that could be carried. During the early Stuart period, his designs were altered to increase buoyancy and so permit a heavier armament to be carried. It was found, however, that this modification led to a far poorer sailing performance. In effect, Hawkins saw ship design as a balancing act between firepower and speed, and his fine-tuning of the fleet perfectly suited the requirements of the Navy Royal at the time.

Another innovation soon followed. Before 1570, every attempt had been made to form the gundeck into a continuous belt running for as far as possible along the length of the ship. Gundecks followed the curve of the hull, and therefore rose sharply towards the bow and stern. Previously, this meant that few guns could be carried in the stern or beneath the forecastle, and the guns were therefore placed in the superstructure. Hawkins' solution was to break the run of the gundeck abaft of the mizzen mast, stepping it down by half a deck, and so creating a lower gunroom. This design allowed heavy guns to be carried lower down in the hull, thereby improving the stability of the ship. It also provided a platform for a pair of sternchase guns, the gunports for which were cut in the transom at its widest point rather than high up in the superstructure, where the guns would fill the available cabin space.

The upper deck was also stepped down abaft the mainmast, creating an additional space that became the upper gunroom. In the larger ships this gunroom was used to house another pair of sternchasers, and even a few extra broadside guns, which therefore would appear roughly in line with those sided in the waist, on the upper deck. The step down also allowed the lowering of the superstructure by providing enough headroom for any stern cabins, but at a lower level in the ship. This allowed Hawkins to reduce the height of the superstructure, and thereby improve the sailing performance of the ship. The end result was the nearest thing to perfection that the Tudor world could produce. Compared to other warships, Hawkins' race-built galleons could sail faster and closer to the wind (up to 45 degrees or four compass points from the wind direction), and they had less leeway – the sideways drift experienced by sailing ships when the wind was on the beam. In short, they were well-designed ships that could outsail the majority of other warships – particularly the carracks that made up the bulk of the Spanish fleet in 1588. When this superiority was combined with the gunnery innovations described later, the result was a winning combination.

When Benjamin Godson died in 1577, Hawkins was appointed as the new Treasurer of the Navy, charged with continuing his good work. For the next 12 years he was the man responsible for building up the Elizabethan fleet, for designing and overhauling its ships, and for preparing it for war. He never received the favours

Another depiction of the *Ark Royal*, the flagship of the English fleet during the Spanish Armada campaign. It had originally been built as a large privateering vessel by Sir Walter Raleigh, and bore the name *Ark Raleigh* before being transferred into royal service (Stratford Archive).

bestowed by the queen on her court favourites and beaux, yet if any one man was responsible for her great victory over the Spanish in 1588 it was Hawkins. During his career he was constantly suspected of corruption, of embezzlement and of profiteering. No formal charges were ever laid, however, and whether the allegations were true or not the fact remains that during his tenure in office the fleet was always fully equipped and prepared for war. The 'cold war' followed by the active conflict with Spain meant that during the period from 1577 to 1589 the Navy Royal went through a phase of considerable expansion, and just as in any historical period, the opportunities for profit were there, as too was the room for suspicion by those not involved in the process.

During those 12 years, Hawkins continued the process of building powerful new ships for the fleet, or supervising the conversion of existing older vessels to better conform to his new design. Three more galleons were built, all displacing less than 500 tons — a size Hawkins saw as ideal for a fleet that relied on speed, manoeuvrability and firepower rather than boarding to win its battles. The *Revenge* (460 tons) was built at Deptford in 1577, followed by the *Rainbow* (380 tons) in 1586, which was constructed under the supervision of Peter Pett. That same year, just down the River Thames at Woolwich, Matthew Baker built the *Vanguard* (450 tons).

All three ships were powerful, well-armed race-built galleons, and all would play a leading part in the coming fight with Spain. They conformed to the lean, racy 3:1 ratio advocated by Hawkins and Lord Burghley, the Lord Treasurer. As it was lost before the survey that recorded ship specifications was drawn up, exact details of the *Revenge* are unknown. However, it is generally assumed that it had a keel length of around 110ft, and a 34ft beam. The *Rainbow* had a keel of 100ft and a beam of 32ft, while the *Vanguard* boasted dimensions of 108ft and 32ft respectively.

A major part of Hawkins' job was to supervise the rebuilding and refitting of the Navy Royal. During his tenure some 12 ships were rebuilt into race-built galleons. The first were the *Tiger* and the *Bull* (both rebuilt in 1570), undertaken as a means of proving that the process would indeed improve the sailing and fighting qualities of these two ships, now no longer recognizable as the small galleasses originally built for Henry VIII in 1546. When war with Spain appeared inevitable, then other larger units underwent the same process. The three galleons ordered by Mary — the *Golden Lion* (refitted in 1582), the *Philip & Mary* (refitted and renamed *Nonpareil* in 1584) and the *Mary Rose* (refitted in 1589) — were only part of the overhaul. The *Aid* underwent the process in 1580, the *Elizabeth Bonaventure* followed in 1581 and then the *Victory* was rebuilt in 1586. Other warships such as the *Elizabeth Jonas*, the *Triumph*, the *Hope* and the *White Bear* were all rebuilt after the Armada campaign, and after Hawkins' tenure ended in 1589.

Then there was the *Ark Raleigh*, an impressive private warship of 550 tons and 55 guns, owned by Sir Walter Raleigh. It had been built in Deptford by Richard Chapman as a private venture, based on Hawkins' design. Although not noticeably larger than its predecessors (it had a 100ft long keel, and a 33ft wide beam), it carried a greater weight of ordnance (some 50 tons), which meant it had the firepower of much larger warships such as the *Victory*. Renamed the *Ark Royal*, it was bought into service in time to participate in the Spanish Armada campaign, it where served as Lord Howard's flagship.

Sir John Hawkins retired in the year following the Armada campaign, but the warships designed according to his specifications continued to be built. The most significant of these were the *Defiance* (440 tons) and the *Garland* (530 tons – also known as the *Guardland*), both of which were built in Deptford in 1590, the first

Revenge, 1588

The most famous of all Elizabethan galleons, the *Revenge* was built at Deptford in 1577, and cost the royal exchequer around £4,000. She proved a sound investment, as the new galleon built according to Hawkins' principles proved to be one of the best-designed galleons in the fleet. Although her builder was never named, it is usually accepted that the man responsible for her construction was Master Shipwright Matthew Baker, the author of *Fragments of Ancient Shipwrightry*. However, Peter Pett was also almost certainly involved in the project. The *Revenge* was noted for being a stoutly built ship, and while her sailing qualities were not as impressive as those of her lighter contemporaries, she was considered probably the best all-round warship in the fleet. During the Spanish Armada campaign of 1588, the *Revenge* served as the flagship of Sir Francis Drake, and consequently she was involved in the fighting from the first engagement off Plymouth on 31 July, until the close-range engagement fought off Gravelines on 8 August. Under Drake's command she forced the surrender of the Spanish galleon *Nuestra Señora del Rosario*, and her crew were first to loot the Spanish prize. Her most famous battle, however, came in 1591, when she was overtaken by a Spanish fleet off the Azores. Her commander Sir Richard Grenville put up a spirited fight, but after 16 hours of battle he was forced to surrender the battered hulk of his ship. The *Revenge* was caught in a storm a few days later, and was wrecked off the island of Terceira (Tony Bryan).

Specifications
Displacement: 464 tons
Keel length: 110ft (33.5m) approx.
Beam: 34ft (10.4m)
Armament: 40 guns
Crew: 240 men
Service notes:
Built 1577. Lost in action, 1591

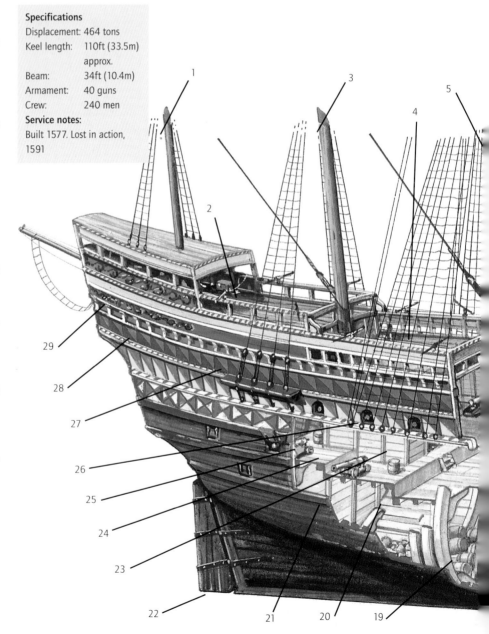

by Richard Chapman and the second by Peter and Joseph Pett. In the same year an even larger galleon, the *Merhonour* (690 tons – also known as the *Mer Honour*), was built at Woolwich by Matthew Baker. Then in 1595 came the *Due Repulse*, a 620-ton replacement for the *Repulse* lost off the Azores four years earlier. It was followed in 1596 by the *Warspite*, a 520-ton galleon built by Edward Stevens at Deptford. It can be argued that Hawkins' legacy lasted long after his death in 1595, as many of his ships remained in active service with the fleet long after the death of his monarch in 1603, and remained as mainstays of the Stuart navy well into the 17th century.

1 Bonaventure mast
2 Poop deck
3 Mizzen mast
4 Quarterdeck
5 Mainmast
6 Waist
7 Ship's boat
8 Fowler (swivel gun)
9 Foremast
10 Forecastle
11 Bowsprit Foremast
12 Beak
13 Main anchor
14 Cable store
15 Boatswain's store
16 Carpenter's cabin
17 Galley
18 Main deck armament
    (demi-culverins)
19 Powder store
20 Orlop deck
21 Lower wale
22 Rudder
23 Surgeon's cabin

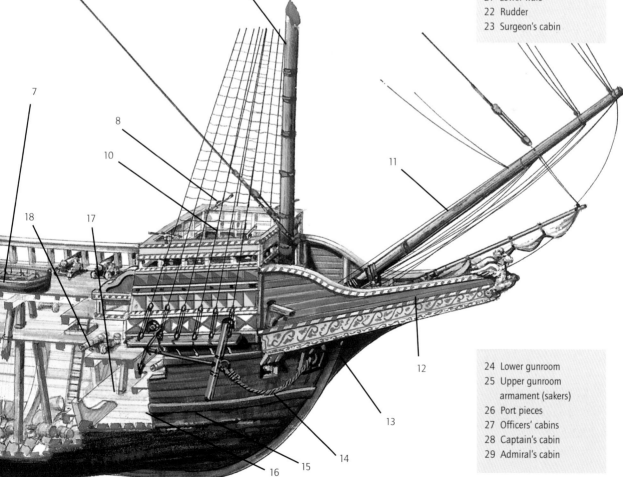

24 Lower gunroom
25 Upper gunroom
    armament (sakers)
26 Port pieces
27 Officers' cabins
28 Captain's cabin
29 Admiral's cabin

Of course, Queen Elizabeth's Navy Royal contained more than just major warships. During her reign 99 warships of various types were commissioned into the fleet, a figure that includes some vessels that remained in service for a year or two at the most. Three of these were prizes captured from the Spanish, the most notable of which was the *Nuestra Señora del Rosario*, a 1,150-ton great ship captured by Sir Francis Drake in 1588. It was never used against its former owners, as it was far too lumbering a vessel for the English, who even classified it as a carrack rather than as a galleon. It became a floating storage hulk on the River Medway in 1594, and was broken up 28 years later.

These 99 warships do not include the numerous armed merchantmen that were hired to augment the Navy Royal in wartime. Ninety-four such ships were hired or volunteered for service in 1588, a total that discounts the 15 or so vessels that displaced less than 90 tons. While the majority of these displaced less than 200 tons, 29 were larger, and included the *Galleon Leicester* and the *Merchant Royal*, both of 400 tons. With the addition of ordnance supplied from royal stores, these ships were almost as powerful as some of the major vessels in the Navy Royal, although they probably lacked the manoeuvrability of comparable warships such as the *Foresight* or the *Dreadnought*.

Other smaller additions to the Navy Royal during the Elizabethan period included nine galleys, four pinnaces, four small galleons and seven small ships, as well as an assortment of small vessels labelled by their sailing rig – pinks, ketches, barks and hoys. The fleet even included seven discovery vessels at various times.

A Tudor Master shipwright at work. Under the guidance of John Hawkins, shipwrights used mathematically produced plans to build their ships, resulting in much more effective hull shapes. From Matthew Baker's *Fragments of Ancient English Shipwrightry* (c.1582) (By permission of the Master and Fellows, Magdalene College, Cambridge).

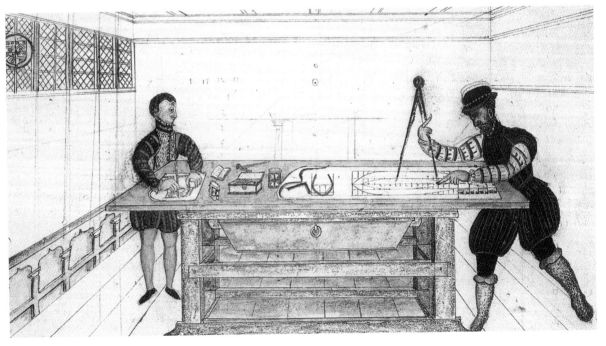

A few of these were bought into service, but the majority were built specifically for the Navy, mainly at the yards at Deptford, Woolwich and Limehouse on the River Thames on the outskirts of London, or at Chatham on the River Medway. These all had their own distinct role in the Tudor fleet – as escorts, guard ships, supply vessels, dispatch boats, tenders, fleet launches and transports.

Building the Ships

Regarding shipbuilding techniques, we are fortunate not only that in Matthew Baker's *Fragments of Ancient English Shipwrightry* (*c.*1582) we are given an insight into Tudor ship construction, but also that we can draw on evidence provided by maritime archaeology, most notably the remains of the earlier Tudor warship *Mary Rose* (1545) and the Elizabethan vessel known as the *Alderney Wreck* (1592). Unlike some earlier Tudor warships, Elizabethan royal ships were built using the carvel method, where a framework was created to form the shape of the hull, then the planking was fastened to it, with each plank laid side by side to form the outer hull. The earlier clinker-built method, where the planks overlapped each other, had fallen into disuse by the early 16th century.

The first step was the laying of the keel, using a series of three or more timbers, joined together using scarf joints. The keel on the *Ark Royal* was 100ft long, a fairly typical length for a vessel displacing around 400–600 tons. The keel was further strengthened by a keelson, which was also formed from several sections. The stem and sternposts rose to form the profile of the vessel – in the case of the *Ark Royal* the stern extending 6ft beyond the end of the keel, while the bow curved outwards for 33½ft.

Next a series of 'C-shaped' frames were raised above the keel, a wooden ribcage that formed the shape of the hull. In Elizabethan ship construction, the key frame was called the main frame, usually located in the centre of the vessel, close to the site of the mainmast. The width and thickness of these frames tapered off towards the stem and stern, as too did the deck beams, which were then set in place to span the frames. The beams themselves were supported by a series of knees that were attached to the frames, rather like a line of modern shelf brackets. Matthew Baker referred to the framing system as 'whole moulding', where the dimensions of each frame, knee and deck beam followed a carefully proscribed mathematical formula. Further supports were provided by futtocks – a series of angled timbers that strengthened the base of the frames, and secured them to the keel and keelson.

The outer hull was formed by a series of wales, wooden beams attached to the outer sides of the frames; these followed the shape of the ship as it would finally lie in the water. The lower wale was sited just above the waterline at the waist, but rose gradually towards the stem and stern. Additional wales were spaced regularly between it and the upper deck of the ship. Between these wales came the planking of the hull, with both planks and wales secured to the frames by means of wooden treenails and iron fasteners. Additional cross bracing known as stringers was provided inside the ship, linking the frames together. The frames bulged outwards just above the lower wale, which meant the ship curved out slightly immediately above the waterline, then a tumblehome brought the sides of the hull inwards slightly as they rose towards the upper deck. The deck beams themselves also rose towards the centreline of the ship, a feature designed to allow water to drain easily into scuppers and so over the side of the ship.

As Royal Master Shipwright, Baker laid out the proportions he used in ship construction, and his formula for ship construction reveals just how scientific the process was. While we have already stated that Sir John Hawkins introduced his design innovations based on his extensive practical experience, he also needed to team up with a first-class shipwright in order to see the project through – in his case Richard Chapman. Baker, along with his compatriot Peter Pett, was a disciple of Hawkins' approach to ship design. Therefore his *Fragments* should best be seen as a means by which the Hawkins' race-built galleon design was explained for all to see.

Unlike earlier galleons, those designed by Hawkins and built by men like Baker and Pett tapered rapidly towards the stern, while the lower wale and consequently the wide point of the hull immediately above it both rose towards the stern, creating a lean, streamlined hull that can be seen clearly in the illustrations supplied by Baker in his treatise. This tapering became more pronounced in the stern superstructure, where the quarterdeck rose gradually as it narrowed, until it reached the top of the narrow transom.

Painted shortly after the event, *The Spanish Armada*, an oil painting of the English School, provides us with a summary of the main events of the campaign, including Elizabeth's address to her troops at Tilbury, the fire beacons on the coast, and the close-quarter fighting off Gravelines. The appearance of the ships themselves suggests that the unknown artist was unfamiliar with maritime subjects (Worshipful Society of Apothecaries, Apothecaries Hall, London).

Arming the Fleet

We are lucky to have fairly detailed ordnance records for the later Tudor period. A comprehensive survey of the Tudor fleet was carried out shortly before the campaign, and we can build up a detailed picture of the fleet's fighting potential. If we compare this with earlier inventories we can see how the number of large bronze guns increased in the years before the Armada, while the number of obsolete wrought-iron guns was reduced. However, as late as the Spanish Armada campaign of 1588, a small number of these obsolete breech-loading weapons – by then classified as port pieces – were carried throughout the fleet as close-range anti-personnel weapons.

Smaller wrought-iron breech-loading bases (or swivel guns) continued to be carried, mounted on the ships' gunwales in a manner reminiscent of more modern machine guns. Their role was also much the same – delivering a hail of anti-personnel rounds at an enemy that was attempting to board. A larger version of the base, known as the fowler, was used in much the same way.

If we compare a list of the guns issued to the *Elizabeth Bonaventure* in 1585, and those that it actually carried during the expedition to the Caribbean that year, we see that Drake altered its suite of ordnance, dropping all its anti-personnel weapons (port pieces, fowlers and bases), and instead carried a handful of extra cannon-periers, culverins and demi-culverins (see table below for definitions). In other words, he had no intention of fighting a boarding action, and preferred to equip his most powerful ship with a formidable broadside. The layout of Hawkins' race-built galleons gave commanders the ability to carry larger, heavier guns than before, and so men like Drake made full use of this opportunity. The cannon-perier was an unusual, short, large-calibre weapon that fired a stone rather than a cast-iron roundshot. Although stone shot was expensive and time-consuming to produce, 16th-century navies retained a few such weapons, which had a limited range but were lethal at close quarters, the shot most probably shattering on impact into a shower of high-velocity stone flakes.

Excluding the handful of light swivel guns and other anti-personnel weapons, the vast majority of ordnance carried on ships of the Navy Royal was cast from bronze. An inventory detailing the ordnance carried by the ships of the fleet in 1603 lists very few iron pieces – less than 8 per cent of the total carried in the fleet, if swivel guns are excluded from the total. Despite improvements in the techniques of cast-iron gunfounding, and the development of a large and reliable iron gunfounding industry in the Wealden area of south-east England, the Navy Board remained unconvinced, and continued to purchase bronze guns for the fleet, the majority supplied by royal founders. Cast-iron ordnance, however, proved popular with private ship owners, largely because the metal was a third of the cost. Merchant vessels usually carried a significantly smaller armament than warships of a comparable size, and so the greater weight of iron guns compared to bronze ones was of less importance. Equally importantly, the Navy Board could exert more control over exactly what kind of weapons the royal gunfounders produced.

The following list of ordnance types is culled from a contemporary artillery manual, *The Arte of Shooting in Great Ordnance*, by William Bourne, published in London in 1578. As a land-based master gunner in the queen's service, Bourne was careful to include a list of the most common contemporary types of gun, and listed their basic specifications.

Table of types of ordnance as listed by William Bourne, c.1578

	Calibre	Length	Weight	Shot size
Cannon	8in.	12 feet	7,500 lbs.	64-pdr.
Demi-cannon	6½in.	10-11 feet	5,500 lbs.	33-pdr.
Culverin	5½in.	12 feet	4,500 lbs.	17-pdr.
Demi-culverin	4½in.	10 feet	2,700 lbs.	10¼-pdr.
Saker	3¾in.	8-9 feet	1,500 lbs.	6-pdr.
Minion	3¼in.	8 feet	900 lbs.	3-pdr.
Falcon	2¾in.	7 feet	700-750 lbs.	2½-pdr.
Falconet	2¼in.	5-6 feet	360-400 lbs.	1¼-pdr.

We can compare Bourne's list with a list of ordnance carried in the Navy Royal in 1585, which gave the number of guns carried on all the major units of the fleet that were then on active service, dividing them by gun type. Cannons were considered too large for shipboard use, as there was insufficient room to mount these weapons in pairs, one on each broadside, even if the gundeck beams could support the weight. This meant that the demi-cannon was the largest practical gun carried on board warships of the Elizabethan fleet, a weapon equivalent to the late 18th century 32-pdr. The list also shows that as late as the 1580s, most ships in the fleet still carried between one and three paired wrought-iron breech-loading guns, similar to the pieces found on the *Mary Rose*. This practice reaffirms the idea, already noted, that although these weapons were considered obsolete compared to modern bronze pieces, their ability to fire rapidly at close range made them a valuable weapon to include in a ship's arsenal. For a similar reason most large warships carried one or two pairs of cannon-periers, which were essentially the modern replacement for the port-piece as a large-calibre anti-personnel weapon.

Taking the *Revenge* as an example, we see that in just three years before the start of the Spanish Armada campaign, it carried 36 large guns, all but two of which were almost certainly bronze pieces. In addition it was fitted out with ten swivel guns (fowlers and bases). Using the terminology of the 18th century, the heavy armament was divided into 32-pdrs, 18-pdrs, 12-pdrs and 6-pdrs – not counting the cannon-periers. The heaviest guns would be carried as low as possible in the ship, leaving the sakers and demi-culverins to be housed on the upper deck, and in the upper gunroom. Given that the *Revenge* had a beam of about 32ft at the position of its main frame (immediately forward of its mainmast), then according to Bourne's table there was barely sufficient room to deploy two guns in broadside, one

on either side of the gundeck. However, the Navy Board had already addressed this problem. During the 1570s, William Winter, the Master of Ordnance for the Navy, developed a new and shorter range of bronze guns designed for sea service, and these were in general use by the time the Spanish Armada sailed up the English Channel.

While the Spanish still mounted their guns on two-wheeled carriages — essentially solid-wheeled and slightly shortened versions of those employed on land — the English had developed their own form of gun carriage. The carriages recovered from the *Mary Rose* in 1545 show that this process was already underway during Henry VIII's reign, and a combination of accounts and a few scant pictorial records suggest that by 1580 the Navy Royal had fully adopted the four-wheeled carriage. The combination of shorter guns and more manoeuvrable carriages was as important to the success of the Elizabethan warship as the design of its hull.

In fact, in 1588, while one English gunner complained about the lack of skilled gunners in the fleet, Spanish observers claimed that the English fired their guns as frequently as the Spanish could fire a musket. The gun and carriage were perfectly designed for the business of naval gunnery, and consequently they easily outdid the Spanish in terms of rate of fire if not in accuracy. If the English fleet closed to within point-blank range of the enemy — just as they did during the final stages of the Armada campaign — then the effect could be devastating.

In this English shipbuilding treatise, the clean underwater lines of a race-built galleon are being likened to the streamlined shape of a fish. Hawkins' innovations resulted in a royal fleet which – for the most part – consisted of fast, nimble and well-armed warships. From Matthew Baker's *Fragments of Ancient English Shipwrightry* (c.1582) (By permission of the Master and Fellows, Magdalene College, Cambridge).

✥ The Campaign

The Launch of the 'Great Enterprise'

On 9 February 1588 the Marquis of Santa Cruz died in Lisbon, the victim of overwork and chronic illness. The king appointed the Duke of Medina Sidonia as his replacement, and issued very specific instructions, emphasizing the need for speed and secrecy. King Philip even added: 'The general opinion here lately has been that it would be as well to spread abroad the report that the galleons are bound for the Indies, so as the more easily to recruit personnel, particularly seamen. Now however, that you are joining the Armada, it may be that the matter wears a different complexion, and that, when it is learned that they will serve with you and under your command, recruits will respond more readily to the call of the Armada, than to that of the Indies. You who are on the spot will be able to judge more easily what course will produce the better results.' Despite this flattery, and the almost laughable suggestion of subterfuge, after initial reservations and excuses, the duke accepted the post.

Preparations for the Armada were in turmoil, and only a handful of the men, ships and stores were ready. Under supervision, Lisbon was transformed as new ships arrived; others were repaired and provisioned, and the Portuguese gun foundries worked at full production. By May each of the 130 ships of the expedition was issued with an adequate provision of ordnance, powder and shot, stores were loaded, pilots issued with the appropriate charts and each ship was inspected, and refitted where appropriate. A total of 18,973 soldiers were embarked, together with their military equipment, including a full siege train. The duke infused the fleet with a new sense of optimism, and on 9 May the fleet was inspected and declared ready for sea.

The king had already sent him his last orders: 'You are to sail with the whole Armada, making for the English Channel, and pass through it until you reach Margate Point, where you will join the Duke of Parma and Placencia, my nephew. You are to remove any obstacles and make secure his passage across the channel, according to the plan pre-arranged and according to my decision, with which you are both acquainted.' Even at this late stage the details of his planned rendezvous with the Duke of Parma

Opposite
Robert Dudley, 1st Earl of Leicester (c.1532–88), an oil by a painter of the English School, c.1586. As commander of the English army gathered at Tilbury, the Earl of Leicester had the task of defeating the Duke of Parma if the Spanish managed to land in Kent (Parham Park, Storrington, West Sussex).

ORDERS,
Set dovvne by the
Duke of Medina, Lord general
of the Kings Fleet, to be obſerued in
the voyage toward England.

Tranſlated out of Spaniſh into Engliſh by T.P.

Imprinted at London by Thomas Orwin for Thomas Gilbert, dwelling in Fleetſtreete neere to
the ſigne of the Caſtle. 1588.

An enterprise as large as the organization and planning of the Spanish Armada was impossible to keep secret. This is the cover of an English pamphlet, culled from a Spanish document, which outlined the composition of the fleet, its rules of engagement and planned dispositions. It was published in England before the Spanish Armada had even left Lisbon (Clyde Hensley Collection, Ashville, NC).

were extremely vague. A second letter clarified things a little: 'When you are at your post off Margate, which you are to endeavour to reach with the Armada, having dealt with any difficulties encountered along the way, you will know where the Duke, my nephew, wishes the soldiers you are giving him to be landed, and there you will land them. It is my desire that Don Alonso de Leyva, my Captain-General of the Light Cavalry of Milan, should take them ashore, and keep them under his command until he delivers them to the Duke. You are to arrange for this to be done.'

Interestingly, the king also gave the Duke of Medina Sidonia an alternative plan. If, after reaching Flanders, the Army of Flanders was for some reason unable to cross, then the Armada was given a new set of orders. The king wrote: 'You will see whether you are able to capture the Isle of Wight, which is not so strongly defended as to appear able to resist you. Once captured, however, it can be defended, and you will have a secure port in which the Armada may take shelter and which, being a place of importance, would open the way for further action by you. It would therefore be well for you to fortify yourself strongly on it.' This was a rather naïve option, as it meant that after reaching Flanders the Armada would have to battle wind and tide to travel back up the English Channel, then force a landing. Not only did the prevailing winds make this all but impossible, but by that stage the intentions of the fleet would have been clear to the English, who would have had a chance to reinforce and fortify the island. Wisely, the duke decided not to point out these points to his king.

Bad weather kept it in Lisbon harbour for another fortnight, but on 28 May the Spanish Armada slipped anchor and headed out into the Atlantic. Philip II's 'Great Enterprise' had begun. From the first the Armada's progress was dogged by weather 'boisterous and bad as if it were December' and the squadron of hulks proved singularly slow. It was soon discovered that many of the ships' provisions were bad, and the duke decided to put into the north-western Spanish port of La Coruña to repair his ships and restock the fleet's provisions. On 19 June the flagship and the leading ships entered La Coruña, but a sudden south-westerly gale scattered the rest throughout the Bay of Biscay. Medina Sidonia considered abandoning the enterprise, but the king ordered him to continue. The ships made their way into the port, the duke supervised their repair.

He also had grave doubts about the efficiency and seaworthiness of many of his ships. He said as much to the king, who replied: 'I see plainly the truth of what you say, that the Levant ships are less free and staunch in heavy seas than the vessels built here, and the hulks cannot sail to windward, but it is still the fact that the Levant ships sail constantly to England, and the hulks hardly go anywhere else but up the English Channel, and it is quite an exception for them to leave it to go to other seas.

The Armada's Progress up the Channel

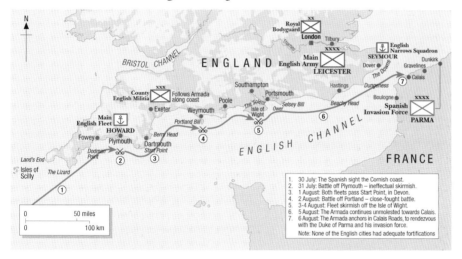

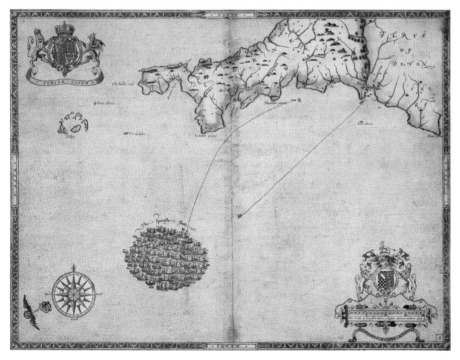

The Spanish fleet off the coast of Cornwall, 29th July 1588, a chart by Robert Adams reproduced in his *Expeditionis Hispanorum in Angliam vera descriptio anno 1588.* This is the first of a dozen such charts in the same series, each showing a different stage of the campaign. The track marked on the chart is that of the Falmouth vessel which first spotted the Spanish Armada, and which raced back to Plymouth with the news (National Maritime Museum, Greenwich, London).

It is true that if we could have things exactly as we wished, we would rather have other vessels, but under the present circumstances the expedition must not be abandoned on account of this difficulty.' The king had spoken, and so the duke threw himself into the task of preparing his fleet for another voyage. Within a month the Armada was once again ready to put to sea. It carried fresh provisions, the men were in good heart, and the enemy were just ten days' sailing away from them.

Medina Sidonia sailed from La Coruña on 21 July, and morale was reportedly high among the crews. Four days later he sent a pinnace ahead to warn Parma of his approach, and a brisk southerly breeze carried the rest of his fleet north towards England. The rough seas in the Bay of Biscay proved too much for the four galleys which accompanied the Armada, and they were forced to run for shelter to a French port. This was a serious blow, as they would have been vital support vessels during the landing in Kent. The *Santa Ana*, flagship of the Biscay Squadron, was also forced to drop out, having lost a mast. A week after leaving La Coruña the rest of the Armada was off Ushant (the western tip of Brittany) and the English coastline lay just beyond the northern horizon. Neither side knew it, but the rival fleets were only 100 miles apart.

Off Plymouth (30–31 July)

It was 1600hrs on Friday 29 July 1588 and 125 ships of various sizes stretched in a ragged line across three miles of ocean. As the flagship hoisted a flag bearing the Virgin Mary and a cross, the sailors gathered to hear mass. The Spanish

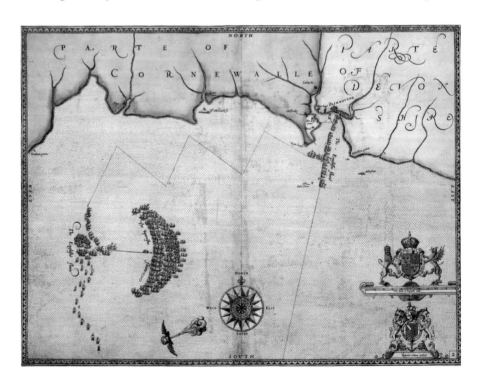

The Spanish and English fleets near Plymouth on 30th-31st July 1588, the fourth in the series of charts by Robert Adams reproduced in his *Expeditionis Hispanorum in Angliam vera descriptio anno 1588* (National Maritime Museum, Greenwich, London).

The Battle off Plymouth (First Shots), 31 July 1588

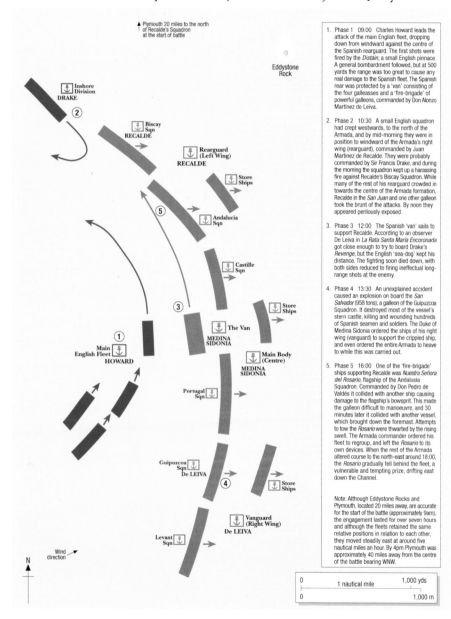

Plymouth 20 miles to the north of Recalde's Squadron at the start of battle

Eddystone Rock

Inshore Division
DRAKE

Biscay Sqn
RECALDE

Rearguard (Left Wing)
RECALDE

Store Ships

Andalucia Sqn

Castille Sqn

Store Ships

The Van
MEDINA SIDONIA

Main English Fleet
HOWARD

Main Body (Centre)
MEDINA SIDONIA

Portugal Sqn

Guipuzcoa Sqn
De LEIVA

Store Ships

Vanguard (Right Wing)
De LEIVA

Levant Sqn

Wind direction

N

1. **Phase 1   09:00** Charles Howard leads the attack of the main English fleet, dropping down from windward against the centre of the Spanish rearguard. The first shots were fired by the *Distain*, a small English pinnace. A general bombardment followed, but at 500 yards the range was too great to cause any real damage to the Spanish fleet. The Spanish rear was protected by a 'van' consisting of the four galleasses and a 'fire-brigade' of powerful galleons, commanded by Don Alonzo Martinez de Leiva.

2. **Phase 2   10:30** A small English squadron had crept westwards, to the north of the Armada, and by mid-morning they were in position to windward of the Armada's right wing (rearguard), commanded by Juan Martinez de Recalde. They were probably commanded by Sir Francis Drake, and during the morning the squadron kept up a harassing fire against Recalde's Biscay Squadron. While many of the rest of his rearguard crowded in towards the centre of the Armada formation, Recalde in the *San Juan* and one other galleon took the brunt of the attacks. By noon they appeared perilously exposed.

3. **Phase 3   12:00** The Spanish 'van' sails to support Recalde. According to an observer De Leiva in *La Rata Santa Maria Encoronada* got close enough to try to board Drake's *Revenge*, but the English 'sea-dog' kept his distance. The fighting soon died down, with both sides reduced to firing ineffectual long-range shots at the enemy.

4. **Phase 4   13:30** An unexplained accident caused an explosion on board the *San Salvador* (958 tons), a galleon of the Guipuzcoa Squadron. It destroyed most of the vessel's stern castle, killing and wounding hundreds of Spanish seamen and soldiers. The Duke of Medina Sidonia ordered the ships of his right wing (vanguard) to support the crippled ship, and even ordered the entire Armada to heave to while this was carried out.

5. **Phase 5   16:00** One of the 'fire-brigade' ships supporting Recalde was *Nuestra Señora del Rosario*, flagship of the Andalusia Squadron. Commanded by Don Pedro de Valdés it collided with another ship causing damage to the flagship's bowsprit. This made the galleon difficult to manoeuvre, and 30 minutes later it collided with another vessel, which brought down the foremast. Attempts to tow the *Rosario* were thwarted by the rising swell. The Armada commander ordered his fleet to regroup, and left the *Rosario* to its own devices. When the rest of the Armada altered course to the north-east around 18:00, the *Rosario* gradually fell behind the fleet, a vulnerable and tempting prize, drifting east down the Channel.

Note: Although Eddystone Rocks and Plymouth, located 20 miles away, are accurate for the start of the battle (approximately 9am), the engagement lasted for over seven hours and although the fleets retained the same relative positions in relation to each other, they moved steadily east at around five nautical miles an hour. By 4pm Plymouth was approximately 40 miles away from the centre of the battle bearing WNW.

0	1 nautical mile	1,000 yds
0		1,000 m

Armada's crewmen had just sighted the Lizard, marking the start of the English coastline. The Duke of Medina Sidonia allowed the sailors to pray, then he ordered his ships to heave to and called his senior commanders together for a council of war. The duke was about to issue his final instructions. Once the English fleet appeared, such an opportunity might not occur again until the Armada reached its rendezvous with the Duke of Parma.

This was also the last chance to redeploy the fleet before the fighting started. The Duke's council included his chief-of-staff, Diego Flores de Valdés, the deputy Armada commander Juan Martinez de Recalde, six squadron commanders and Don Francisco de Bobadilla, commander of the embarked Spanish troops. Also present was a volunteer, Don Alonso de Leiva, charged with secret orders to take command of the Armada in the event of the duke's death. All these men were key players in the drama which was about to unfold.

While King Philip of Spain demanded that the Armada maintain a defensive formation as it travelled up the English Channel towards the Flemish coast, some of the commanders argued for a more aggressive approach. Both de Leiva and de Recalde proposed a direct assault on Plymouth, the main gathering point of the English fleet. If the English could be confined in the narrow harbour by part of the Spanish fleet, the rest of the Armada could sail down the Channel unimpeded. The duke rejected the plan, emphasizing that the Spanish objective was to reach Flanders, not become embroiled in a direct attack on the English fleet.

He also made the last arrangements to his order of battle: Don Alonso de Leiva would command the vanguard, or left wing, consisting of the 20 major ships of the Levant and Guipúzcoa squadrons. Juan Martinez de Recalde would lead the rearguard, or right wing, which was made up primarily of the 20 major warships of the squadrons of Biscay and Andalusia. The duke himself would control the main body or centre. He emphasized the importance of maintaining a tight defensive formation, and created a 'van'; a powerful ad hoc squadron which could act as a 'fire-brigade'. It could race to support any portion of the defensive formation that was threatened by the English. This task was assigned to Juan Martinez, who was the most experienced naval commander in the fleet. With the plans made, the commanders returned to their ships, and the Armada was readied for battle.

By the next morning the Armada was sailing north-eastwards, following the line of the Cornish coastline for some dozen or so miles. It was certainly an impressive sight, spanning more than two miles of sea. An English observer wrote: 'We never thought that they could ever have found, gathered and joined so great a force of puissant ships together, and appointed them with their cannon, culverin and other great pieces of brass ordnance.' Along the coast beacons were lit, a string of signals that stretched the length of the south coast.

The news of the Armada's arrival had already reached Lord Howard in Plymouth because the previous night a scouting ship – probably the *Golden Hinde* – had caught sight of the Spanish fleet through Friday's rain squalls and raced into Plymouth that afternoon with the news. According to tradition, Lord Howard, Francis Drake and other senior commanders were playing a game of bowls. There is little to substantiate this myth, or to corroborate Drake's line about 'having time to finish the game, and beat the Spanish too.' However, a few hours of inactivity could not be helped. The fleet were unable to sail until the incoming tide slackened and turned that evening. In theory there was actually time to spare.

Worse, the arrival of the Spanish had come at a bad time. The fleet had attempted to launch a raid on La Coruña, but the same bad weather which hindered the Spanish had also forced Lord Howard to abandon the enterprise. The fleet had only returned to Plymouth a week before, and was still replenishing its stores. Rather than playing a leisurely game of bowls, most of the seamen in the fleet would have spent those precious few hours frantically loading food and water onto their ships. That evening Howard and Drake managed to warp 54 ships out of Plymouth harbour; an impressive display of seamanship in the face of contrary winds and tides. By dawn the following morning a total of 105 ships had cleared the harbour, and were beating their way to windward, and towards the Spanish.

Throughout Saturday morning the last of the English fleet cleared the tricky entrance to Plymouth Sound, and the growing number of ships gathered off the Eddystone Rocks, some ten miles south of Plymouth. Howard planned to split his force into two: a main body and an inshore squadron. They would pass on either side of the Armada and rendezvous to the west of the Spaniards. This would give the English the weather gauge. This almost mystical fighting term from the age of sail involved one fleet being upwind of the other. That allowed it to swoop down on the enemy at will. Conversely, the enemy were virtually unable to work their way to windward to close with the enemy. The admiral who held the weather gauge could dictate the course of the battle.

During the Spanish Armada campaign, the English held the weather gauge for most of the week-long fight up the English Channel. When the wind briefly shifted and gave the Spanish this advantage, Medina Sidonia tried to close with the English fleet off Portland (2 August), but the local tidal race prevented the Spanish from closing, and so the English maintained their tactical advantage – one they held for the rest of the campaign.

The Armada would have been in sight by 3pm, but rain squalls hid the two fleets from each other. During the afternoon the Spanish deployed from 'line of march' into 'line of battle', spreading into a crescent formation, with de Recalde's rearguard on the left wing and de Leiva's vanguard on the right. As the Duke of Medina Sidonia noted in his diary, 'Our Armada put itself in combat formation'. The Spanish fleet reduced sail during the night to prevent straggling. This also allowed the two sections of the English fleet to sail past the Armada on either side (north and south).

(Note: Throughout most of the narrative, the left wing of the Armada was opposite the left wing of the English fleet: the Armada was essentially fighting a rearguard action, and both fleets travelled in the same direction).

During the night a small Spanish scouting vessel captured a Falmouth fishing boat. Once the crew had been interrogated it became apparent that the English

Drake's Pursuit of the *Rosario*. During the first battle of the campaign off Plymouth (31 July), the *Nuestra Señora del Rosario* served as the flagship of Don Pedro de Valdés, commander of the Andalusia Squadron. She damaged her bowsprit and foremast in the fight, and she fell behind the main Armada formation. By dusk she was well to the south of the Spanish fleet, which had changed course to the north-east. Sir Francis Drake in the *Revenge* was ordered to shadow the Armada during the night, showing his stern lantern so the English fleet could follow him. Instead he extinguished all lights and headed south to intercept Don Pedro. The Englishman, who had made his name as a privateer, claimed he forgot about the lantern and that on seeing strange sails to the south he pursued them. At dawn he was two to three cables to windward of the *Rosario*. As Frobisher later retorted, this was because 'you were within two or three cables length ... all night!' Don Pedro duly surrendered to Drake, and the rich prize was towed into Falmouth. While the incident made the English privateer a rich man, it did little to further the English cause in the campaign, and amounted to a gross dereliction of duty. The plate shows Drake abandoning the Armada during the night, and setting course for the crippled *Rosario* (Howard Gerrard).

knew of the Spanish presence and there was no possibility of surprise. The English were at sea, and the following day would bring about the first battle of the campaign. During the night the wind veered slightly, blowing west-north-west. The sea was also becoming rougher, and the rain squalls continued to pass up the Channel.

At dawn, lookouts in the Armada saw the English ships to the south-west. Both the inshore and main squadrons had passed the Spaniards during the night and were taking up a position to windward, although the smaller inshore wing was still tacking westward to join Howard and the main body. Medina Sidonia ordered his hulks to form into three groups ahead of the main fleet, protecting his supply vessels with the rest of his fleet. To the English the Armada must have been an imposing sight. One observer reported the Spanish ships deployed 'like a half-moon, the wings thereof spread out ... sailing very slowly, with full sails ... and the ocean groaning under their weight'.

Another more phlegmatic chronicler was less impressed. The Florentine Petruccio Ubaldino wrote: 'This enemy too, was very sure of his own strength, so we can realize how true it is in sea matters that the fleet of any prince desiring to attack any State or foreign kingdom cannot hope to gain the victory, however honourably commanded, when it comes across a fleet which depends on itself in such a way as the English did; while the attacking fleet is manned by crews of different race, with strange officers and a variety of customs and languages, and ideas.'

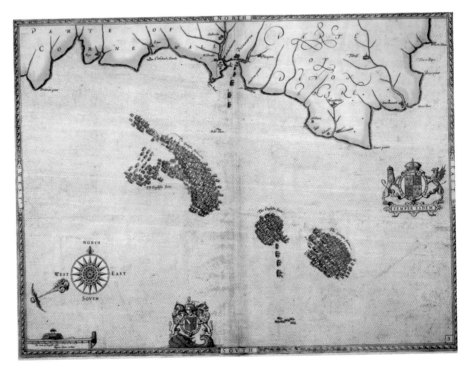

The English engage the Spanish fleet near Plymouth on 31st July 1588, the fifth in the series of charts by Robert Adams reproduced in his *Expeditionis Hispanorum in Angliam vera descriptio anno 1588*. This shows the skirmish off Plymouth, and the subsequent departure of Drake when he broke away from the pursuit to corner the damaged galleon *Rosario* (National Maritime Museum, Greenwich, London).

Lord Howard was accompanied by the small 80-ton bark *Distain*, and, probably because no formal declaration of war had ever been made, he decided to open the battle with a chivalric gesture — his way of laying down the gauntlet to the Duke of Medina Sidonia. He ordered it to sweep down towards the centre of the Spanish formation and to fire an opening shot at the Spanish flagship. The 'flagship' turned out to be de Leiva's *La Rata Santa María Encoronada*, but the ceremonial shot fired by the appropriately named *Distain* prompted Medina Sidonia to unfurl his command flag on the real flagship, the *San Martín*. Chivalric honour had now been satisfied by both sides. It was shortly after 9am, and the battle was now underway.

Lord Howard led his fleet in an attack on the centre and rear of the Spanish formation. Spanish witnesses describe the English attack as being *en ala*, or 'in file' (line astern). This in itself was unusual, as ships usually fought by 'caracole', firing a broadside, and then turning to fire the other, then retiring to reload, firing the stern guns in the process. The cycle would then be repeated. With so many ships under his command, it made sense for Howard to order the rest of the fleet to follow him. In effect he was writing a manual for naval warfare as he went along.

At the same time a handful of latecomers to the inshore squadron tacked within range of the Armada's northerly (left) wing. Two parts of the Armada formation were therefore under attack, the 'van' guarding the centre rear and the extreme tip of the left wing, a position held by the Squadron of Biscay, 'the windermost ships', as Sir Walter Raleigh described them.

When the Squadron of Biscay came under attack, most of the naos instinctively veered away from the enemy, closing in on the Squadron of Andalusia to starboard. This crowding left the two most northern ships exposed, de Recalde's *San Juan de Portugal* and the *almiranta* (vice-flagship), *Gran Grin*. By this time more of the English inshore squadron were firing on the Spanish, with most of the shots being concentrated on the two naos. The records are unclear, but it has been suggested that Drake commanded the inshore squadron. Drake is also mentioned leading a detachment of eight ships against de Recalde, including Frobisher's and Hawkins' ships, which presumably formed part of the main body. Whoever commanded the attack, the fire was largely ineffective, since Spanish accounts mention that only 15 men were killed on de Recalde's flagship that afternoon.

As Howard's main battle line passed the Spanish 'van' they fired in succession at long range (about 500 yards), then continued north towards de Recalde's wing. Witnesses in Plymouth describe hearing the sound of the guns in the distance and seeing the mass of ships and smoke on the horizon as the action slowly passed by, at a steady three or four knots. Medina Sidonia saw the danger of having the enemy concentrate its force against his left wing so he ordered the 'van' to turn to port and steer north on a course parallel to the English. Don Alonso de Leiva, in *La Rata Santa María Encoronada*, took charge of the 'van' (abandoning his supervision of the unengaged right wing) and accompanied by the *San Mateo*, two other galleons and the galleasses, he tried to close with Drake and his ad hoc squadron of eight vessels.

The English 'sea dog' kept his distance and veered to port, avoiding becoming trapped between the powerful 'van' and the left wing of the crescent-shaped Spanish formation. Once the Spanish 'van' reached de Recalde the crisis had passed, and the English were content to keep their distance, firing from windward at long range. Lord Howard later wrote that: 'we durst not adventure to be put in amongst them', while one of his commanders – Captain Henry Whyte of the *Bark Talbot* – was a little more blunt: 'the majesty of the enemy's fleet, the good order they held, the private consideration of our own wants did cause, in mine opinion, our first onset to be more coldly done than became the value of our nation and the credit of the English navy.' In other words, the English were unable or unwilling to close within effective range of the Armada's powerful defensive formation.

As the main battle was being fought around the Spanish wing, an unexpected disaster struck the Spanish in the vanguard, or right wing. Around 1.30pm a huge explosion ripped the sterncastle and part of the after decks out of the *San Salvador*, a large nao of the Squadron of Guipúzcoa. Although the exact cause remains unknown, it is probable that a powder barrel on the sterncastle exploded, setting off other powder barrels nearby. The blast killed or wounded hundreds of the crew and wrecked the vessel's steering mechanism. Medina Sidonia instantly ordered the Armada to heave to, and neighbouring ships came to the *San Salvador's* aid, including the fleet flagship. Survivors were plucked from the water, and the fires on the *San Salvador* were extinguished while the wounded were transferred to other ships. By late afternoon the burnt and limping vessel was under way, escorted by the rest of its squadron.

Around 4pm a second disaster befell the Armada. One of the principal warships on the left wing was the *Nuestra Señora del Rosario*, the *capitana* of the Squadron of Andalusia, commanded by Don Pedro de Valdés. The neat formation of the Armada was disrupted as the 'van' and the two left wing squadrons crowded together. In the confusion Don Pedro's nao collided with a ship of the Squadron of Biscay and damaged its bowsprit. This affected the steering of the ship, and while repairs were being carried out the *Rosario* collided again, this time with the *Santa Catalina* of its own squadron. This second collision brought down its foremast.

The sea was becoming rougher all the time, so Don Pedro sent a small ship to Medina Sidonia to ask for help. His ship was now virtually unmanoeuvrable. Counselled by Don Pedro's cousin Diego Flores de Valdés, Medina Sidonia decided that to rescue the *Rosario* would be to place the Armada in jeopardy. As the Dominican friar Bernardo de Góngora put it: 'The Duke continued on his way and left the good Don Pedro and his company ... in the power of the enemy, who were never more than a league behind us ... God knows what happened to them.' Petruccio Ubaldino claimed that the decision to abandon this great vessel was 'to the great surprise of the English fleet.'

Consequently the furious Don Pedro was abandoned and the *Rosario* drifted off to the east, while the rest of the Armada altered course slightly to the north-east. Dusk and increasingly rough seas brought the first day's action to a close. While the Spanish had two ships damaged, neither was as a result of English attack. The defensive tactics of the Armada had been tested and proven, and the integrity of its formation had never been seriously threatened.

Drake was ordered to shadow the Armada while the rest of the English fleet regrouped then followed on behind. This was presumably because following the English fleet's experiment with line ahead tactics, Drake was closest to the enemy. Howard sent a pinnace with orders that Drake was to light his stern lanterns to serve as a guide for the other ships. At around 9pm a small armed merchant vessel probed the wounded *Rosario* and was driven off by artillery fire. Drake was aware of the Spanish ship's plight and of its position. Instead of following the main fleet, he quietly altered course to starboard and shadowed the *Rosario* for the rest of the night.

Without their guide, Howard in the *Ark Royal* followed by the *Mary Rose* and the *White Bear* tried to shadow the Armada in the darkness, but the rest of the fleet lagged behind. In the mounting seas, the English ships became scattered in the darkness. Drake has been roundly criticized for his action, which placed his own desire for plunder before the needs of his nation, but he had built his reputation on privateering and would simply have found the opportunity too good to resist. Although he later claimed that he was pursuing strange sails and that he forgot to light his stern lantern, there is little doubt of his true actions or motives. Even one of his apologists, Petruccio Ubaldino, wrote: 'the vice-Admiral had left his place to follow five strange ships which were sighted very late in the evening'. It was no accident. Ever the 'sea dog', Drake was abandoning the fleet in search of plunder.

Off Dartmouth (I August)

Dawn on Monday I August found the Armada some 20 miles to the south of Start Point, and although still in its defensive formation, the fleet had become somewhat straggled during the night. The English were in a far worse position, as only Howard in the *Ark Royal* and his two consorts remained in position behind the Spanish and to windward. The English commander spent most of the morning hove to, waiting for his scattered fleet to gather around him, while the Armada a few miles away used the respite to heave to themselves, allowing Medina Sidonia time to reorganize its formation. With Don Pedro de Valdés and the *Rosario* lost

The English pursue the Spanish fleet east of Plymouth on 31st July-1st August 1588, the sixth in the series of charts by Robert Adams reproduced in his *Expeditionis Hispanorum in Angliam vera descriptio anno 1588.* It shows how Drake's actions led to a temporary scattering of the English fleet. In the bottom of the map, Drake is occupying himself with the capture of the *Rosario* (National Maritime Museum, Greenwich, London).

The Campaign off Devon and Cornwall

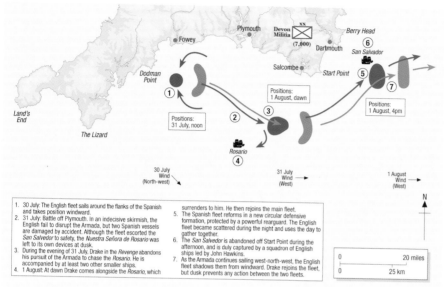

1. 30 July: The English fleet sails around the flanks of the Spanish and takes position windward.
2. 31 July: Battle off Plymouth. In an indecisive skirmish, the English fail to disrupt the Armada, but two Spanish vessels are damaged by accident. Although the fleet escorted the *San Salvedor* to safety, the *Nuestra Señora de Rosario* was left to its own devices at dusk.
3. During the evening of 31 July, Drake in the *Revenge* abandons his pursuit of the Armada to chase the *Rosario*. He is accompanied by at least two other smaller ships.
4. 1 August: At dawn Drake comes alongside the *Rosario*, which surrenders to him. He then rejoins the main fleet.
5. The Spanish fleet reforms in a new circular defensive formation, protected by a powerful rearguard. The English fleet became scattered during the night and uses the day to gather together.
6. The *San Salvedor* is abandoned off Start Point during the afternoon, and is duly captured by a squadron of English ships led by John Hawkins.
7. As the Armada continues sailing west-north-west, the English fleet shadows them from windward. Drake rejoins the fleet, but dusk prevents any action between the two fleets.

somewhere to the south, his deputy, Don Diego Enríquez, became the new commander of the Squadron of Andalusia.

The problem with the horned or crescent-shaped defensive formation of the previous day was that it was cumbersome, and the extreme tips of the crescent had been vulnerable to attack. Medina Sidonia expected the English to bar his progress up the Channel, and his formation was perfectly designed to envelop and surround the smaller English fleet. Since the English ships kept the weather gauge and refused to allow the Spaniards to come near enough to board them, a new approach was needed. The duke's solution was to join the horns together, forming a defensive circle rather than a crescent. Like the *tercio* formation used on land, the main body would be surrounded by smaller units. On land these would be musketeers, but at sea Medina Sidonia used his most powerful and well-armed ships, supported by his galleasses, which could tow the sailing warships if the wind failed.

While de Recalde busied himself with repairs to his flagship, Don Alonso de Leiva in *La Rata Santa María Encoronada* commanded the rearguard and the duke controlled the main body of the fleet. The formation was partly a response to the 'flinching' under fire, which had threatened to disrupt the Armada's defensive formation the day before. To avoid a repetition of this, Medina Sidonia sent small boats throughout the fleet, threatening that any captain who broke formation would suffer death by hanging. An executioner and provost marshal in each boat helped to emphasize the threat.

Further to the south, dawn found Don Pedro de Valdés and the *Rosario* alone but for one other ship, which was accompanied by a few small escorts. During the

Drake's capture of the Spanish squadron flagship *Nuestra Señora del Rosario*, on 1 August 1588, as depicted in a detail from *The English pursue the Spanish Fleet east of Plymouth* – an engraving based on a contemporary series of tapestries which were destroyed during a fire in the House of Lords in 1834 (Stratford Archive).

night Drake in the *Revenge* had shadowed the damaged galleon, and as the sun rose the sea dog was less than 500 yards to windward. He later expressed surprise at finding the *Rosario* at first light, prompting the sceptical Frobisher to comment: 'Ay marry, you were within two or three cables length [at dawn, as] you were no further off all night.' Although Drake could make excuses to his queen and his fleet commander, his fellow 'sea dogs' and privateers knew exactly what his motives were.

The *Rosario* was virtually defenceless, since the *Revenge* could rake the Spanish vessel at will. Drake called on Don Pedro to surrender, and after an initial refusal the Spanish commander agreed to discuss terms with Drake on board the *Revenge*. After some contemplation, Don Pedro agreed to surrender his ship. The *Rosario* carried part of the Armada's pay chest – 50,000 gold ducats (or escudos), and the personal wealth of the ship's officers probably amounted to as much again. Although Drake was usually careful to prevent personal looting, his critics claim that only a portion of the plunder was handed over to the crown.

While the armed merchantman *Roebuck* towed the *Rosario* into Dartmouth (some accounts say Weymouth), Drake sailed north with his high-ranking prisoners and the plunder to rejoin the main battle. By that afternoon Drake had rejoined Howard, who met Don Pedro and expressed sympathy for his plight. Howard was probably less sympathetic towards his own vice-admiral, who had deserted his post in search of plunder. The reorganization complete, the Armada was slowly sailing north-east, past Dartmouth, Berry Head and the entrance to Torbay. The Spanish had already lost one powerful warship, and they were about to lose another.

The rough seas of the previous night had made it impossible to repair the *San Salvador*, and in the morning it was clear that it was taking on water from the damaged stern. At 11am Medina Sidonia ordered the crew and valuables to be transferred to other ships, and as it was holding up the rest of the fleet, with the English force gathering to windward, he then ordered it to be abandoned or sunk. Not all the injured crewmen could be recovered in time, and by mid-afternoon the nao was cast adrift, as the Armada resumed its slow progress to the east.

Around 4pm John Hawkins in the *Victory* and Lord Thomas Howard in the *Golden Lion* came alongside the *San Salvador*. A witness described what they found: 'The deck of the ship had fallen down, the steerage broken, the stern blown out and about 50 poor creatures burnt with powder in most miserable sort. The stink in the ship was so unsavoury, and the sight within board so ugly, that Lord Thomas Howard and Sir John Hawkins shortly departed.' Thomas Flemyng in the small *Golden Hinde* took it under tow and eventually brought it into Weymouth.

Both fleets crept along within sight of each other during the late afternoon and early evening, but the wind had dropped to almost a whisper and progress was more with the tide than the wind. The rear of the Armada was protected by *La Rata Santa María Encoronada*, the *Florencia*, the *San Mateo*, the *Santiago* and three of the galleasses, but the English never attempted to come within range. With the Armada maintaining a tight, powerful formation, the English were unable or unwilling to attempt any attack. Howard preferred to bide his time and wait for an opportunity to attack on his own terms. He also remained unsure about the Armada's ultimate destination. Although Devon was safe, he could not rule out the possibility of a landing in Weymouth Bay or in the Solent. He needed to conserve his force for a battle to prevent any amphibious landing.

The *San Salvador* exploding during the battle off Plymouth, fought on 31 July 1588. Detail from *The English and Spanish Fleets off Berry Head*, one of the House of Lords Tapestries which were destroyed by fire in 1834. The following day the shattered vessel was captured, and towed into Weymouth, still smelling of charred flesh and timber (Stratford Archive).

While the Armada was safe from any immediate English threat, Medina Sidonia was becoming increasingly concerned about his rendezvous with the Duke of Parma. He had no idea whether Parma was ready to embark his troops, or even whether Parma was aware that the Armada had sailed from La Coruña on 21 July. He therefore sent a Spanish officer – Juan Gil – in a fast pinnace with a message for Parma, outlining the events of the previous day and asking for pilots to help guide the Armada through the shoals which lay off the Flemish coast. 'Without them I am ignorant of the places where I can find shelter for ships so large as these, in case I should be overtaken by the slightest storm.' Gil was charged with arranging the union between Parma's invasion flotilla and the Armada, which was to protect the invasion barges. Medina Sidonia also changed the location of his rendezvous, from off Margate to Calais, where he would be able to form a tight protective ring around the barges for their short journey across the Channel.

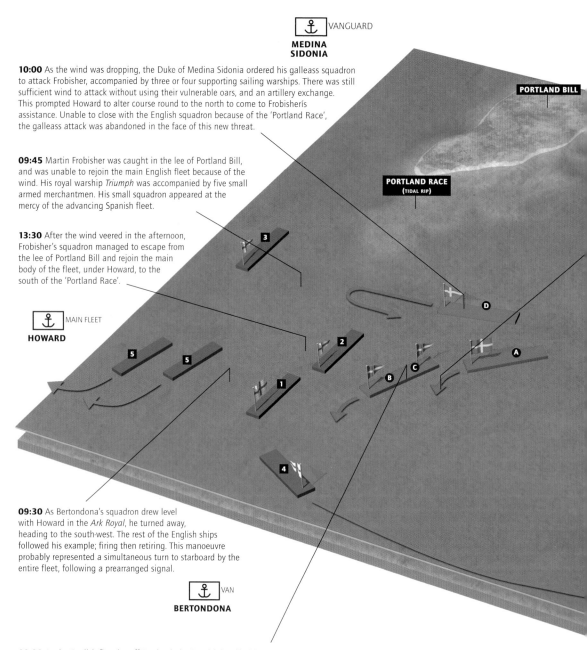

10:00 As the wind was dropping, the Duke of Medina Sidonia ordered his galleass squadron to attack Frobisher, accompanied by three or four supporting sailing warships. There was still sufficient wind to attack without using their vulnerable oars, and an artillery exchange. This prompted Howard to alter course round to the north to come to Frobisher's assistance. Unable to close with the English squadron because of the 'Portland Race', the galleass attack was abandoned in the face of this new threat.

09:45 Martin Frobisher was caught in the lee of Portland Bill, and was unable to rejoin the main English fleet because of the wind. His royal warship *Triumph* was accompanied by five small armed merchantmen. His small squadron appeared at the mercy of the advancing Spanish fleet.

13:30 After the wind veered in the afternoon, Frobisher's squadron managed to escape from the lee of Portland Bill and rejoin the main body of the fleet, under Howard, to the south of the 'Portland Race'.

PORTLAND BILL

PORTLAND RACE
(TIDAL RIP)

MAIN FLEET

HOWARD

09:30 As Bertondona's squadron drew level with Howard in the *Ark Royal*, he turned away, heading to the south-west. The rest of the English ships followed his example; firing then retiring. This manoeuvre probably represented a simultaneous turn to starboard by the entire fleet, following a prearranged signal.

VAN
BERTONDONA

09:00 As the English fleet lay off Portland, the Spanish 'van' led by Martin de Bertendona in the *Regazona* turned to avoid the tidal anomaly known as the 'Portland Race'. They swept down on the English from the north-east, steering south-south-west. Both sides exchanged broadsides at close range.

Battle off Portland Bill
(Medina Sidonia offers battle), 2 August, 1588

Viewed from the south, the relatively slow and limited manoeuvring which took place allows us to show the development of the battle in relation to P... Bill, the nearest point of land. A change in the wind allowed the Duke of Medina Sidonia to gain the weather gauge, and he used the opportunity to t... force a close-range engagement on the English fleet.

Note: The times given here are estimates, as the participants kept no accurate records.

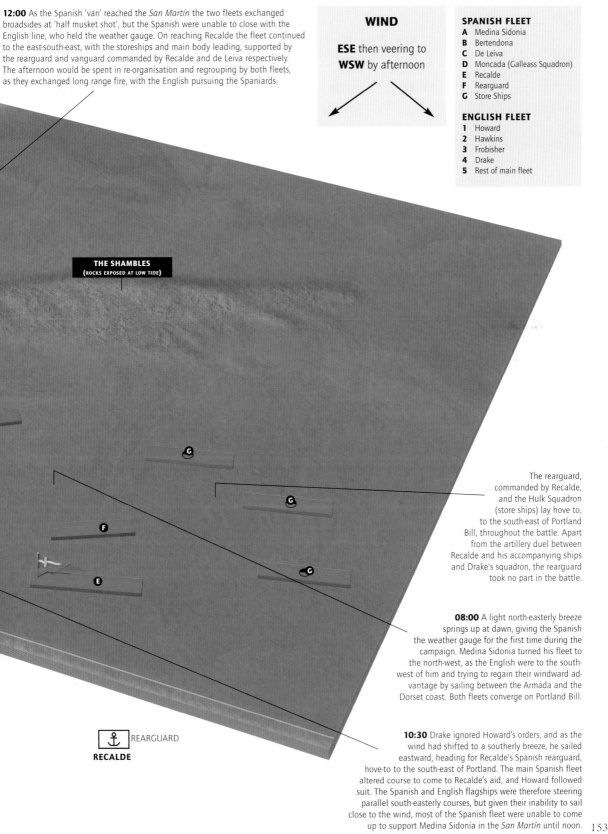

12:00 As the Spanish 'van' reached the *San Martín* the two fleets exchanged broadsides at 'half musket shot', but the Spanish were unable to close with the English line, who held the weather gauge. On reaching Recalde the fleet continued to the east-south-east, with the storeships and main body leading, supported by the rearguard and vanguard commanded by Recalde and de Leiva respectively. The afternoon would be spent in re-organisation and regrouping by both fleets, as they exchanged long range fire, with the English pursuing the Spaniards.

WIND

ESE then veering to **WSW** by afternoon

SPANISH FLEET
A   Medina Sidonia
B   Bertendona
C   De Leiva
D   Moncada (Galleass Squadron)
E   Recalde
F   Rearguard
G   Store Ships

ENGLISH FLEET
1   Howard
2   Hawkins
3   Frobisher
4   Drake
5   Rest of main fleet

THE SHAMBLES
(ROCKS EXPOSED AT LOW TIDE)

REARGUARD
RECALDE

The rearguard, commanded by Recalde, and the Hulk Squadron (store ships) lay hove to, to the south-east of Portland Bill, throughout the battle. Apart from the artillery duel between Recalde and his accompanying ships and Drake's squadron, the rearguard took no part in the battle.

08:00 A light north-easterly breeze springs up at dawn, giving the Spanish the weather gauge for the first time during the campaign. Medina Sidonia turned his fleet to the north-west, as the English were to the south-west of him and trying to regain their windward advantage by sailing between the Armada and the Dorset coast. Both fleets converge on Portland Bill.

10:30 Drake ignored Howard's orders, and as the wind had shifted to a southerly breeze, he sailed eastward, heading for Recalde's Spanish rearguard, hove-to to the south-east of Portland. The main Spanish fleet altered course to come to Recalde's aid, and Howard followed suit. The Spanish and English flagships were therefore steering parallel south-easterly courses, but given their inability to sail close to the wind, most of the Spanish fleet were unable to come up to support Medina Sidonia in the *San Martín* until noon. 153

Off Portland (2 August)

During the night the wind dropped completely, but shortly before dawn on Tuesday 2 August a breeze sprang up from the east-south-east. As the Spanish were to the east of the English fleet, this gave Medina Sidonia the advantage of the weather gauge for the first time, and he intended to use it to its best advantage. Howard was following the Armada on an easterly heading, and he immediately ordered his fleet to alter course and head north-north-east towards the coast. The duke had already turned the Armada to port, and was heading on a north-north-westerly course, directly towards the peninsula of Portland Bill. For the first time the two fleets began to close with each other, and it looked as if the decisive encounter was about to take place. Within an hour it became clear that the Spanish had won the race. Unable to creep between the Spanish and the shore to regain the weather gauge, Howard ordered his ships to come about and headed slowly to the south-south-west within four miles of the tip of Portland Bill.

The Armada had already formed into two distinct groups: the vanguard directly commanded by Medina Sidonia and a rearguard under de Recalde, whose orders were to protect the supply ships and to support the vanguard if required. The vanguard was further divided into a 'van' consisting of the most powerful galleons, led by Martín de Bertendona of the Levant Squadron in *La Regazona*, and a main body led by Medina Sidonia in the *San Martín*. Howard's change of course gave Bertendona the opportunity to come to grips with the English fleet, and he turned his ships in a curve off the peninsula, mimicking the *en ala* tactics that had been used by his adversary off Plymouth two days before.

Avoiding the tidal rip off the peninsula known as the Portland Race, Howard's and Bertendona's squadrons converged at around 9am. What happened next is still unclear, but certainly for the first time the protagonists were within close range of each other; *La Regazona* and the *Ark Royal* were within musket range, as accounts mention small arms being used. According to Petruccio Ubaldino: 'A certain number or squadron of Her Majesty's ships and others assailed the Spanish fleet so closely to the westward that the Spanish ships were obliged to give way, whereupon the Lord Admiral, considering the distress of the *Triumph* and the five other ships were in, called a few of the other royal ships, then near to hand, and ordered them to follow him closely and to attack the enemy with all their power, ordering all to go within musket range of the enemy, before firing a gun, because that was the true method of helping friendly ships with the greatest damage to the enemy, which was well performed by the *Ark*, the *Elizabeth Jonas*, the *Galleon of Leicester*, the *Golden Lion*, the *Victory*, the *Mary Rose*, the *Dreadnought* and the *Swallow*.'

Behind Bertendona's flagship were the *San Mateo*, *La Rata Santa María Encoronada* and the *San Juan de Sicilia*. After an initial broadside, where the English 'stood fast and abode their coming', the *Ark Royal* turned to starboard, a change of course which was immediately followed by the other ships in the English line. In effect this was a simultaneous manoeuvre, presumably prompted by a pre-arranged signal, as the English fleet turned away from the enemy. This was part of the caracole manoeuvre, and although the English presented their sterns to the enemy, they prevented the Spanish from bringing on the boarding action they longed for. As Ubaldino put it, the Duke of Medina Sidonia 'came forward with sixteen of his best galleons to foil the English manoeuvre, and to prevent the defence of the *Triumph*'.

The English probably continued to fire on the Spanish from a distance, and records indicate that Howard's flagship was accompanied by the *Victory*, the *Elizabeth Jonas*, the *Nonpareil* 'and divers others'. The Spanish 'were content to fall astern of the *Nonpareil*, which was the sternmost ship'. The firefight was therefore confined to a single close-range broadside, followed by sporadic fire at longer range, with the exchange continuing until around 10am. Petruccio Ubaldino claimed: 'the fight having been at very close quarters – as should be in such a case – the Spaniards at last were forced to leave the field and to retire in their battle order.'

While the main body of the English fleet managed to avoid a close-range mêlée and boarding, another smaller part of the fleet found itself in grave danger. When the fleet had given up its attempt to cut between the Spanish Armada and the land, the six most leeward (inshore) ships had found themselves boxed in by Portland Bill and the Portland Race, unable to attempt to join the main fleet until the wind changed direction or freshened. The isolated group consisted of Martin Frobisher's *Triumph*, the warships *Golden Lion* and *Mary Rose* and the armed merchant vessels *Merchant Royal*, *Margaret & John* and *Centurion*. Frobisher later claimed his whole plan had been to lure a portion of the Spanish fleet into the shoals and tidal rips found off Portland, but he was more probably 'in distress', as Howard recounted after the battle.

The 'van' of the Spanish Armada led by Bertendona was already too far to the south to attack this isolated group, as was the main body of the fleet under Medina Sidonia. Further to the east, off the tip of Portland Bill, lay the Galleass Squadron commanded by Don Hugo de Moncada. Since the wind was dropping steadily, these four oared vessels were ideally suited for the attack against Frobisher. Medina Sidonia sent a pinnace to Moncada with orders to attack Frobisher using sails and oars, and commanded the closest three or four sailing warships to support the attack. The duke had not considered the Portland Race in his calculations.

Moncada's galleasses came close enough to Frobisher to engage in an artillery duel, and 'assaulted them sharply'. The English ships used the light winds for defensive caracole tactics, while the Spanish crept forward as far as the tidal rip. The Portland Race was a patch of water where strong tides moved concurrently in opposite directions; the same natural phenomenon which pinned Frobisher against the lee of Portland Bill also protected his ships. Moncada's galleasses were unable to enter the rip without being dragged to the side, and their commander was too cautious to close with Frobisher using full oars, as they were vulnerable in combat. Using sails alone, he lacked the mobility to close with Frobisher. Medina Sidonia

Opposite

Martin Frobisher's fight with the Spanish Armada off Portland, 1588. The 'invincible Armada' was sighted off Plymouth on 30 July 1588, and the English fleet set sail to give battle. Over the next few days a running battle ensued as the Armada continued it stately course eastward, with the English fleet harassing, but failing to break the Spanish defensive formation. By the morning of 2 August the Armada was off Portland. While the main English fleet pursued the Spaniards, a small squadron under Martin Frobisher lay inshore, charged with preventing any landing attempt near Weymouth. When the wind dropped the Spanish commander saw a golden opportunity to destroy a portion of the English fleet and sent a force of oared galleasses supported by sailing warships to attack Frobisher. The Spanish lacked Frobisher's local knowledge of the waters around Portland, and the tidal race which lay like a hidden river between the protagonists. Only the galleasses could cross it using their oars, and their attempt was supported by long-range fire from the other Spanish warships. By concentrating his fires on the enemy oar banks, Frobisher managed to disable the galleasses, which were swept away to the south-east by the 'Portland Race'. The Spanish abandoned their attack and rejoined the main body of the Armada. The reconstruction is viewed from the decks of Frobisher's flagship *Triumph* as it fires on the galleasses. The four-wheeled truck carriage gave the English a decisive edge over the Spanish who were unable to easily reload their guns once they had been fired. By denying the Spaniards the opportunity to board their vessels, the English could disrupt the enemy with gunfire at little risk to themselves (Angus McBride).

sent a tart message to his galleass commander, containing 'certain words which were not to his honour'.

Just as the attack petered out, the wind changed. A mild southerly breeze sprang up, which gave Howard the chance to support Frobisher. Howard reversed course, turning the main body of his fleet to the north to rendezvous with the isolated contingent.

The change in wind also altered the tactical situation. The 'van' of the Armada under Medina Sidonia and Bertendona was strung out in a line on a roughly southerly course, heading away from Portland Bill. The change of wind would have forced them to alter course slightly to either the south-east or south-west, but it is almost impossible to reconstruct Bertendona's actions from this point on. Howard and the English fleet were some distance to the west, while Drake and a handful of ships were ahead of both Howard and the Spaniards. De Recalde and the Spanish rearguard were hove to further to the east of Medina Sidonia, with a line of warships protecting the vulnerable supply hulks.

To the north and rear of Medina Sidonia the private fight between Frobisher and Moncada was just ending. Howard's change of course had presented him with the option of cutting between Portland Bill and the rear of the Armada's main body. This was risky since it would have placed him between the Armada and a lee shore, where his fleet could have been trapped. It could also have precipitated a decisive close-range engagement. Howard opted for the safer course, steering to the west of the Portland Race. He did encourage his commanders to close the range to Medina

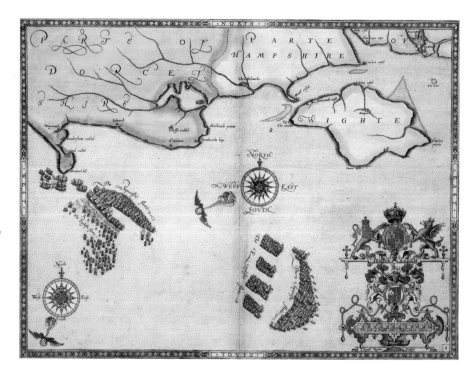

Sidonia's ships, and 'to go within musket shot of the enemy before they should discharge any one piece of ordnance'. Howard's ships engaged the rear of the Spanish 'van', but the English fleet had become badly disorganized and only part of the formation could come to grips with the enemy.

To the south, Drake appeared to be taking matters into his own hands. The change of wind had placed him slightly to windward of Medina Sidonia, and level with the southern tip of de Recalde's rearguard further east. He ignored Howard's orders to alter course to the north and instead steered to the east, closing with de Recalde's *San Juan de Portugal*. Drake's and de Recalde's formations were fighting in isolation of the main battle, with the Spanish formation representing an inverted horseshoe and the English in an L-shaped formation around its outside.

As accounts are vague and often contradictory, this stage of the battle remains difficult to follow in anything other than the broadest terms. Seeing that his rearguard was under threat, Medina Sidonia ordered several of his most powerful warships to sail to de Recalde's support. In all probability this meant that the ships around de Recalde at the rear of the 'van' were ordered to alter course to starboard and sail on an east-south-easterly heading. Bertendona's command probably remained in position to windward of the English fleet and waited for further orders. *La Rata Santa María Encoronada* is mentioned as coming to de Recalde's aid, and earlier in the day Don

Opposite

The English and Spanish fleets between Portland Bill and the Isle of Wight, on 2nd-3rd August 1588, the eighth in the series of charts by Robert Adams reproduced in his *Expeditionis Hispanorum in Angliam vera descriptio anno 1588.* This shows the confused fighting off Portland, then the subsequent engagement further up the Channel. By that time the English fleet had divided itself into four squadrons, as shown here (National Maritime Museum, Greenwich, London).

Alonso de Leiva's ship was reported to have been following Bertendona's *Regazona*. It is probable that Don Alonso was simply acting on his own initiative, although he may have led a general regrouping of the 'van', bringing it round to form a tighter formation in support of de Recalde. An English witness described the Spanish as flocking together like sheep. This probably meant they were tightening up their defensive formation after the failure of Bertendona's 'van' to bring the enemy to close quarters.

This left Medina Sidonia in the *San Martín* at the apex of the horseshoe formation, now rapidly becoming a circle. Howard realized that his opponent was exposed, and ordered part of his fleet to reverse course once again and head south-east towards the Spanish flagship. The Spanish were now subjected to a two-pronged attack, with a southerly group led by Drake attacking de Recalde, and a north-westerly group under Howard attacking Medina Sidonia. At this stage both Howard and the Spanish 'van' were probably on a south-easterly heading, under light sail. Medina Sidonia even lowered his topsails, encouraging Howard to close and fight a boarding action, a chivalric gesture which Howard ignored.

The *Ark Royal* was followed in line astern by the *Elizabeth Jonas*, *Galleon Leicester*, *Golden Lion*, *Victory*, *Mary Rose*, *Dreadnought* and *Swallow*. Presumably the rest of the English fleet were further to the north-west and were bystanders to the action. The English advantage lay in gunnery, and their main fleet pounded the *San Martín* at 'half-musket shot', shrouding the Spanish ship in smoke. As one Spanish witness put it: 'The galleon *San Martín*, being to windward of the Armada and near the enemy's ships, the latter attacked her with the whole of their cannon, she returning the fire with so much gallantry that on one side alone she fired of hundred shots, and the enemy did not care to come to close quarters with her although she was alone, and her consorts were unable to aid her for one and a half hours.'

At some point in the early afternoon Don Alonso de Leiva and a 'fire brigade' of Spanish ships managed to work their way through their own fleet to support the flagship. Along with the *San Marcos* and the *Santa Ana*, Leiva screened the flagship and escorted it to the comparative safety of the main body of the Armada.

Deprived of their victim and faced by a solid line of powerful Spanish warships, the English altered course to the south-west, and headed out to sea to regroup, accompanied by the handful of ships around Frobisher. Further to the south, Drake gave up his half-hearted attack on de Recalde's wing, presumably because Bertendona's 'van' had managed to come up to support the rearguard. After the fury of the morning and early afternoon, both sides retired to patch their vessels and to determine their next move.

The action centred on the *San Martín* had demonstrated the basic differences between the Spanish and English tactics. The Spanish flagship had made several attempts to board the English vessels, but the English had kept their distance. Both sides had fought a fierce artillery duel, but by almost all accounts the English had fired three shots for every one from the Spanish. This English advantage in gunnery came about through their adoption of four-wheeled truck carriages, as opposed to the larger two-wheeled sea carriages of the Spanish. The English carriages were easier to use, and allowed the guns to be reloaded at a faster rate. The Spanish also lashed their carriages to the side of the ship, while the English used a system of blocks and tackles to run their guns in and out and to hold them in position. This also meant that the English ships expended more powder and shot. Howard sent a messenger ashore with a request for more munitions, and he suggested removing powder from the two Spanish vessels captured the previous day. The effectiveness of the English fleet was temporarily reduced because of this lack of powder.

The damage inflicted by the English gunnery was surprisingly light. The *San Martín* had borne the brunt of the fighting, but although its hull had been pierced and its rigging cut up, the damage was largely superficial. The English had demonstrated their superiority in gunnery, but they had failed to harm the Armada, or to disrupt its formation. Total Spanish casualties for the battle were estimated at 50 men throughout the entire fleet, and English losses were minimal. As the English gunner William Thomas put it: 'What can be said but our sins was the cause that so much powder and shot (were) spent, and so long a time in (the) fight, and in comparison thereof, so little harm (done to the enemy)'.

Long-range skirmishing continued throughout the rest of the afternoon but neither side would be drawn into another major engagement. Howard and Drake both thought that Medina Sidonia's objective was the Isle of Wight, and with their powder stocks dangerously low, they felt they would be hard-pressed to prevent the Spanish landing troops on the island or entering the Solent. The Hampshire Militia stood to arms, and beacons flared along the coast. For his part, Medina Sidonia was becoming increasingly concerned about his impending rendezvous with the Duke of Parma. Once past the Isle of Wight there was no safe anchorage for the Armada, and it would be committed to a rendezvous off Calais. Heading into the Solent would delay the campaign but it would also give Parma time to prepare his troops for embarkation.

During the evening Medina Sidonia reorganized the Armada, and his orders reflected his new doctrine: 'The important thing for us is to proceed on our voyage, for these people do not mean fighting, but only to delay our progress.' Clearly the lack of effectiveness of the English gunnery had made him contemptuous of their ability to prevent him from reaching his objective. His new formation consisted of two fighting squadrons: the 'rearguard' commanded by de Recalde and the 'vanguard' under de Leiva. These squadrons would protect the main body led by Medina Sidonia, which also protected the supply hulks. As night fell the wind changed once again, this time reverting to the westerly wind which had predominated during the previous few days. Both fleets were sailing east-south-east, with the English behind and to windward of the Spanish. The following day would determine whether the battle would be continued in the approaches of the Solent or whether the Armada would continue its progress down the Channel.

Off the Isle of Wight (3–4 August)

At dawn on Wednesday 3 August the English fleet pursuing the Armada noticed that one of the Spanish vessels had fallen behind the rest of the fleet, at the southern tip of the Armada formation. It was the *El Gran Grifón*, the flagship of Juan Gómez de Medina, commander of the squadron of hulks. Several English ships raced forward to attack her, led by Drake in the *Revenge*. Drake fired a broadside at close range, then raked the hulk and loosed a second broadside. The *Grifón* was struck by over 40 roundshot, but no serious damage was inflicted. Musket balls flattened by impact recovered in the 1970s from the wreck of the Spanish vessel suggest that the combatants fought within range of small-arms fire. Although the *Revenge* and its consorts were able to outmanoeuvre the *Grifón* and batter it with gunfire, they could not to stop her.

Medina Sidonia sent support for Juan Gómez: Don Hugo de Moncada and the Galleass Squadron, with de Recalde's rearguard at long range. The galleasses managed to tow the battered hulk of the *Grifón* back into the safety of the Armada's defensive formation, and then de Recalde and de Leiva were ordered to close with the English ships and try to initiate another engagement. Instead the *Revenge* and its consorts withdrew, and the rest of the English fleet hove to well to windward of the Spanish, avoiding an engagement.

Howard's reluctance to fight was probably caused by his chronic lack of munitions. For the rest of the day the two fleets wallowed along in extremely light airs, and the Armada crept towards the Isle of Wight. As the day wore on it became

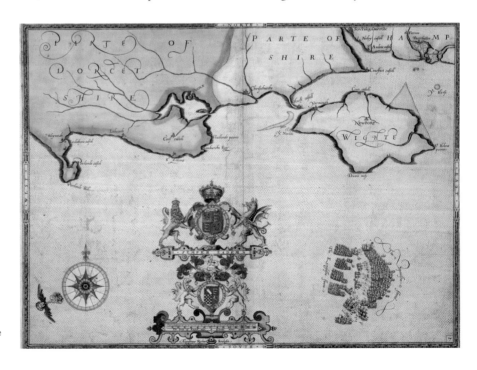

The battle off the Isle of Wight, 4th August 1588, the ninth in the series of charts by Robert Adams reproduced in his *Expeditionis Hispanorum in Angliam vera descriptio anno 1588*. By this stage the English fleet is shown in its four squadrons, harassing the rear of the Spanish formation (National Maritime Museum, Greenwich, London).

The Campaign off Dorset and Hampshire

Devon Militia
(4,000)

Hampshire Militia
(6,000)

Southampton

Exeter

Dorset Militia
(5,000)

Poole

Portsmouth

Carisbrooke Castle

Selsey Bill

Isle of Wight

Owers

Weymouth

FROBISHER 2 Sqn
Portland Bill Galleass Sqn

St Catherine's Point

1

Berry Head

3

Sqn MEDINA SIDONIA Sqn MEDINA SIDONIA

Dartmouth

HOWARD Sqn MEDINA SIDONIA 4 Sqns 4

FROBISHER HAWKINS HOWARD DRAKE

4 Sqns FROBISHER HAWKINS HOWARD DRAKE 5

Positions: 2 August, noon

Positions: 3 August, noon

Positions: 4 August, noon

2 August Wind (South)

3 August Wind (South-west)

4 August Wind (West)

N

1. Dawn on 2 August: Change of wind gives Spanish the weather gauge. The English manoeuvre inshore to regain position to windward. The Spanish then attack the English fleet prompting a brief close-range mêlée.
2. Frobisher with a small squadron is trapped in the lee of Portland Bill. The Spanish launch an attack against his ships spearheaded by the galleass squadron. A tidal race off Portland prevents the Spanish closing with Frobisher's ships. Howard reverses course to rescue Frobisher.
3. Around 10.30am, Drake launches an attack on the Spanish rearguard, commanded by Recalde. Medina Sidonia sails

to support Recalde, but is attacked by Howard's main fleet. The Armada regroups into a defensive formation and continues sailing east.
4. Dawn on 3 August: Howard divides English fleet into four squadrons, under himself, Drake, Frobisher and Hawkins. Skirmishing continues throughout the day.
5. 4 August: Skirmishing continues although the wind drops away forcing the English to tow their ships into action. By nightfall it becomes apparent that the Spanish have no intention of landing near Portsmouth, but are heading towards Flanders.

0   20 miles
0   25 km

apparent that Medina Sidonia had little intention of making for the western entrance of the Solent, but Howard still suspected that the Armada planned to anchor in the shelter of the eastern side of the Isle of Wight. That evening he called his senior commanders together on board the *Ark Royal*. It was decided that the English fleet should be reorganized into four squadrons, to be commanded by Howard, Drake, Hawkins and Frobisher. Instead of simply following the flagship, the new structure allowed the fleet to operate in smaller, more manoeuvrable formations. Howard stressed that the principal aim of any battle the following day was to prevent the Spanish from entering the Solent or attempting to land.

During the night two more Spanish ships dropped behind the Armada, and at dawn on Thursday 4 August the *San Luís* and the *Duquesna Santa Ana* lay between the two fleets. The wind had died away completely during the early hours and any attempt to attack the two Spanish stragglers would mean towing the English warships into range. Hawkins' squadron was closest to the two ships, and he immediately ordered his ships to lower their boats. As the English were towing their ships into position, de Recalde detached two galleasses to protect the stragglers; a third towed de Leiva's becalmed *La Rata Santa María Encoronada* to safety.

Hawkins' ships opened fire on the galleasses and, according to Hawkins, they managed to damage one of the three oared vessels. In turn Hawkins was forced to withdraw his boats when they were peppered by Spanish small-arms fire. The *Ark*

161

Royal and the *Golden Lion* were towed into the fray, but the English were unable to prevent Moncada from rescuing the two Spanish ships. The three galleasses rejoined the Armada formation, each towing a sailing ship behind it.

By mid-morning a slight south-westerly breeze gave the English the weather gauge again, allowing Frobisher on the English left (northern) wing to run before the wind, placing his leading ships between the Armada and the eastern edge of the Solent. The *Triumph* fired on the *San Martín*, which had become isolated for the second time in as many days. The Spanish flagship was holed twice below the waterline before it could be escorted to safety. Several Armada ships were despatched to attack Frobisher, possibly the vanguard formation commanded by de Leiva himself. A freak of the wind deprived Frobisher of sail-power, while the Spanish to the south were still able to close the range. In desperation he lowered the *Triumph*'s boats and tried to tow his ship to safety. At the last minute his sails caught the wind and he escaped to the north.

Hawkins and Howard launched another attack against de Recalde on the Armada's southern flank. A brisk engagement followed, and as one Spaniard put it, 'If the Duke had not gone about with his flagship ... we should have come out vanquished that day.' From this it seems that elements of the main body were forced to break formation and return to assist the rearguard commanded by de Recalde. It has been argued that Drake led this attack, slowly working his unengaged squadron to seaward of the rest of the fleets, then, as they became engaged, he

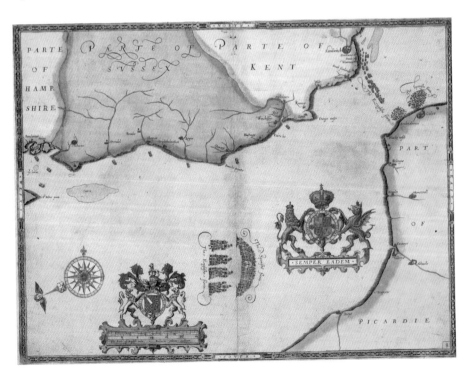

The pursuit to Calais, 4th–6th August 1588, the tenth in the series of charts by Robert Adams collated into his *Expeditionis Hispanorum in Angliam vera descriptio anno 1588*. It shows the relatively uneventful last stage of the voyage up the Channel, and the sortie by Lord Seymour's squadron when it was ordered to join the main fleet off Calais (National Maritime Museum, Greenwich, London).

turned against de Leiva's flank. Whoever masterminded the attack, it succeeded in diverting the Spanish for two crucial hours. By the time the English fleet regrouped in mid-afternoon, Medina Sidonia had missed his opportunity to turn towards the Solent. He now had no option but to continue sailing up the Channel towards Calais. That night he sent another pinnace racing ahead with a message for the Duke of Parma.

If Medina Sidonia had planned to anchor in the Solent or off the eastern side of the Isle of Wight, he kept his plans to himself. His formation remained intact, and as the English drew back to a safe distance, the Armada was allowed to continue its progress up the Channel. Another boat was sent ahead to Dunkirk, this time asking for 40 to 50 small light craft to help harass the English fleet. For their part the English needed reinforcements and supplies if they were to continue the fight. Howard wrote: 'Forasmuch as our powder and shot was well wasted, the Lord Admiral thought it was not good in policy to assail them any more until their coming near unto Dover.'

After a rendezvous with Seymour and the squadron of supply ships sent from the Thames, Howard would continue the fight somewhere between Calais and the Kent coast. For all of the following day (5 August) the two fleets continued their progress, heading north-north-east towards the Straits of Dover in very light winds. In another meeting on board the English flagship, Howard knighted Hawkins and Frobisher for their services during the campaign.

At 10am on Saturday 6 August the Armada came within sight of the French coast near Boulogne. It maintained a tight defensive formation and by the late afternoon had dropped anchor in Calais Roads. The Duke of Medina Sidonia had sailed the full length of the English Channel with his fleet relatively intact and its defensive integrity maintained. All that remained was to arrange a rendezvous with the Duke of Parma's troops at Dunkirk and to escort them across the Channel. His frustration at not being met by the Duke of Parma's messengers was apparent in a letter he penned to the army commander that evening: 'I have constantly written to your Excellency, and not only have I received no reply to my letters, but no acknowledgement of their receipt.' Until the duke responded, and his laden invasion barges were ready to sail, the Armada would be forced to remain where it was, lying off a potentially hostile shore, and shadowed by an even more threatening enemy fleet.

Medina Sidonia held a council of war that evening, when it was decided to remain in the exposed anchorage off Calais until Parma's small fleet had joined the Armada. For their part the English anchored some miles to the west, maintaining their windward advantage. That evening Howard was joined by Seymour's squadron, bringing much-needed supplies and munitions from the Thames. The English fleet now numbered around 140 ships, but Howard planned to expend some of these vessels in order to break the tactical deadlock. He had one great turn of the cards to play, and his hand would be a truly devastating one.

Off Calais (7 August)

Late on Friday night Howard sought the advice of Sir William Winter of the *Vanguard*, who reportedly suggested using fireships against the Spanish fleet. Howard was enamoured with the idea, and early the following morning he called his senior commanders together for a council of war on board the *Ark Royal*. Seymour, Drake, Hawkins and Frobisher approved the plan, and its execution was set for midnight that night. Howard sent Sir Henry Palmer of the *Antelope* to Dover to commandeer suitable vessels and combustible materials. Seymour had already gathered a store of brushwood and pitch at Dover for exactly this purpose. The freshening south-westerly wind made their arrival before midnight unlikely, so Howard was forced to sacrifice vessels from his own fleet. After further consultation with his squadron commanders, eight armed merchantmen were selected for conversion into fireships.

The ships selected were the *Bark Talbot* and *Thomas Drake* (both of 200 tons), the *Hope Hawkins of Plymouth* (180 tons), the *Bark Bond* and *Cure's Ship* (both of 150 tons), the *Bear Yonge* (140 tons), the small *Elizabeth of Lowestoft* (90 tons) and one other even

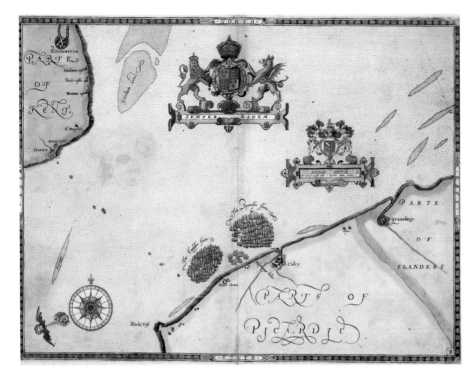

Opposite
The Fireship attack at Calais. During the morning of 7 August, Howard decided to launch a midnight fireship attack against the Spanish fleet at anchor off Calais. The English were to windward (upwind), so the fireships could be sailed straight towards the mass of Spanish shipping, aided by the flooding tide. Behind the Armada lay the treacherous sandbars of the Banks of Flanders. During the day English shipwrights converted eight small vessels for the attack, loading them with combustibles and powder. Around midnight Spanish scout ships saw the fireships and raised the alarm. They managed to tow two of the fireships clear of the fleet, but the remainder continued unimpeded. The Spanish commander ordered his ships to cut their anchors and escape to safety. Although no ships were damaged by the fireships, without their main anchors the Armada was unable to remain in position off Calais, and by dawn the fleet was disorganised and drifting to the north-east of Calais. It was now impossible for the Armada to rendezvous with the Duke of Parma's army. The plate shows the initial launch of the fireships; small English merchant vessels, seen from the west. In the distance the Armada is still at anchor in Calais Roads, its commanders unaware of the English attack (Howard Gerrard).

smaller vessel. Petruccio Ubaldino claimed: 'This was carefully done under the supervision of Captain Yonge and Captain Prouse, both daring men.' For the rest of the day carpenters worked on the vessels, strengthening rigging, altering or removing the gunports and possibly cutting exit ports in the stern for the skeleton crew to escape through. Other seamen gathered all the combustible materials which could be found in the fleet (old sails, cordage, hemp, tar, pitch, etc.), and soaked the ships in oil. They also loaded and double-shotted the guns, so that when the heat ignited the charges, they would fire into the enemy fleet and increase the confusion.

A handful of volunteers were selected to steer each ship towards the Armada. At the last moment the tiller or whipstaff would be lashed and the crew would escape over the stern into a waiting longboat which was towed behind each fireship. While the English were busy preparing for their night-time attack, the Duke of Medina Sidonia was trying to determine his next move. Although he had sent two messages to Parma as the Armada sailed up the Channel, he had not received any reply. On 2 August Parma was informed that the Armada had left La Coruña, but he only heard it was approaching Calais on 5 August, the day before the fleet anchored in Calais Roads. For the first time, the two commanders could communicate with each other.

A messenger reported that the Duke of Parma was still at his headquarters in Bruges, and most of his troops and stores were still in their camps. Many had not even started to board the invasion barges which would transport them to Kent.

Petruccio Ubaldino saw the threat a little differently: 'He had already embarked a certain number of his soldiers and was in a hurry to embark the others, so that they should be ready to seize any chance of leaving, having taken in abundant supplies of ammunition, victuals and water.' Meanwhile word also came of a Dutch coastal squadron blockading Dunkirk and Nieuport, making it difficult for Parma to put to sea. The barges would have to creep towards Gravelines using the Flemish network of small canals and rivers, and it was estimated that the process would take anything up to two weeks.

Medina Sidonia's fleet was in an unsheltered anchorage off a neutral port, with a powerful English fleet to windward and the mass of sandbanks known as the Banks of Flanders to leeward. It was an unenviable position, but he had little option but to remain in place and wait for Parma. The French Governor of Calais was Giraud de Mauleon, Seigneur de Gourdan. As a Catholic who had lost a leg fighting the English 30 years earlier, his sympathies lay with Spain. Presents were exchanged between the governor and Medina Sidonia, and a Spanish delegation went ashore to liaise with the French and buy provisions for the fleet. It was headed by the Duke of Ascoli, who also established firm lines of communication with Parma in Bruges. Throughout the day French boats ferried food and supplies out to the waiting Spanish ships, supervised by the Armada's paymaster-general, Don Jorge Manrique. That evening Don Jorge was ordered to ride to Bruges to persuade the Duke of Parma to speed up his embarkation.

During the evening the wind changed from the south-west to the west, the same direction as the tidal flow. That Sunday it was also a full moon, so the spring tides were at their strongest. Both the wind and the flood tide were therefore in the

A detail from an 18th-century engraving by John Pine, based on the House of Lords Tapestries, which were destroyed by fire in 1834. It shows the English fireships drifting towards the Spanish fleet as it lay off Calais (Stratford Archive).

English favour, and as final preparations were made for the fireships, the rest of the fleet prepared for a naval attack on the Armada the following day. For his part Medina Sidonia placed a screen of light craft (carvels, patches, falúas or zabras) to the west of his anchorage, between the Armada and the English fleet. Similar screening vessels were presumably deployed to the east, to prevent any surprise attack by the Dutch. Soon after midnight Spanish lookouts on these screening craft spotted two glowing ships heading towards them from the English fleet two miles away. What had happened was that the fireship attack had been launched on schedule, but on two of the eight vessels either the fires had been ignited prematurely or the vessels had proved particularly combustible. This gave the Spanish some advanced warning of the impending attack, and the alarm was raised.

To the Spanish, fireships had a particularly alarming association, since just over three years before, the Dutch rebels had launched an attack against a Spanish pontoon bridge across the River Schelde, near Antwerp. The Dutch fireships had been packed with explosives, and the resulting devastation destroyed the bridge and cost the lives of 800 Spanish soldiers. The Dutch engineer who had created them was known to have moved to England, and could well have been behind this attack.

In fact the English fireships were far less lethal and consequently far less effective. Around midnight the flood tide moved east at three knots, and although they carried minimal sails, the fireships would be among the Armada within 15 or 20 minutes. The small screening ships managed to grapple and tow two of the eight vessels out of the path of the Armada, but the other six were presumably blazing too fiercely to approach. Medina Sidonia reacted swiftly to the threat, and issued the only sensible order he could. Pinnaces were sent through the fleet ordering the ships to cut their anchor cables, raise their sails and escape to seaward. He hoped that once the threat had passed, the Armada would be able to regroup and anchor in the same position again.

Subsequent English accounts have suggested that the Spanish panicked and fled, but this has since been refuted. Like almost all evolutions undertaken by the Armada, it was a seamanlike manoeuvre, accomplished with almost complete success. Of the mass of craft that made up the fleet, only one vessel collided with another in the darkness. The galleass *San Lorenzo* broke its rudder in the collision and

Fireships such as these were used to good effect during the attack by the English on the Spanish Armada as it lay at anchor off Calais on the night of 7–8 August 1588. The holds of small vessels like these were filled with dry wood and pitch, then set alight by their skeleton crews. After aiming the fireships at the enemy the crew then swiftly abandoned their vessel. Engraving from a maritime manual of 1590 (Stratford Archive).

spent the night trying to creep back towards Calais under oars. The remainder of the fleet avoided the fireships but were unable to regain their original anchorage in Calais Roads. The strong flood tide, combined with a seabed which provided poor holding, meant that most of the ships were unable to anchor and they drifted to the north-east, towards Gravelines and the Banks of Flanders.

Petruccio Ubaldino put it simply: 'the enemy were forced to abandon their anchorage at the first onslaught of the fireships, being unable to find in that brief period of time any other and safer or more admirable remedy than to cut the cables, losing anchors and raising sail in order to save the fleet from the fireships.' He added: 'On account of this unexpected tumult and of the great confusion – which indeed, was very great – the flag galleass got entangled with another ship whose anchor cable jammed her rudder and she could not get clear during the night, on account of the confusion of her company.'

This turned out to be the single most decisive incident of the campaign. The Armada had been driven from its anchorage, and its ships had been forced to sacrifice their best and strongest anchors. These were irreplaceable, and the remaining smaller anchors would be unable to provide a purchase in the tidal waters off Calais. Although the Armada remained undamaged, it was scattered, and for the first time since the campaign began it was strung out over miles of sea; it had lost the tight defensive formation that had enabled it to cross the Channel in relative safety.

The loss of the anchorage also meant that the Armada was now unlikely to be able to rendezvous with the Duke of Parma. One English historian called the purchase of the eight fireships for just over £5,000 'the cheapest national investment the country has ever made'. It was also one of the most effective. The Spanish lay off some of the most dangerous coastal waters in Europe, and without anchors their position was precarious. Only five galleons managed to anchor in their original position, including Medina Sidonia's *San Martín* and de Recalde's *San Juan de Portugal*. The rest of the Armada lay scattered in the darkness, and to windward the English fleet was preparing to fight the climactic battle of the campaign.

Off Gravelines (8–9 August)

At dawn Medina Sidonia in the *San Martín* found himself accompanied by only four other galleons: the *San Juan de Portugal*, the *San Marcos*, the *San Juan Bautista* and the *San Mateo*. The English fleet moved in for the attack and Medina Sidonia fired his guns as a signal for the Armada to regroup for battle. It would take some considerable time before they would be able to re-establish their defensive formation, and in the meantime these five galleons were all that stood between the scattered fleet and the English. The battle began around 7am and would last throughout the day, the most intensive and bloody action of the campaign.

The galleass *San Lorenzo*, which had damaged its rudder during the fireship attack, had grounded on a sandbar off Calais during the night. It was the *capitana* of the Galleass Squadron, the flagship of Don Hugo de Moncada, and therefore was seen as too tempting a prize for the English to ignore. Howard himself led his squadron in an attack on the lone ship, leaving the rest of the fleet to engage Medina Sidonia.

The shoals prevented the English warships from coming in close, so ships' boats were used to attack the galleass, supported by long-range fire. The fighting was fierce for almost an hour, until Don Hugo was shot through the head with a musket ball. With their commander killed, the Spaniards lost heart and either surrendered or fled in boats towards the shore. As Ubaldino put it: 'the greatest part threw themselves into the water to gain the port, but many died in the water; therefore, on account of the disorder among the enemy, the English fleet saw this, and took and looted the ship to their profit.'

It was true. The English sailors began to pillage the *San Lorenzo*, and while Bernabe de Pedroso, the senior Spanish officer in Calais, rallied the survivors, his appeals for French assistance were ignored. Eventually the Spaniards managed to drive off the English with small-arms fire (some accounts mention artillery, which is unlikely), but soon after the looters retreated, the French rowed out to plunder the vessel. When they were threatened by returning English seamen, the French reputedly threatened to fire on the English boats.

Opposite

The English Fleet off Calais, 1588. In early August 1588, as the Spanish Armada worked its way up the English Channel, a reserve fleet based off Dover prepared itself for battle. This force – the Narrow Seas Squadron – was commanded by Lord Henry Seymour, a veteran naval leader, and the cousin of Lord Howard, the English fleet commander. On 6 August Sir Henry led his vessels out from the Downs, the anchorage between Sandwich and Dover that had long been a mustering point for the fleet. Two days previously, reinforcements consisting of 17 armed merchantmen had sailed from London to join his squadron, and once they arrived, Seymour sailed across the narrows of the Channel to join the rest of the English fleet off Calais. Seymour's fleet of 31 ships was spearheaded by seven vessels of the Navy Royal: the 500-ton galleons *Rainbow* and *Vanguard*, the 400-ton *Antelope*, the two 200-ton converted galleasses *Tiger* and *Bull*, and two smaller vessels, the *Tramontana* and the *Scout*. The plate shows Seymour flying his flag in the *Rainbow*, the flagship followed by the other ships of the Navy Royal in his squadron. They are pictured sailing in the order given above (Tony Bryan).

The whole action lasted some two hours and diverted almost half of the English fleet from the initial phase of the main battle, which was raging to the north. Eventually the *San Lorenzo* was returned to the Spanish authorities, together with its armament of 50 guns. The armament was removed, but the galleass was abandoned where it lay. By Ubaldino's account, the English also 'looted 22,000 golden ecus which were there, belonging to the King, and 14 chests of very noble spoil, belonging to the Duke of Medina Sidonia, together with other monies ands spoils and several prisoners, among them Don Rodrigo de Mendoza and Don Giovanni Gonsalez de Solorzano, the true captain of the galleass.' Still, the whole incident benefited the Spanish, as it gave the Armada a brief respite to reorganize its defences.

Medina Sidonia decided to stand and fight with his five warships, buying time for the rest of his fleet to organize themselves into some kind of defensive formation. Presumably Don Alonso de Leiva was charged with this reorganization, as both Medina Sidonia and Juan Martinez de Recalde were in the 'forlorn hope' or small blocking force facing half the English fleet. It seems that the duke was willing to sacrifice his own ship and its consorts in order to save the rest of his fleet.

The *San Martín* withstood several hours of close-range fighting at 'half musket shot'. Drake in the *Revenge* led the first attack, an honour which would have been

The battle off Gravelines, from The Armada's progress from Plymouth to Gravelines, a series of contemporary engravings by Claes Jansz Visscher. Although it was fought as a close-range engagement, the Spanish fleet still managed to maintain some degree of defensive formation, and so the loose mêlée of ships pictured here is somewhat fanciful (Stratford Archive).

given to Howard had he not been preoccupied with the attack on the *San Lorenzo*. At one point the Spanish flagship was surrounded by Drake in the *Revenge*, Hawkins in the *Victory* and Frobisher in the *Triumph*, while other English ships lined up to take their turn. It was estimated that during the two-hour action the *San Martín* was hit over 200 times by roundshot. Its hull and rigging were badly damaged, its decks 'awash with blood'.

Petruccio Ubaldino said of the *San Martín* battle: 'A great Spanish galleon was seen and attacked on the one side by George Raymond in the *Bonaventure*, who had with him the Earl of Cumberland, and at the same time attacked on the other side and keenly contested by Lord Henry Seymour in his ship the *Rainbow* and by Sir William Winter in the *Vanguard*; however, she saved herself, gallantly regaining the body of her own fleet, but with such ill fortune that, having been damaged in the terrible conflict, and torn by the hits of hostile artillery, the following night, being separated from her consorts, she was swallowed by the sea, but it is believed that the crew were saved.' This was a slight exaggeration. Unlike many of her companions, the battered but unbowed fleet *capitana* managed to return safely to Spain.

The other Spanish ships of the 'forlorn hope' fared almost as badly, but gradually they managed to creep northward to rejoin the rest of the fleet, which by then had managed to form into some semblance of order. By 10am the *San Martín* and its consorts were safely inside a ring of Spanish warships, and the English prepared themselves for an attack against the main body of the Armada. What followed would essentially be a running fight, with the Spanish trying to maintain a tight defensive formation while striving to keep as close as possible to the Flemish coast. The English objective was to concentrate on attacking the wings of the formation using close-range fire, and to try to force the Armada onto the sandbanks to the east.

According to Sir William Winter in the *Vanguard*, the Armada 'went into a proportion of a half moon. Their admiral and vice-admiral, they went in the midst … and there went on each side, in the wings, their galleasses, armados of Portugal, and other good ships, in the whole to the number of sixteen in a wing, which did seem to be of their principal shipping.' In other words, they resumed their old defensive posture, with a centre protected by a rearguard, and flanked by two powerful wings. The supply hulks took up position in front of the Armada, between the warships and the English.

Shortly after 10am Drake launched the first close-range attack in the *Revenge*, leading his squadron towards the Armada's left (western) wing. Soon Sir John Hawkins joined the battle with his squadron, echeloned on Drake's right. One of his ships was the *Mary Rose*, and an observer on board noted: 'As soon as we that pursued the fleet were come up within musket shot of them, the fight began very hotly.' Petruccio Ubaldino claimed that the fight continued for the rest of the morning, and that: 'In this assault truly every Captain rendered honourable service, but Captain Beeston (in the *Dreadnought*) without any doubt deserving particular

10:30 A general mêlée ensued, with the English fleet being reinforced by stragglers arriving from the scene of the *San Lorenzo* action, including Seymour. These newcomers attacked the right flank of the Armada formation, which was slowly sailing north-north-east. The running battle continued at close range.

07:30 The Duke of Medina Sidonia's flagship the *San Martìn* and four other galleons lay between the English and the scattered Armada. For two hours they fought a rearguard action, buying time for the main Spanish fleet to reorganise their defensive formation. Although badly battered, the five galleons succeeded in rejoining the rest of the Armada.

10:00 Sir Francis Drake in the *Revenge* led the first close-range attack on the Armada formation, assaulting the western side of the Spanish fleet. John Hawkins then led in a second division, and Martin Frobisher a third. Soon both sides were firing at each other from within 'musket shot'.

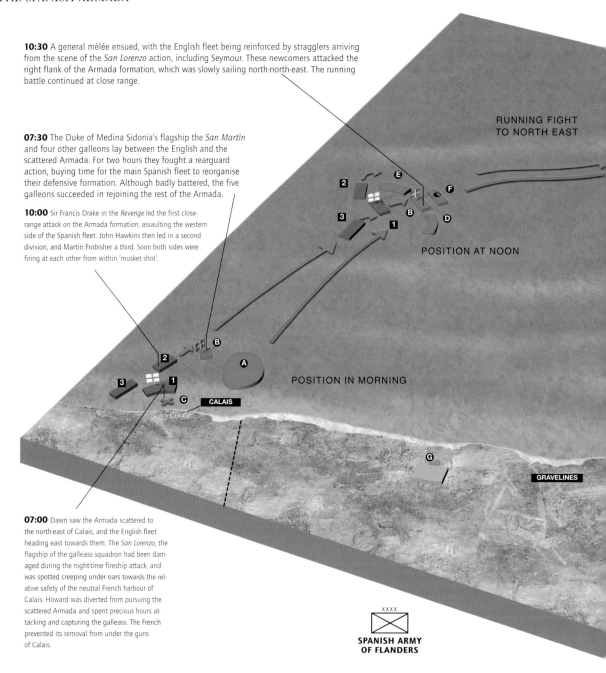

RUNNING FIGHT
TO NORTH EAST

POSITION AT NOON

POSITION IN MORNING

CALAIS

GRAVELINES

07:00 Dawn saw the Armada scattered to the north-east of Calais, and the English fleet heading east towards them. The *San Lorenzo*, the flagship of the galleass squadron had been damaged during the night-time fireship attack, and was spotted creeping under oars towards the relative safety of the neutral French harbour of Calais. Howard was diverted from pursuing the scattered Armada and spent precious hours attacking and capturing the galleass. The French prevented its removal from under the guns of Calais.

SPANISH ARMY
OF FLANDERS

Battle off Gravelines
(The decisive close-range engagement), 8 August, 1588

Viewed from the Flemish Coast (south), this decisive fight took the form of a running battle, heading from the Calais Roads north around the Banks of Fla and into the North Sea. The relative positions of all elements of the two fleets have been shown at various crucial stages of the engagement.

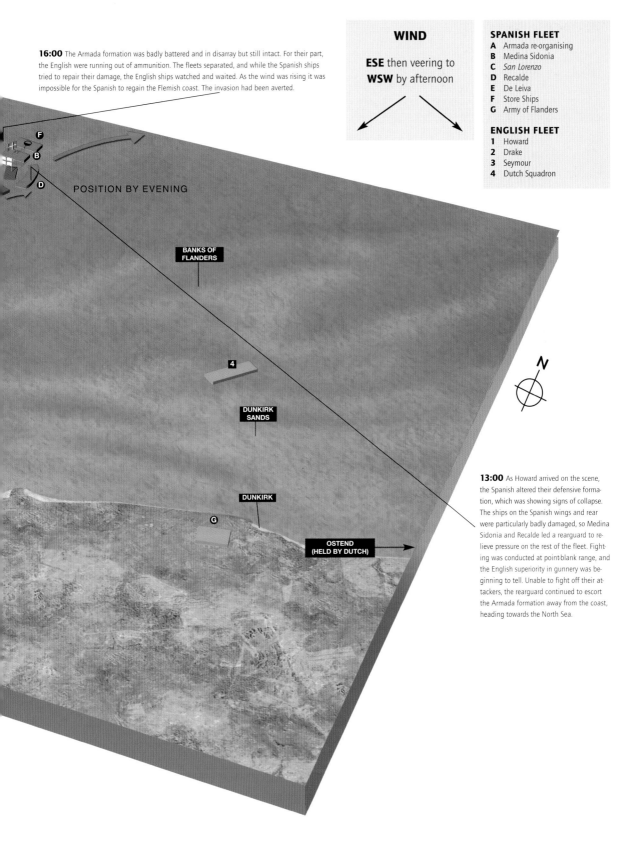

16:00 The Armada formation was badly battered and in disarray but still intact. For their part, the English were running out of ammunition. The fleets separated, and while the Spanish ships tried to repair their damage, the English ships watched and waited. As the wind was rising it was impossible for the Spanish to regain the Flemish coast. The invasion had been averted.

WIND

ESE then veering to **WSW** by afternoon

SPANISH FLEET
- **A** Armada re-organising
- **B** Medina Sidonia
- **C** *San Lorenzo*
- **D** Recalde
- **E** De Leiva
- **F** Store Ships
- **G** Army of Flanders

ENGLISH FLEET
- **1** Howard
- **2** Drake
- **3** Seymour
- **4** Dutch Squadron

POSITION BY EVENING

BANKS OF FLANDERS

DUNKIRK SANDS

DUNKIRK

OSTEND (HELD BY DUTCH)

N

13:00 As Howard arrived on the scene, the Spanish altered their defensive formation, which was showing signs of collapse. The ships on the Spanish wings and rear were particularly badly damaged, so Medina Sidonia and Recalde led a rearguard to relieve pressure on the rest of the fleet. Fighting was conducted at point-blank range, and the English superiority in gunnery was beginning to tell. Unable to fight off their attackers, the rearguard continued to escort the Armada formation away from the coast, heading towards the North Sea.

173

praise for his work.' He added: 'Sir Francis Drake's ship was pierced through by several cannon balls of all sizes which were flying everywhere between the two fleets, seeming as thick as arquebuses usually are.' He then claimed: 'It is true that his cabin was twice pierced by cannon balls'. This was one of the most closely fought engagements of the whole campaign.

Behind Hawkins and probably further to the east came Sir Martin Frobisher's squadron. All three squadrons began a fierce close-range engagement, with the Spanish ships continually trying to board their English assailants and the smaller Tudor warships trying to avoid coming too close. Once again the battle was fought within musket shot, so that the English gunnery advantage could be used to its greatest effect. The battle soon degenerated into what appeared to observers to be a general mêlée. This was an illusion, since although the English attacks were causing massive damage to individual Armada ships, the integrity of the Spanish battle formation remained largely intact.

During the late morning the English were reinforced by stragglers returning from the action against the *San Lorenzo* off Calais. Seymour led these ships in an assault

The battle off Gravelines, 8th August 1588, the last in the series of tactical charts by Robert Adams, reproduced in his *Expeditionis Hispanorum in Angliam vera descriptio anno 1588*. While part of the English fleet chases the Spanish, other vessels are shown attacking the crippled galleass *San Lorenzo* off Calais (National Maritime Museum, Greenwich, London).

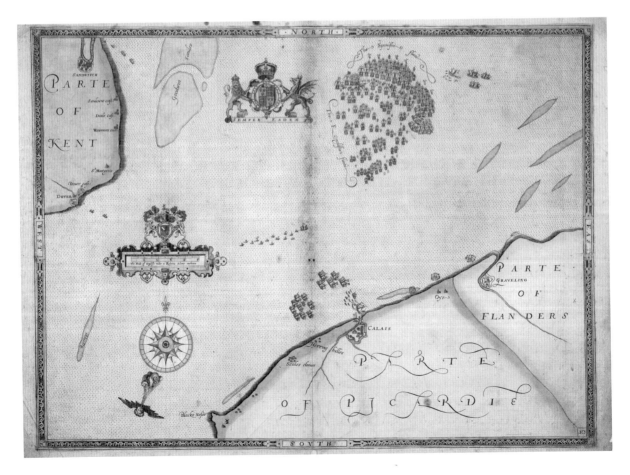

on the unengaged right (east) flank of the Armada formation, so that by noon the entire Armada formation was engaged in the battle. Over on the left flank Sir William Winter reported firing at 120 paces, and that the English fire caused the left wing of the Armada to crowd in towards the centre, repeating the tendency first shown in the battle off Plymouth. He also claimed that four of the Spanish warships collided with each other and were badly damaged.

When Howard rejoined his fleet at around 1pm the Spanish formation was showing signs of disintegration. Howard engaged the Spanish rearguard. As a witness recorded: 'My Lord Admiral with the rest of the fleet came up and gave a very fresh onset.' The damage and casualties were concentrated in the most powerful of the Spanish warships, the galleons and naos which had formed the 'van' or rearguard during the fighting in the Channel. Witnesses claimed that by the end of the battle some of these ships were so low in powder and shot that the only reply to the English barrage was small-arms fire.

Evidence from Armada shipwrecks tells a different story. Spanish guns were slow to reload, and any attempt to do so would have disrupted the organization of the ship. The Spanish posted one gunner to each large gun, assisted by six or more soldiers. Once the gun had been fired, the soldiers would return to their normal duty, which was to wait for a boarding action. In order to reload they would have to lay aside their weapons and manhandle a gun on an awkward two-wheeled

A colourful and wholly inaccurate depiction of the battle off Gravelines – although the fighting was often conducted at close quarters, the two sides never fought hand-to-hand during the engagement. *Defeat of the Spanish Armada*, a late 18th-century oil painting by Philippe-Jacques de Loutherbourg (National Maritime Museum, Greenwich, London).

The *San Martin* at Gravelines. Dawn on 8 August found the Armada in disarray following a night-time fireship attack, the fleet was completely vulnerable, and the English fleet closed with them to give battle. The Duke of Medina Sidonia's fleet flagship lay between the two fleets, and formed a rallying point for four other galleons. These five galleons held off the English attack for two hours, buying time for the rest of the Armada to regroup into a defensive formation. Fortunately for the Spaniards, half of the English fleet were trying to capture the damaged galleass *San Lorenzo* off Calais.. The *San Martín* eventually fought her way back to the Armada, her hull pierced over 200 times, and her decks reportedly running with blood (Howard Gerrard).

carriage. In the 15 minutes or so it would have taken for a skilled crew to reload a Spanish culverin, a similar-sized gun and crew using an English four-wheeled truck carriage could have fired two or three times. On the other hand, evidence from the Armada shipwrecks suggests that these ships had expended almost all of their close-range armament of light guns and swivel guns ('*versos*'). In other words, the smaller the gun, the more likely it was to have been fired.

This supports the English assertion that the fighting off Gravelines was fought at very close range. Sir William Winter stated: 'When I was furthest off in discharging any of the pieces, I was not out of the shot of their harquebus, and most times within speech of one another.' One of the galleons on the Armada's left (west) flank was the *San Felipe*, and when its commander, Don Francisco de Toledo, tried to board an English ship, the enemy were close enough for Spanish soldiers to fire on to its decks before the English vessel turned away. Ubaldino claimed that: 'Seymour and Winter made such excellent hits upon two other Spanish galleons – the *San Mateo* and *San Felipe* – from among the best and better provided, that they were obliged to withdraw to the coast of Flanders, because they had been so badly mauled, both because of the deaths of the crews and because the ships were leaking everywhere.'

Medina Sidonia scraped together what reserves he could find and formed a new rearguard, probably led by Don Alonso de Leiva in *La Rata Santa María Encoronada* and Juan Martinez de Recalde in the battered *San Juan de Portugal*. His aim was to protect the more battered ships of the Armada and shepherd the fleet away to the north-east. The three Portuguese galleons – the *San Mateo*, *San Felipe* and *San Luis* – were among the most badly battered ships in the Armada, apart from Medina Sidonia's *San Martín*. According to a Spaniard, the *San Juan de Sicilia* was damaged so heavily by English fire that it was forced to 'repair the damage from many shots which the ship had received alow and from the prow to the stern'. A Spaniard on board the *San Salvador* reported: 'The enemy inflicted such damage upon the galleons *San Mateo* and *San Felipe* that the latter had five guns on the starboard side and a big gun on the poop put out of action.'

By late afternoon the two warships were forced to fall out of the Armada formation, and drifted off towards the Banks of Flanders to the south and east. During the night they grounded close to the Flemish coast and were captured by the Dutch coastal fleet. Ubaldino stated: 'They were taken and looted by the Zeelanders and taken to Flushing, together with the survivors that were taken in them. Among those made prisoner the most important was Don Diego Pimentel, a man very well known in his country.' One other Spanish ship was lost during the day. The nao *La María Juan* of the Biscay Squadron was sunk by the concentrated fire of several English ships. It went down as negotiations to surrender were under way, and only one boatload of men escaped.

Ubaldino recounted another incident: 'Captain Fenton in the *Mary Rose* and a Spanish galleon met, the one from the east and the other from the west, so near to each other that the gunners could take sure aim and pierce through the ship's side. Captain Fenton and his men were deservedly praised for their daring which had such a happy result ... Particularly praised too was Captain Robert Crosse, who, in the ship *Hope*, showed fruitful results no less great than those of the ship in which he sailed whose name made men hope. Others also showed their worth and for their labours received the same praise.'

By 4pm the ferocity of the battle had begun to diminish, as the English ships became increasingly short of powder and shot. Accounts listing some of the armed merchant vessels which accompanied Seymour's squadron say that the ships carried only 20 rounds for each gun, plus a few extra rounds of barshot (to cut down rigging) and 'diced shot' (a form of grapeshot). Sir William Winter estimated that his ship, *Vanguard*, fired over 500 rounds, roughly 12 shots per gun. As the battle had already lasted over eight hours, this was hardly surprising.

Although the Spanish Armada was badly battered during the day and its formation was in some disarray, it remained intact as a fleet. The English slowly fell behind the Spanish rearguard, and as firing died away both sides tried to repair the damage they had suffered. The lack of ammunition was a grave concern to Howard and the other English commanders, who thought their fleet would be unable to renew the fight unless more munitions were brought from England. For his part, Medina Sidonia was perfectly willing to renew the battle the next day, as it was the only way he would be able to link up with the Duke of Parma. He must also have been aware that the English were short of ammunition. Spanish casualties had been heavy – estimated at around 1,000 killed and 800 wounded – but Spanish morale was still high.

It was the wind that sealed the Armada's fate. In the early evening a strong north-westerly sprang up, threatening to push the Armada ships back towards the Banks of Flanders. As darkness fell, Medina Sidonia's advisers suggested heading north-north-east into the safety of the North Sea. Instead he preferred to wait for morning, so he ordered his ships to try to maintain their position. Through the rest of the night the Armada edged closer to the Banks of Flanders, and the duke sent experienced pilots throughout the fleet in small pinnaces, advising the ships to stay as close to the wind as possible.

At dawn on Tuesday 9 August the two fleets were within a mile of each other, somewhere to the north of the sandbanks, some 25 miles north-north-east of Calais. Once again the *San Martín* was closest to the enemy, supported by five large warships and the remaining three galleasses. Medina Sidonia formed a rearguard that turned to face the English, but by that time the wind had died away almost completely, and Spanish morale was at last starting to break, causing him to accuse several of his captains of cowardice. One of these men was hanged a few days later.

For their part the English were willing to wait and see what happened, since the tide was still carrying the Armada towards the Banks of Flanders. Just when disaster seemed inevitable, the wind sprang up again, this time from the south-west. It allowed the Spaniards to claw themselves away from the sandbanks, but it also made it impossible to approach the English fleet.

As his ships drifted north-east, the duke called another council of war. He expressed his desire to return to Calais if the weather permitted, but he realized that if the breeze continued to freshen, he would be drawn further and further away into the North Sea. His more experienced naval commanders thought it almost impossible that they would be able to defy wind, tide and the English fleet and regain their anchorage off Calais. By the end of the meeting, it had been decided that there was little option but to continue on into the North Sea, then circumnavigate the British Isles in order to return to La Coruña.

Throughout the day the ships tried to prepare themselves for the long voyage home, and the bread, water and other victuals were redistributed throughout the Armada. For the most part the fleet was still intact, and although it faced a long voyage around Scotland and Ireland, the Armada was still a viable force, which could fight another day. The planned invasion of England would have to be postponed for another year. Unbeknown to both Medina Sidonia and Howard, a storm was forming in the Atlantic which would decimate by means of natural fury the fleet which English gunnery had failed to destroy.

✤ The Aftermath

The Long Voyage Home

The decision by the Duke of Medina Sidonia to return to Spain by way of the North Sea and the Atlantic Ocean was based on a sound grasp of the strategic situation. His decision had been supported by his leading commanders – de Recalde, Flores, Oquendo and de Leiva. Unable to return to Calais or sail down the Channel due to contrary winds, he had little option. On 10 August he determined a course for the entire fleet which took it around the Shetlands into the Atlantic; then, giving the Irish coast a wide berth, it would steer south towards La Coruña. As his orders put it: 'The course that is first to be held is to the north-north-east, until you be found under 61½ degrees.' Rather prophetically it then warned 'to take great heed lest you fall upon the island of Ireland, for fear of the harm that may happen to you upon that coast.'

By this stage there was little doubt that the 'Great Enterprise' had failed. Several Spanish vessels had already been lost, and many of those that remained were badly battered. One some vessels, only ceaseless work at the pumps kept the ships afloat. Most of the ships in the Armada were also short of water. Many casks had been damaged by enemy shot, and on the majority of ships water was now rationed. Food stocks were also depleted, as there had been no chance to take on fresh supplies off Flanders. Finally there was the problem of sickness. While many of the crew were listless through the effects of their exertions and lack of rations, hundreds of men had been wounded in the battle, while a growing number were also falling sick – victims of disease caused by the poor sanitary conditions aboard, as well as from chronic seasickness.

The Armada was in no real condition to renew the fight, and so the duke's only option was to return home to try again – circumnavigating the British Isles in the process. Still, morale generally remained high. It was clear that most of the men would have been willing to return to the fight if they had the chance. The duke's other problem was discipline. Off Calais his orders to remain together in the face of the fireship attack had been ignored, as captains ensured their own safety at the

expense of the cohesion of the fleet as a whole. The duke was unwilling to risk another similar breach of discipline. Twenty of his captains were charged, and while a few, like Francisco de Cuellár, commanding the galleon *San Pedro*, were relieved of their command, most were released with a stern warning from the duke. One unlucky individual was selected to be Medina Sidonia's scapegoat. He needed an execution to make his point. The unfortunate captain was Don Cristobal de Ávila, a captain from a ship in the squadron of hulks. Despite the pleading of the Judge Advocate Martín de Aranda, Don Cristobal was hanged from the yardarm of the flagship as it wallowed northwards through the North Sea.

The North Sea journey was an unpleasant one: temperatures dropped and fog banks and squalls disrupted the unity of the fleet. The English fleet was short of ammunition and supplies, but Lord Howard followed the Spanish as they sailed north, although he ordered Seymour's squadron back to the Downs to shield against any further invasion attempt by the Duke of Parma. The watershed for the English came on 13 August. The Armada had travelled the whole east coast of England without attempting to land, so when the Spanish passed the Firth of Forth in Scotland, Lord Howard ordered his ships to turn back to the ports of north-east England. The English admiral lamented: 'If our want of victuals and munitions were supplied, we could pursue them to the furthest that they durst have gone.' He could still not be sure that the Armada would return, but he simply lacked the supplies to stay at sea any longer.

Most of the Spanish fleet remained together, trying to make headway against a strong north-westerly wind, veering to the south-west for days on end. Medina Sidonia's flagship and the bulk of the fleet passed between Orkney and Shetland on 20 August and entered the Atlantic. By then the wind had changed to a north-easterly, ideal for running past the northern coast of Ireland before heading south for Spain. A day later the duke sent a pinnace flying ahead with news of the Armada's progress. Other parts of the fleet were not so fortunate. As North Sea squalls turned into light gales, ships were driven as far east as the Norwegian coast and as far north as the Faroe Islands. On entering the Atlantic, most ships held a west-south-westerly course from Fair Isle, but the poor-sailing hulks and the most damaged ships were unable to hold such a southerly course and were forced further north.

The plan was that, after passing into the Atlantic Ocean, the Spanish ships would alter course to the west-south-west, until they reached the latitude of 58 degrees, somewhere beyond the island of Rockall. Then they would change their heading to the south-west until they reached the latitude of 53 degrees North – in mid-Atlantic to the south of Iceland and well to the west of Ireland. From there they would head back to Spain on a south-easterly course. Naturally, as longitude could not be worked out, the navigators in the fleet had no way of knowing for certain how far west of Ireland they actually were. Even the calculation of latitude depended on clear skies, to allow the accurate use of the mariner's astrolabe.

Without accurate plotting the ships could just as easily be heading into danger as sailing towards a safe haven.

By 24 August the wind had freshened and veered from the south. A Spanish officer recalled: 'From the 24th to the 4th September we sailed without knowing whither, through constant storms, fogs and squalls.' The bad weather caused the fleet to scatter a little, and the damage caused by the English gunnery placed strains on the seams and hulls of the most badly battered ships. As their seams opened up ships started to founder, including the 750-ton hulk *La Barca de Hamburg*, whose crew were transferred to *La Trinidad Valencera* and *El Gran Grifón* just before it sank. Of these, *La Trinidad Valencera* was in a bad way, having been damaged during the fight off Gravelines. Its crew had to man its pumps to keep it afloat, and they were fast becoming exhausted.

To avoid further ships opening their hulls, others could just sail where the wind took them. On 3 September Medina Sidonia wrote in his journal: 'I pray God in his mercy will grant us fine weather so that the Armada may soon enter port; for we are so short of provisions that if for our sins we are long delayed, all will be irretrievably lost. There are now a great number of sick and many die.' In a letter sent ahead to the king, the duke declared that his casualty lists included approximately 3,000 sick and wounded. He also wrote that of the ships under his command, excluding the four galleys which had been detached from the fleet, he still had 112 of his 126 ships, and so although the campaign had been a failure it was certainly not a disaster.

By the second week in September Medina Sidonia was somewhere to the west of Ireland, with the rest of the fleet scattered for hundreds of miles north. The wind was changing direction almost daily, and with no chance to estimate their position, most of the Spanish had no accurate idea of their location. By 12 September a new storm was approaching, and the seas became increasingly rough. This fresh gale roared up from the south and scattered the fleet even further. Although Medina Sidonia and the main body of the fleet passed the southernmost tip of Ireland by 14 September with about 60 ships, the rest of the fleet remained somewhere off the Irish coast.

One by one, the leaking or sinking ships gave up and ran inshore, trying to find shelter on the Irish coast. One of the first was the *La Trinidad Valencera*, which beached in Kinnagoe Bay in Donegal. The ship broke up two days later, but most of the crew had managed to reach the shore, where they found themselves at the mercy of the Irish. The survivors marched inland, but were trapped by an English patrol, and eventually forced to surrender. They were duly stripped of their belongings, money and even their clothes. Then all but the senior officers were massacred. The English were well aware of the dangers of an Irish insurrection, and were taking no chances.

A similar fate befell other shipwreck survivors from Ulster to County Kerry. The three Levant Squadron ships – the *Lavia*, *Juliana* and *Santa Maria de Visón* – anchored

The Armada's Voyage around the British Isles

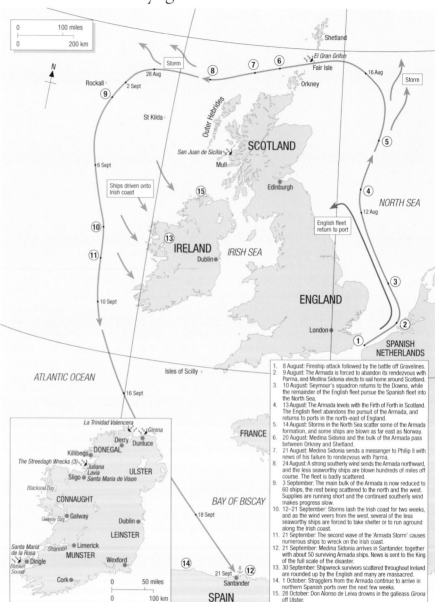

0 100 miles
0 200 km

N

Shetland

El Gran Grifon
Storm
28 Aug
8
7
6
Fair Isle
16 Aug
Storm
Rockall
2 Sept
9
Orkney

St Kilda

Outer Hebrides

SCOTLAND

5

6 Sept
San Juan de Sicilia
Mull

15
Edinburgh
4
12 Aug
NORTH SEA

Ships driven onto
Irish coast

10
13
IRELAND
Dublin
IRISH SEA
English fleet
return to port

11
10 Sept

3

ENGLAND

London
2
1

ATLANTIC OCEAN
Isles of Scilly
SPANISH
NETHERLANDS

16 Sept

1. 8 August: Fireship attack followed by the battle off Gravelines.
2. 9 August: The Armada is forced to abandon its rendezvous with Parma, and Medina Sidonia elects to sail home around Scotland.
3. 10 August: Seymour's squadron returns to the Downs, while the remainder of the English fleet pursue the Spanish fleet into the North Sea.
4. 13 August: The Armada levels with the Firth of Forth in Scotland. The English fleet abandons the pursuit of the Armada, and returns to ports in the north-east of England.
5. 14 August: Storms in the North Sea scatter some of the Armada formation, and some ships are blown as far east as Norway.
6. 20 August: Medina Sidonia and the bulk of the Armada pass between Orkney and Shetland.
7. 21 August: Medina Sidonia sends a messenger to Philip II with news of his failure to rendezvous with Parma.
8. 24 August: A strong southerly wind sends the Armada northward, and the less seaworthy ships are blown hundreds of miles off course. The fleet is badly scattered.
9. 3 September: The main bulk of the Armada is now reduced to 60 ships, the rest being scattered to the north and the west. Supplies are running short and the continued southerly wind makes progress slow.
10. 12–21 September: Storms lash the Irish coast for two weeks, and as the wind veers from the west, several of the less seaworthy ships are forced to take shelter or to run aground along the Irish coast.
11. 21 September: The second wave of the 'Armada Storm' causes numerous ships to wreck on the Irish coast.
12. 21 September: Medina Sidonia arrives in Santander, together with about 50 surviving Armada ships. News is sent to the King of the full scale of the disaster.
13. 30 September: Shipwreck survivors scattered throughout Ireland are rounded up by the English and many are massacred.
14. 1 October: Stragglers from the Armada continue to arrive in northern Spanish ports over the next few weeks.
15. 28 October: Don Alonso de Leiva drowns in the galleass *Girona* off Ulster.

La Trinidad Valencera
Girona
Derry
Dunluce
DONEGAL
Killibegs
FRANCE
The Streedagh Wrecks (3)
Juliana
Lavia
Sligo
Santa Maria de Vison
ULSTER
Blacksod Bay
CONNAUGHT
Galway
Galway Bay
Dublin
LEINSTER
BAY OF BISCAY
Santa Maria
de la Rosa
Shannon
Limerick
18 Sept
Blasket
Sound
Dingle
MUNSTER
Wexford
14
21 Sept
12
Cork
0 50 miles
Santander
0 100 km
SPAIN

off Streedagh Strand in County Sligo. They had been trapped in Donegal Bay by the wind, and were unable to escape back out to sea. A few days later another westerly gale hit them, driving the ships ashore. Francisco de Cuellár, formerly captain of the *San Pedro*, was now a prisoner on board the *Lavia*. He survived the order, and was able to tell his tale: 'the cables could not hold nor the sails serve us, and we were driven ashore with all three ships upon a beach, covered with very fine sand, shut in on one side and the other by great rocks. Such a thing was never seen, for within the space of an hour all three ships were broken to pieces, so that there did not escape three hundred men, and more than a thousand were drowned, among them many persons of importance – captains, gentlemen, and other officials.' Over 600 bodies were washed up on the beach of Streedagh Strand, ten miles north of Sligo.

Those who survived were stripped and killed by the English and their Irish auxiliaries. Only a handful escaped into the hinterland, and most of these were captured and executed. Again, Francisco de Cuellár recalled what happened. The beach was lined with enemy soldiers and their Irish auxiliaries: 'When any of our people set foot on the shore, two hundred savages and other enemies fell upon him and stripped him of what he had on until he was left in his naked skin. All of this was plainly visible from the battered ships.' De Cuellár made it as far as the sand dunes, accompanied by a naked Spanish officer. From there he managed to reach the relative safety of the Irish hinterland, and eventually made his way back to Spain.

The brutality of the English troops in Ireland was largely due to the policy of the local commander, Sir Richard Bingham, the governor of Connaught. The shipwrecks caused a great deal of confusion in Ireland, and many – including Bingham – suspected that the reports of Spanish on the coast heralded an invasion. Consequently he gave the order to: 'Apprehend and execute all Spaniards found, of what quality soever. Torture may be used in prosecuting this enquiry.' This brutal

Engagement between Spanish galleons and Dutch warships, by unknown Spanish artist, early 17th century (Museo Naval, Madrid).

The wreck of the Amsterdam, an oil painting by Cornelis Claesz van Qieringen. This dynamic painting captures some of the horrors of a shipwreck, when the wooden home of hundreds of men was torn apart on the rocks. This was the fate of several Armada vessels, including the *Girona*, and *El Gran Grifón* (National Maritime Museum, Greenwich, London).

policy was more the result of fear than unnecessary cruelty. The real threat was that these Spaniards might incite a general Catholic insurrection in the country, which was only weakly garrisoned by English troops.

El Gran Grifón, carrying the survivors of *La Barca de Hamburg*, had become separated from *La Trinidad Valencera* on 4 September, and like its former consort it too was badly damaged, and taking on water. Three days later it was driven eastwards by the gale, but clawed its way towards the north in an attempt to avoid the Irish coast. Instead it was driven ashore on Fair Isle on 27 September, and was dashed to pieces on the rocky south-east corner of the island. Most of its crew managed to scramble up the foremast and onto the cliff top, and miraculously, only seven men were lost. The survivors were sheltered by the local islanders, although 50 of them died of sickness before they could be rescued. The survivors were eventually taken to Edinburgh, and from there the majority were eventually repatriated back to Spain.

This new gale, which raged from 21–25 September, finished off many of the leaking Armada ships, including the *La Santa María de la Rosa*, which sank off County Kerry, and *El Gran Grin*, which was wrecked off Connaught. A nobleman on board the *San Juan de Portugal* which was sheltering from the gale in Blasket Sound saw the first of these two ships founder: 'The flagship of Juan Martinez drifted down on ours, cast anchor and other cable, and having smashed our lantern and our mizzen tackle and rigging, the flagship secured itself. At mid-day the *Santa María de la Rosa*, of Martín de Villafranca, came in by another entrance, nearer land on the north-west side. She fired a shot on entering, as if asking help, and another further on.

All her sails were in shreds except the foresail. She cast her single anchor, for she was not carrying more, and with the tide coming in from the south-east side and beating against her stern she stayed there until two o'clock. Then the tide waned, and as it turned the ships began dragging on our two cables, and we with her, and in an instant we could see that she was going down, trying to hoist the foresail. Then she sank with all aboard, not a person being saved – a most extraordinary and terrifying thing.'

An even worse tragedy was the loss of Don Alonso de Leiva. He survived the wrecking of his flagship *La Rata Santa María Encoronada* in Blacksod Bay (County Mayo) on 21 September and transferred his men to the *Duquesna Santa Ana*. He put to sea, but another gale drove this second ship ashore in Donegal. Don Alonso and the other survivors marched overland to Killibegs on Donegal Bay, where he found the galleass *Girona*. The commander supervised repairs to the ship for three weeks, then elected to continue north around Ulster to Scotland and a neutral harbour. The galleass was crammed with 1,300 men: the survivors of two shipwrecks as well as the original crew. On 28 October the *Girona* damaged its rudder fighting through heavy seas off Dunluce in Ulster. In the face of a northern gale and heavy seas the galleass was helpless, and it struck Lacada Point, a rocky outcrop at the base of a 400-foot cliff. All but a handful of the crew perished, including Don Alonso.

The first Armada ships began to straggle into the northern Spanish ports from 21 September and news of the disaster was sent to King Philip II. Most of the crew were suffering from advanced scurvy and malnutrition, while the incapacitated Medina Sidonia retired to his estates. Juan Martinez de Recalde survived to reach Bilbao, only to die a few weeks later while in a monastery hospital. As news of the

A late 16th-century representation of Irish warriors. It reflects the 'savages' who met many shipwrecked Spaniards on the beaches of Ireland. Many local chieftains then sold or handed over the Spanish survivors to the English (Ashmolean Museum, Oxford).

187

A true description of the Norwest partes of Irelande, a chart drawn by Baptista Boazio. It shows the coast of County Sligo, and marks the location of three Spanish shipwrecks – *La Juliana*, *La Lavia* and the *Santa Maria de Visón*. All of these vessels were from the Levant squadron, and wrecked on the shore of Streedagh Strand (National Maritime Museum, Greenwich, London).

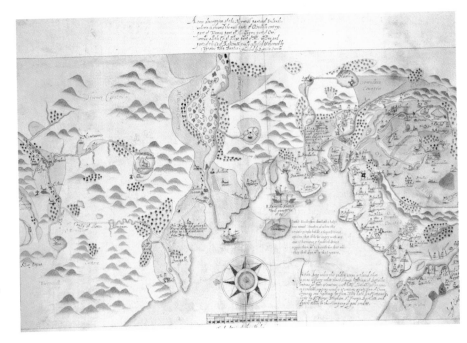

Below

A Spanish mariner's astrolabe, of the late 16th century. It was found on Valencia Island on the south-west corner of Ireland, and almost certainly came from a Spanish shipwreck in Blasket Sound – possibly the *Santa Maria de la Rosa*. Astrolabes were used to determine latitude of the observer by measuring the height of the sun (National Maritime Museum, Greenwich, London).

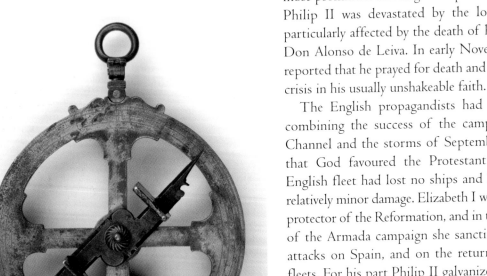

losses mounted, the full extent of the disaster made itself apparent. In all, 65 ships made it back to Spain, which meant that at least 45 were lost, including 27 of the most prominent and largest ships in the Armada. Philip II was devastated by the loss, and was particularly affected by the death of his favourite, Don Alonso de Leiva. In early November it was reported that he prayed for death and underwent a crisis in his usually unshakeable faith.

The English propagandists had a field day, combining the success of the campaign in the Channel and the storms of September as proof that God favoured the Protestant cause. The English fleet had lost no ships and had suffered relatively minor damage. Elizabeth I was seen as the protector of the Reformation, and in the aftermath of the Armada campaign she sanctioned further attacks on Spain, and on the returning treasure fleets. For his part Philip II galvanized the nation by ordering replacement ships, ordnance and men. As one of his councillors said: 'What matters is that we should show great courage, and finish what we have started.' Despite the disaster, the war would go on.

The War Continues

Queen Elizabeth followed up her success by sending Drake and Sir John Norris to Santander in April 1589 with 126 ships and 21,000 men. The objective of this 'Armada in reverse' was the destruction of the remaining Spanish fleet. Drake and Norris decided that both San Sebastian and Santander were too dangerous to attack, so instead they landed their troops at La Coruña and sacked the port. The English fleet then sailed to Lisbon where the Englishmen attacked ships anchored in the Tagus River and captured 60 German ships, which eventually had to be returned to avoid a diplomatic incident. The English troops landed but were unable to take Lisbon, so they re-embarked and the fleet sailed north, attacked and sacked Vigo, then sailed for the Azores.

The aim was to intercept the annual treasure fleet, but the English missed it and Drake returned home, his ships rotten and half of his men dying from disease. The queen privately castigated Drake for looting rather than attacking enemy ships, and the former hero remained in disgrace in Plymouth for the next five years.

For the rest of that year squadrons under Sir Richard Grenville and George Clifford, Earl of Cumberland, raided the Azores and intercepted Spanish ships off

The Shipwreck of the *Girona*. Following the storm that scattered much of the Armada, the galleass *Girona* put into Killibegs in County Donegal. She spent much of October repairing her damaged hull, and took on survivors from two other ships. On 26 October she sailed with over 1,300 men crowded on board. The senior officer was Don Alonso Martínez de Leiva, who decided to sail towards neutral Scotland rather than risk the journey to Spain with the battered ship. She was off Dunluce in Antrim when her jury rudder broke and she was forced against Lacada Point. Only five men survived the disaster and it was said that King Philip mourned the loss of Don Alonso more than the rest of the fleet. The wreck was found in 1968 by Robert Sténuit, and all the artefacts recovered now reside in Ulster Museum, Belfast (Howard Gerrard).

the Iberian coast. In April 1591, Lord Thomas Howard put the fleet with a large Tudor squadron to intercept the returning treasure fleet off the Azores, while the Earl of Cumberland cruised off the Spanish coast. Howard and his squadron sailed around the Azores for three months, but never managed to sight the treasure *flota*. Instead they were caught by a superior enemy fleet of over 50 warships, sent to the Azores to rendezvous with the treasure galleons. The commander of the Spanish fleet, Don Alfonso de Bazan, decided to surprise the English fleet, sneaking up on them by using the island of Flores for cover.

On 30 August 1591, the *Revenge* was lying off the island of Flores in the Azores, part of Lord Thomas Howard's English fleet. Commanded by the veteran sea captain Sir Richard Grenville, the 500-ton galleon carried a crew of about 250 men. Dawn revealed the approach of a Spanish fleet of over 30 warships, the majority of which were large galleons. All but one of Howard's fleet escaped to the north, but Grenville's galleon was delayed as many of his crew were ashore on the island. Unable or unwilling to escape, Grenville ordered the *Revenge* to turn towards the enemy. Grenville forced his way into the middle of the powerful

The Defeat of the Armada - Elizabeth I at Tilbury, an oil-painted wooden panel by an unknown English artist of the early 17th century. It depicts Queen Elizabeth, reviewing her troops at Tilbury following the defeat of the Spanish Armada. The Spanish ships are shown burning in the background (St Faith Church, Gaywood, near King's Lynn, Norfolk).

Castillian Squadron, repeatedly firing both broadsides as he went. His ship broke through the Spanish formation and headed north, with the Spanish galleons in pursuit.

The galleon *San Felipe* overhauled the *Revenge* on its starboard side, stealing its wind. As the Spaniard tried to board, Grenville fired a broadside that all but crippled the enemy galleon, which fell away astern. However, the Spanish vessel had slowed the *Revenge* down sufficiently for the *San Barnabe* to come alongside its port side. The two ships locked together. The English were unable to fire their heavy guns for fear of sinking the Spaniard, which would probably have taken the *Revenge* down with her. The Spanish upper deck guns concentrated on the masts and sails of the *Revenge*, denying it the opportunity to escape even if it could free itself. Meanwhile, Spanish sea soldiers took advantage of their vessel's height and whittled down the English defenders using firearms and grenades.

Howard made several attempts to break through the ring of Spanish ships that now surrounded the *Revenge*, but to no avail. Grenville and his men were on their own. Just as darkness fell, the galleon *San Cristobal* crashed into the stern of the *Revenge*, and a wave of Spaniards scrambled onto its quarterdeck. Although the attackers cut their way forward as far as the mainmast, the crew of the *Revenge* rallied and drove them back to the *San Cristobal*. Grenville himself was mortally wounded in the mêlée. Meanwhile, English gunners fired their sternchasers into the Spanish galleon, holing it below the waterline. The *San Cristobal* pulled away, its commander signalling for assistance.

The next ship to attack was the *La Asuncion*, whose crew boarded the *Revenge* over its port bow. The attack was driven back, as were several more attempts to storm the *Revenge*'s forecastle. The *La Serena* was next, but the English defenders hung on grimly, and repulsed all assaults. Three Spanish galleons were now grappling with the *Revenge*, and Spanish reinforcements were ferried over to these three ships, thereby adding a fresh impetus to the fight. Only the starboard side of the *Revenge* remained clear of enemy ships, which were kept at bay by repeated broadsides from the English guns. The Spanish fired back during lulls in the boarding action. At some point during the night, the battered *San Barnabe* cut its losses and limped away. However, English losses continued to mount, and the deck of the *Revenge* was beginning to resemble a charnel house.

As dawn rose the true extent of the damage was revealed. Most of the ship's upper works had been shot away, but its lower deck guns were still firing intermittently. Daylight also offered the Spanish soldiers fresh targets, and before long few of the English defenders remained standing. The dying Grenville ordered his ship to be blown up, but was convinced by his surviving officers that his ship was already sinking, and that he needed to surrender in order to save his crew. He did so reluctantly, despite being offered full honours by the Spanish commander General Alfonso de Bazan. Grenville died three days later. As for the *Revenge*, it sank in a storm a few days later, as did the five Spanish ships that had been badly damaged during the engagement.

While a stirring piece of English naval history, the last fight of the *Revenge* also demonstrates the ability of Howard's race-built galleons to fight and to absorb damage. The engagement shows the heavy volume of firepower available to Elizabethan naval commanders, as well as the way in which the Spanish preferred to fight a naval action by boarding rather than by gunnery. A key element in the fighting was the sheer determination of Grenville's crew. According to Sir Walter Raleigh, we may assume that as many as 90 of the English crew were already too sick to participate in the action. That left Grenville with a crew of just 160 men. At least half of these were killed during the 16-hour battle, and most of the remainder were badly wounded. While books such as this may talk about the technical aspects of ships and their armament, we must remember that warships are only as effective as the men who served aboard them. In this respect, it appears that Grenville, Drake, Hawkins, Frobisher and their like were extremely fortunate to have both the ships and the men they deserved.

Fighting in European waters during the Armada campaign provided a lull in hostilities in the Spanish Main, and Spain took the opportunity to strengthen its

Sir Richard Grenville (c.1542-91), an oil painting by an unknown artist of the English School, late 16th century. Grenville participated in Raleigh's attempts to establish a colony in the Carolinas, and fought in the Armada campaign. However, he is best remembered for his last fight on board the *Revenge*, fought off the Azores in 1591 (National Maritime Museum, Greenwich, London).

fortifications. Consequently, Spanish ports in the Caribbean were well prepared for a new series of attacks. In 1595 Drake and Hawkins jointly commanded a fresh expedition to the Caribbean, with 26 ships and 2,500 men. A private venture supported by investors, the aim was plunder rather than strategic gain. Drake attacked Las Palmas in the Canary Islands before crossing the Atlantic, but the assault failed, and captured sailors told the Spanish about Drake's plan to assault Puerto Rico. Drake and Hawkins quarrelled bitterly over the attack, and this animosity continued until Hawkins' death on 12 November 1595.

Drake launched two attacks on Puerto Rico in November, both of which were repulsed. Abandoning the attempt, Drake sailed for South America, and cruised along the Caribbean coast heading west. He sacked Rio de la Hacha and Santa Marta before crossing to the Darien Peninsula, where he captured Nombre de Dios on 6 January 1596. Once again the Spanish had warning of his arrival, and moved the treasure in the town to safety. Two days later he sent a force of 600 men up the mule trail towards Panama hoping to find the hidden treasure, but weather and Spanish resistance forced them to return to the coast within a week. Drake then sailed up the coast of Honduras in search of Spanish shipping, but within weeks he became ill from a fever, and died at sea off Porto Bello on 28 January 1596.

Across the Atlantic a large Anglo-Dutch naval force of 30 warships and 30 transports assembled under the command of Lord Thomas Howard and Sir Walter Raleigh, with an amphibious element of 8,000 men led by Robert Devereaux, Earl of Essex. The allies arrived off Cadiz on 21 June 1596, and the next evening a council of war was held to decide the best course of action. The naval commanders decided to attack the enemy fleet in the harbour before any landing was attempted, so the next morning Raleigh spearheaded an attack on the inner harbour. In a fierce battle against Spanish ships and shore batteries, Raleigh devastated the Spanish fleet, burning, capturing or forcing aground over 40 ships of various sizes. An amphibious landing was made, supported by a naval bombardment, and Cadiz fell to the allies, who held the port for another six weeks before returning home.

Philip II's attempts to send a second Armada against England were defeated by bad weather in 1596, and this bad weather was then repeated in 1597, forcing the

Sir Richard Grenville and the last fight of the *Revenge*, 1591. Although the defeat of the Armada was a devastating blow to Spanish naval power and prestige, the Spanish empire still possessed considerable resources of ships and men. In 1591 Lord Thomas Howard led a small English fleet to the Azores where it lay in wait for the annual treasure fleet en route from Havana to Seville. The Spaniards learned of the ambush and sent a large fleet to attack Howard's force. The hunters had become the hunted, and when the Spanish appeared, Howard ordered his fleet to flee to the north. Howard's second-in-command was Sir Richard Grenville on board the *Revenge*, who waited to recover a shore party who had been filling water casks on the island of Flores. Surprised by a second squadron of Spaniards who used Flores as cover, Grenville found himself cut off from the rest of the English fleet. Instead of escaping into the Atlantic, Grenville steered the *Revenge* towards the Spanish fleet. Soon the *Revenge* was ringed by 22 Spanish ships, but fought off all boarding attempts. The fight continued into the night, and at dawn, the mortally wounded Grenville had no choice but to surrender his sinking ship. Two Spanish vessels also sank in the night. The scene is set during the early evening on the deck of the *San Barnabe*, a Spanish galleon of 1,000 tons (Angus McBride).

abandonment of the project. Philip II died in 1598, having just made peace with France, but refusing to do so with England. After his death the war fizzled on for another six years, but following the death of Queen Elizabeth in 1603, England was ready to make peace. The two sides duly met at Somerset House in London during 1604. A peace treaty was signed in August that year.

The Somerset House Conference, an oil painting by Pantoja de la Cruz, c.1604. Peace between England and Spain was ratified in August 1604. In this painting the Spanish delegation sit on the left, while the English face them to the right. Lord Howard is the second figure from the window on the right (National Maritime Museum, Greenwich, London).

The era of the 'sea dogs' drew to a close, and national privateering at sea was replaced by a less glamorous but ultimately more productive era of mercantile and colonial expansion for the English and overseas exploitation and economic stagnation for the Spanish.

For the Spanish, the Armada marked the high-water mark of her political and military aspirations in Europe. The loss of prestige following the defeat of the Armada did Spain irreparable harm, and although the war with the Dutch would continue intermittently until 1648, Spain was increasingly seen as a secondary player in European politics. For the English, they emerged with a greatly enhanced reputation. Although the Armada had been defeated by fireships and storms rather than by the English navy, England's status as a leading maritime power was assured, a position she would retain for the next three and a half centuries.

The Fleets

The Spanish Armada

Note: A *capitana* is a squadron flagship, and an *almiranta* is a second-in-command's ship. All vessels marked (*) were regarded as front-line vessels and were often deployed in a special 'van', a form of 'fire brigade' which could relieve pressure on threatened sections of the Armada formation.

Squadron of Portugal

Commander: The Duke of Medina Sidonia (who was also the Armada commander)

Ship Name	Ship Type	Tonnage	Guns	Crew	Fate
San Martín (fleet *capitana*)	Galleon (*)	1,000	48	469	Returned
San Juan de Portugal (fleet *almiranta*)	Galleon (*)	1,050	50	522	Returned
Florencia	Galleon (*)	961	52	383	Returned
San Felipe	Galleon (*)	800	40	439	Lost
San Luis	Galleon (*)	830	38	439	Returned
San Marcos	Galleon (*)	790	33	386	Lost
San Mateo	Galleon (*)	750	34	389	Lost
Santiago	Galleon	520	24	387	Returned
San Bernardo	Galleon	352	21	236	Returned
San Crístobal	Galleon	352	20	211	Returned
Julia	Zabra	166	14	135	Returned
Augusta	Zabra	166	13	92	Returned

Squadron of Biscay

Commander: Juan Martinez de Recalde (Also Armada deputy commander, with flag in *San Juan*). A nominal squadron commander in the *Santiago* commanded the squadron in de Recalde's absence.

Ship Name	Ship Type	Tonnage	Guns	Crew	Fate
Santiago (capitana)	Nao	666	25	312	Returned
El Gran Grin (almiranta)	Nao (*)	1,160	28	336	Lost
Santa María de Montemayor	Nao	707	18	202	Returned
La María Juan	Nao	665	24	399	Lost
La Magdalena	Nao	530	18	274	Returned
La Manuela	Nao	520	12	163	Returned
La Concepción Mayor	Nao	468	25	219	Returned
La Concepción de Juan del Cano	Nao	418	16	225	Returned
San Juan	Nao	350	21	190	Returned
La María de Miguel de Suso	Patache	96	6	45	Lost
San Esteban	Patache	78	6	35	Returned
La Isabela	Patache	71	10	53	Returned
La María de Aguirre	Patache	70	6	43	Lost

Note: The original squadron *capitana* was the *Santa Ana*, but it was forced to seek shelter in a French port due to bad weather in the Bay of Biscay, and took no part in the campaign. The *Santiago* became the new *capitana* of the squadron.

Santa Ana de Juan Martinez	Nao (*)	768	30	412	

Squadron of Castille
Commander: Don Diego Flores de Valdés

Ship Name	Ship Type	Tonnage	Guns	Crew	Fate
San Cristóbal (capitana)	Galleon (*)	700	36	303	Returned
San Juan Bautista (almiranta)	Galleon (*)	750	24	296	Returned
Nuestra Señora de Begoña	Galleon	750	24	300	Returned
San Pedro	Galleon	530	24	274	Returned
San Juan el Menor	Galleon	530	24	284	Lost
Santiago el Mayor	Galleon	530	24	293	Returned
San Felipe y Santiago	Galleon	530	24	234	Returned
La Asunción	Galleon	530	24	240	Returned
Nuestra Señora del Barrio	Galleon	530	24	277	Returned
San Medel y Celedón	Galleon	530	24	273	Returned
Santa Ana	Galleon	250	24	153	Returned
La Santa Catalina	Nao	882	24	320	Returned
La Trinidad	Nao	872	24	241	Lost
San Juan Bautista ('Ferrandome')	Nao	652	24	240	Lost
Nuestra Señora del Socorro	Patache	75	12	35	Lost
San Antonio de Padua	Patache	75	12	46	Lost

Squadron of Andalusia
Commander: Don Pedro de Valdés

Ship Name	Ship Type	Tonnage	Guns	Crew	Fate
Nuestra Señora del Rosario (capitana)	Nao(*)	1,150	46	559	Lost
San Fransisco (almiranta)	Nao	915	21	323	Returned
San Juan Bautista	Galleon	810	31	333	Returned
San Bartolomé	Nao	976	27	240	Returned
Duquesna Santa Ana	Nao	900	23	273	Lost
La Concepción	Nao (*)	862	20	260	Returned
Santa Catalina	Nao	730	23	289	Returned
Santa María de Juncal	Nao	730	20	287	Returned
La Trinidad	Nao	650	13	210	Returned
San Juan de Gargarín	Nao	569	16	193	Returned
El Espírito Santo	Patache	70	6	33	Lost

Squadron of Guipúzcoa
Commander: Miguel de Oquendo

Ship Name	Ship Type	Tonnage	Guns	Crew	Fate
Santa Ana (capitana)	Nao (*)	1,200	125	400	Returned
Santa María de la Rosa (almiranta)	Nao (*)	945	26	323	Lost
San Salvador	Nao (*)	958	25	371	Lost
San Esteban	Nao	936	26	274	Lost
La Santa Cruz	Nao	680	18	165	Returned
Santa Marta	Nao	548	20	239	Returned
Santa Bárbara	Nao	525	12	182	Returned
La Urca Doncella	Nao	500	16	141	Returned
San Buenaventura	Nao	379	21	212	Returned
La María San Juan	Nao	291	12	135	Returned
San Bernabé	Patache	69	9	34	Lost
La Asunción	Patache	60	9	34	Lost
Nuestra Señora de Guadalupe	Pinnace	-	1	12	Lost
La Madalena	Pinnace	-	1	14	Lost

Squadron of the Levant
Commander: Martín de Bertendona

Ship Name	Ship Type	Tonnage	Guns	Crew	Fate
La Regazona (capitana)	Nao	1,200	30	371	Returned
La Lavia (almiranta)	Nao (*)	728	25	302	Lost
La Trinidad Valencera	Hulk (*)	1,100	42	413	Lost
La Trinidad de Scala	Nao	900	22	408	Returned
La Juliana	Nao	860	32	412	Lost
San Nicolas Prodaneli	Nao	834	26	294	Returned
La Rata Santa María Encoronada	Nao (*)	820	35	448	Lost
San Juan de Sicilia	Nao	800	26	332	Lost
La Anunciada	Nao	703	24	266	Lost
Santa Maria de Visón	Nao	666	18	284	Returned

Squadron of Hulks (Supply and Transport Ships)

Commander: Juan Gómez de Medina

Ship Name	Ship Type	Tonnage	Guns	Crew	Fate
El Gran Grifón (capitana)	Hulk	650	38	279	Lost
San Salvador (almiranta)	Hulk	650	24	271	Returned
El Castillo Negro	Hulk	750	27	103	Lost
La Barca de Hamburg	Hulk	600	23	287	Lost
La Casa de Paz Grande	Hulk	600	26	-	Returned (*)
Santiago	Hulk	600	19	65	Returned
San Pedro el Mayor	Hulk	581	29	144	Lost
El Sansón	Hulk	500	18	125	Returned
San Pedro el Menor	Hulk	500	18	198	Lost
El Falcon Blanco Mayor	Hulk	500	16	216	Returned
La Barca de Danzig	Hulk	450	26	178	Lost
David	Hulk	450	7	-	Returned (?)
San El Ciervo Volante	Hulk	400	18	172	Lost
Andres	Hulk	400	14	65	Returned
El Gato	Hulk	400	9	71	Returned
Santa Bárbara	Hulk	370	10	130	Lost
La Casa de Paz Chica	Hulk	350	15	175	Returned
El Falcon Blanco Mediano	Hulk	300	16	80	Lost
San Gabriel	Hulk	280	4	47	Lost
Esayas	Hulk	260	4	47	Returned
Paloma Blanca	Hulk	250	12	-	Returned (?)
El Perro Marino	Hulk	200	7	96	Returned
La Buena Ventura	Hulk	160	4	64	Returned

Note: The crew levels of many of these vessels are unusually high because they were used to transport Spanish soldiers, reinforcements for the Duke of Parma's main amphibious landing force.

Galleass Squadron

Commander: Don Hugo de Moncada

Ship Name	Ship Type	Tonnage	Guns	Crew	Fate
San Lorenzo (capitana)	Galleass (*)	-	50	368	Lost
Zúñiga	Galleass (*)	-	50	298	Returned
La Girona	Galleass (*)	-	50	349	Lost
Napolitana	Galleass (*)	-	50	321	Returned

Attached Small Vessel Squadron

Commander: Augustín de Ojeda

Note: De Ojeda succeeded Don Antonio Hurtado de Mendoza, who died during the voyage from Spain to the English coast.

Only four of these vessels were over 100 tons:

Ship Name	Ship Type	Tonnage	Guns	Crew	Fate
Nuestra Senora del Pilar de Zaragoza	Nao	300	-	173	Lost
La Caridad Inglesa	Hulk	180	-	80	Returned (?)
San Andrés	Hulk	150	-	65	Returned (?)
El Santo Crusifijo	Patache	150	-	64	Lost

Of the remaining 34 vessels under 100 tons, ten were carvels, ten were pataches, seven were falúas and seven were zabras. Of these, at least nine were lost during the campaign and its aftermath.

An additional squadron of four galleys was forced to retire due to bad weather during the voyage from Spain to the English coast and took no part in the campaign.

The English Fleet

The Main Fleet (Plymouth)

Commander: Charles Howard, the Lord Admiral

Note: This includes the squadrons of Frobisher and Hawkins as well as the one directly controlled by Howard. No records survive which allow us to split the fleet down further into individual squadrons, probably because the commands were 'ad hoc' and were never committed to paper. English records are less complete than those of the Spanish, and information on some vessels is not available. The total of guns includes all weapons over a 1in bore and comes from a list of 1585. Those marked (*) are derived from a list of 1602.

Royal Ships (14)

Ship	Commander	Tonnage	Guns	Crew
Ark Royal	The Lord Admiral	550	38*	430
Triumph	Sir Martin Frobisher	740	46	500
White Bear	Lord Sheffield	730	66	490
Elizabeth Jonas	Sir Robert Southwell	750	54	490
Victory	Sir John Hawkins	800	44	450
Mary Rose	Edward Fenton	600	36	250
Elizabeth Bonaventure	Earl of Cumberland	600	34	250
Golden Lion	Lord Thomas Howard	500	34	250
Dreadnought	Sir George Beeston	360	26	190
Swallow	Richard Hawkins	360	26	160
Foresight	Christopher Baker	300	26	150
Scout	Henry Ashley	100	18	80
Achates	Gregory Riggs	100	16	70
George Hoy	Richard Hodges	100	-	20

Armed Merchant Vessels (33)

Ship	Commander	Tonnage	Guns	Crew
Hercules of London	George Barne	300	-	120
Toby of London	Robert Barrett	250	-	100
Centurion of London	Samuel Foxcraft	250	-	100
Galleon	Dudley James Erisay	250	-	96
Minion of Bristol	John Sachfield	230	-	110
Ascension of London	John Bacon	200	-	100
Mayflower of London	Edward Bancks	200	-	90
Primrose of London	Robert Bringborne	200	-	90
Margaret & John of London	John Fisher	200	-	90
Tiger of London	William Caesar	200	-	90
Red Lion of London	Jervis Wilde	200	-	90
Minion of London	John Dale	200	-	90
Edward of Maldon	William Pierce	186	-	30
Gift of God of London	Thomas Luntlowe	180	-	80
Bark Potts	Anthony Potts	180	-	80
Royal Defence of London	John Chester	160	-	80
Bark Burr of London	John Serocold	160	-	70
Brave of London	William Furthow	160	-	70
Nightingale	John Doate	160	-	16
John Trelawney	Thomas Meek	150	-	30
Cure's Ship	-	150	-	-
Crescent of Dartmouth	-	140	-	75
Golden Lion of London	Robert Wilcox	140	-	70
Thomas Bonaventure ofLondon	William Aldridge	140	-	70
Samuel of London	John Vassall	140	-	50
White Lion	Charles Howard	140	-	50
Bartholomew of Topsham	Nicholas Wright	130	-	70
Unicorn of Bristol	James Langton	130	-	66
Angel of Southampton	-	120	-	-
Robin of Sandwich	-	110	-	-
John of Barnstable	-	100	-	65
Galleon of Weymouth	Richard Miller	100	-	-
Charity of Plymouth	-	100	-	-

Howard also commanded the small royal ships *Charles* (70 tons, 8 guns) and *Moon* (60 tons, 13 guns), plus 87 smaller vessels of between 30 and 99 tons. Almost half were less than 50 tons, making them almost useless in battle. They were probably used to carry messages or stores, although little information is available on these small craft, the equivalent of the 45 pataches, zabras, falúas and carvels accompanying the Spanish fleet.

Drake's Squadron (Plymouth)
Commander: Sir Francis Drake

Royal Ships (5)

Ship	Commander	Tonnage	Guns	Crew
Revenge	Sir Francis Drake	460	36	250
Hope	Robert Crosse	420	33	280
Nonpareil	Thomas Fenner	500	34	250
Swiftsure	Edward Fenner	350	28	180
Aid	William Fenner	240	23	120

Armed Merchant Vessels (21)

Ship	Commander	Tonnage	Guns	Crew
Galleon Leicester	George Fenner	400	-	160
Merchant Royal	Robert Flicke	400	-	140
Roebuck	Jacob Whiddon	300	-	120
Edward Bonaventure	James Lancaster	300	-	120
Gold Noble	Adam Seager	250	-	110
Galleon Dudley	James Erisey	250	-	96
Hopewell	John Merchant	200	-	100
Griffin	William Hawkyns	200	-	100
Minion of London	William Winter	200	-	80
Thomas Drake	Henry Spindelow	200	-	80
Spark	William Spark	200	-	80
Bark Talbot	Henry Whyte	200	-	80
Virgin God save Her	John Greynvile	200	-	70
Hope Hawkins of Plymouth	John Rivers	180	-	70
Bark Mannington	Ambrose Mannington	160	-	80
Bark St Leger	John St Leger	160	-	80
Bark Bond	William Poole	150	-	70
Bark Bonner	Charles Caesar	150	-	70
Bark Hawkyns	William Snell	140	-	70
Bear Yonge of London	John Yonge	140	-	70
Elizabeth Founes	Roger Grant	100	-	60

Drake also commanded the small royal ship *Advice* (50 tons, 9 guns) plus 13 smaller vessels of between 30 and 80 tons.

The Narrow Seas Squadron (off the Downs)
Commander: Lord Henry Seymour

Royal Ships (7)

Ship	Commander	Tonnage	Guns	Crew
Rainbow	Lord Henry Seymour	380	24*	250
Vanguard	Sir William Winter	450	42*	250
Antelope	Sir Henry Palmer	400	24	170
Tiger	John Bostocke	200	20	100
Bull	Jeremy Turner	200	17	100
Tramontana	Luke Ward	150	21*	80
Scout	Henry Ashley	100	18	80

Armed Merchant Vessels (7)

Ship	Commander	Tonnage	Guns	Crew
Grace of Yarmouth	William Musgrave	150	-	70
Mayflower of Lynn	Alexander Musgrave	150	-	70
William of Colchester	Thomas Lambert	140	-	50
William of Ipswich	Barnaby Lowe	140	-	50
Katharine of Ipswich	Thomas Grymble	125	-	50
Primrose of Harwich	John Cardinal	120	-	40
Elizabeth of Dover	John Litgen	120	-	70

Seymour also commanded four small royal vessels: *Achates* (90 tons), *Merlin* (50 tons), *Sun* (39 tons) and *Cygnet* (29 tons). The *Spy*, *Fancy*, *George Hoy* and the *Bonavolia Galley* were detached on other duties. He also retained the use of eight armed merchant vessels displacing 70 tons or less.

English Reinforcements

Armed merchant vessels who voluntarily joined the English fleet during the campaign (6)

Ship	Commander	Tonnage	Guns	Crew
Sampson	John Wingfield	300	-	108
Samaritan of Dartmouth	-	250	-	100
Frances of Fowey	John Rashley	140	-	60
Golden Ryall of Weymouth	-	120	-	50
William of Plymouth	-	120	-	60
Grace of Topsham	Walter Edney	100	-	50

In addition, 15 smaller vessels under 90 tons also volunteered during the campaign.

Note: Most of these ships joined the fleet on 31 July and 1 August, during the fighting off the Devon coast.

Armed merchant vessels sent from London to reinforce Lord Seymour, 4 August 1588 (17)

Note: The first seven ships were commanded by Nicholas Gorges, Esquire, of London. The last ten ships were supplied by the Merchant Adventurers Guild of London, and were commanded by Henry Bellingham ('George Noble').

Ship	Commander	Tonnage	Guns	Crew
Susan Parnell of London	Nicholas Gorges	220	-	80
Violet of London	Martin Hawkes	220	-	60
George Bonaventure of London	Eleazer Hickman	200	-	80
Anne Francis of London	Charles Lister	180	-	70
Solomon of London	Edward Musgrave	170	-	80
Vineyard of London	Benjamin Cooke	160	-	60
George Noble of London	Richard Harper	120	14	60
Antelope of London	Abraham Bonner	120	13	60
Prudence of Leigh	Richard Chester	120	12	60
Jewel of Leigh	Henry Rawlyn	110	13	55
Salamander of Leigh	William Goodlad	110	12	55
Dolphin of Leigh	William Hare	110	11	55
Toby of London	Robert Cuttle	100	13	60
Anthony of London	Richard Dove	100	12	50
Rose Lion of Leigh	Robert Duke	100	10	50
Pansy of London	William Butler	100	10	50
Jane Bonaventure of London	Thomas Hallwood	100	-	80

Supply Vessels

Ship	Commander	Tonnage	Guns	Crew
Mary Rose	Francis Burnell	100	-	70
John of London	Richard Rose	100	-	70
Richard Duffield	William Adams	100	-	70
Bearsabe	Edward Bryan	100	-	60
Elizabeth Bonaventure	Richard Start	100	-	60
Elizabeth of Leigh	William Bower	100	-	60
Solomon	George Street	100	-	60
Pelican	John Clarke	100	-	50
Pearl	Lawrence Moore	100	-	50
Marigold	Robert Bowers	100	-	50
Jonas	Edward Bell	100	-	50
Gift of God	Robert Harrison	100	-	40
Hope	John Skinner	-	-	40
Unity	John Moore	-	-	40
White Hind	Richard Browne	-	-	40

These were despatched from the Thames Estuary to rendezvous with Howard's main fleet on 1 August. They reached Howard off the Isle of Wight on 3 August.

✤ The Archaeological Legacy

There is an old saying that 'No flowers bloom on a sailor's grave', but anyone who has dived on historic shipwrecks will contest this. There are no military cemeteries relating to the Spanish Armada campaign and no neatly preserved battlefields, while the English Channel, where the campaign was fought, is now one of the busiest shipping lanes in the world, particularly between Calais and Dover. What has survived over the centuries is evidence from shipwrecks, the remains of the Spanish Armada ships which held off the English fleet only to succumb to the elements off the coasts of Ireland and Scotland. Over 30 ships were known to have been lost during the storms which hit the Armada in September 1588.

At the time of publication, eight of these wrecks have been located and examined, and the information they have produced has greatly helped our understanding of the Spanish Armada, its ships and the men who sailed in them. In 1968 Sidney Wignall discovered the remains of the *almiranta* of the Guipúzcoa Squadron, *La Santa María de la Rosa*. Over the next two years Wignall and a team of amateur archaeologists examined the remains of the vessel in the eye of a tidal rip 100ft below the surface of Blasket Sound, County Kerry (south-west Ireland).

At the same time Dr Robert Sténuit discovered and excavated the remains of the galleass *Girona* near Dunluce, County Antrim (Northern Ireland). There were 1,300 men on board when it sank, many of whom were survivors of two other shipwrecks. All but five were drowned, including Don Alonso de Leiva, one of the Armada's most celebrated commanders.

In 1970 Dr Colin Martin excavated the remains of the supply hulk *El Gran Grifón* at the base of a cliff at Fair Isle, a small island midway between Orkney and Shetland. Over the next few years he also worked in conjunction with the Derry Sub Aqua Club to excavate the remains of another hulk, *La Trinidad Valencera*, which broke up in Kinnagoe Bay, County Donegal (north-west Ireland). In 1985 three more wrecks were discovered, the *Lavia*, *Juliana* and *Santa Maria de Visón*, all located off Streedagh Strand, County Sligo (western Ireland). Martin liaised with the divers who discovered the wrecks and with the Irish Government to uncover more vital information about the ships of the Spanish Armada.

The eighth wreck is the *San Juan de Sicilia*, which blew up at anchor in the remote Scottish harbour of Tobermory in Mull on 5 November 1588. Unfortunately little or nothing remains of the wreck after some four centuries of salvage and treasure-hunting.

No English warships have been located dating from this period. The *Mary Rose* which sank in the Solent (off Portsmouth) in 1545 has yielded useful information on the ships and men of the Tudor navy. Another shipwreck discovered off Alderney in the Channel Islands was excavated during the 1980s and appears to have been a transport vessel, carrying men and munitions to the island around the time of the Armada campaign.

Taken together, the Spanish vessels cover many of the types which composed the Spanish Armada, from the 'fire brigade' ships which helped protect the rest of the fleet to the transport and supply vessels which carried soldiers and siege equipment, supplies and munitions. The *Girona* is unique as a galleass, a hybrid vessel that became obsolete shortly after the campaign. Unfortunately little remains of the hulls of these vessels, although the wreck site of *La Trinidad Valencera* yielded substantial organic and timber remains in good condition. Of all the objects recovered it is the ordnance carried on these Armada ships which offers the best insight into the campaign.

Artillery during the period was almost exclusively cast from bronze, although the English had begun experimenting with cast-iron production from the mid-16th century, and some vessels still used the older wrought-iron breech-loading guns, which were considered obsolete by 1588. Over 20 pieces of ordnance have been recovered from Armada wrecks and have been catalogued and classified by Martin & Parker (1988). Two significant features stand out: the range of nationalities and types of guns, and the variation in quality found among this sample, which is probably representative of the armament of the Armada as a whole. The German hulk *El Gran Grifón* was the *capitana* of the squadron of hulks, and carried 38 guns. Many of these were recovered during the archaeological excavation of the wreck, and they included a high proportion of wrought-iron guns. Significantly, one of the more modern bronze guns recovered (or at least a fragment of its barrel) showed it had been poorly cast and had a misplaced bore. Similar faults were found in other Armada guns, including a *sacre* (saker) from the *Juliana* that had a section of its bronze barrel blown out.

The equipping of the Armada was a vast undertaking which stretched the resources of Philip II to the utmost. Contemporary accounts mention hurried production of ordnance and may be indicative of a trend throughout the less powerful ships of the fleet. Gunners would be unwilling to risk firing these weapons more than necessary. Guns also came from a wide range of foundries: Flanders,

Spain, Germany, Austria, Italy, France and Sicily. Of these, the German and Flemish guns had the reputation for excellence.

Even more revealing is an analysis of the shot recovered. By cross-referencing this with the shot recorded in manifests, we can gain a rough approximation of the number of shots fired. In a summary of all of the wrecks excavated before 1985, Martin & Parker (1988) demonstrated that while the large guns were not fired much during the campaign, the smaller swivel guns and breech-loading weapons were fired so much that ammunition stocks were low. This supports the notion that Spanish guns were mounted on unwieldy carriages, and therefore took an inordinately long time to reload. Although the navigational instruments, golden jewellery and coins recovered are of great interest, this information about the arming of the fleet is of far greater historical value, as it highlights the constraints faced by the Spanish gunners on board the Armada ships.

One further group of artefacts recovered from *La Trinidad Valencera* was particularly significant. The vessel carried part of a siege train, destined to support the Duke of Parma in his advance through Kent. The siege guns and their carriages, which were earmarked to be used against strongholds such as Dover Castle and the walls of London, were found virtually intact on the seabed off Donegal.

The Twists of Fate:

What if the Spanish had Won?

Ever since those events of 1588, the propaganda of generations of English and then British historians has made the failure of the 'Great Enterprise' all but inevitable. A combination of English pluck and seamanship, better and more manoeuvrable ships, and a breed of 'sea dogs' who became national heroes meant that – according to most history books – the Spanish never stood a chance. The Spanish were less convinced – the fact that Philip II immediately laid plans to launch another Armada is proof enough that he and his advisors thought the invasion was feasible. What then if the dice of fate hand landed differently, and the Spanish had been successful?

The best chance the Spanish had of success was the plan created by the Marquis of Santa Cruz. He envisioned an amphibious force which embarked in Lisbon, and which was escorted to the English coast by the fighting ships of the Armada. This meant that there was no need for a rendezvous with the Duke of Parma, and consequently there was less chance of things going wrong. He argued that the fleet commander could choose a landing site anywhere along the south coast of England, from Falmouth to the Downs, and the fleet itself would have the strength and firepower to protect the troops as they disembarked.

The rejection of this plan in favour of a compromise greatly reduced the chances of success for the 'Great Enterprise'. However, if the Armada had managed to join forces with the Duke of Parma, and if the duke had been ready to launch his invasion from Flanders, then the whole enterprise might well have ended in success. Parma chose a landing site at Ramsgate, in the north-east corner of Kent. It was possible that the Duke of Medina Sidonia could escort Parma's invasion transports across the 40 miles of sea between the Flemish ports and the shore at Ramsgate, and protect the landings as they took place. After all, the Spanish managed to maintain their defensive formation throughout their stately progress up the English Channel, regardless of anything the English tried to disrupt them.

One of Parma's excuses for not being ready when the Armada arrived off Calais was that he had insufficient warning to complete his embarkation. His argument was that the invasion boats and barges were small, and consequently they would be extremely overcrowded. He wanted to reduce the time the troops actually spent on the boats to a minimum. Of course, when the time came his men had not even begun to embark, and the whole process would have taken weeks rather than days. In the end this played into the hands of the English. Still, according to the Duke of Medina Sidonia's staff, 'The German, Italian and Waloon troops, to the number of 18,000 were embarked, and the Spanish infantry together with the cavalry were at Dunkirk ready for embarkation. As they were boarding, the news arrived that the Armada had gone away; but everything remains in the same state, and the Duke of Parma is present in person and will make no changes until there is certain news of our fleet.'

In other words, Parma claims to have been ready – it was the Armada that let him down. Let us suppose, then, that Parma had been able to embark his troops, and after a few days the invasion barges were manned and ready. The next supposition is that Lord Howard never launched his fireship attack, or that the Spanish ship commanders obeyed orders and maintained their formation, rather than cutting their anchors and making for the open sea. In the crowded waters of Calais Roads the fireships might well have caused damage to the fleet – possibly resulting in the loss of half a dozen major warships. These were losses which the Duke of Medina Sidonia considered acceptable. He could have weathered the fireship storm if his captains had held their nerve.

That leaves the problem of escorting the invasion barges across the English Channel. The Dutch ships which had been harassing the Flemish coast withdrew when the Spanish Armada arrived off Calais. The small Dutch ships lacked the fighting potential to threaten the Spanish. Worse, in the confined waters of the Flemish banks, they would have little room to manoeuvre, making it more likely that the Spanish would have been able to board the Dutch ships. The Dutch prudently withdrew. That left the problem of the English. There is little doubt that the English fleet would have thrown itself against the Spanish with the same resolve and ferocity that it displayed off Gravelines. However, in that battle the Spanish fleet had been dispersed, and therefore it was unable to manoeuvre into the defensive formation which had served it well during the running battle up the English Channel.

The wind was in the Spanish favour, and if the invasion barges had managed to form up within the defensive formation, then there is no reason to doubt that they would have suffered any significant casualties during the crossing, which would have taken a day. By the following morning the fleet would have been off Ramsgate, and the Duke of Parma's troops could begin the business of landing on a hostile

shore. This was a manoeuvre which the Spanish had practised before, both in the Mediterranean and during the Azores campaign just six years earlier. Small ships – ideally galleys – would provide naval gunfire support, while the rest of the fleet covered the operation from seaward. The first troops ashore would be Spanish sword and bucklermen, who would drive off any enemy in their path, and clear an area for the rest of the army to land. Next would have come the missile troops, followed by pikemen, and finally the cavalry and artillery would be brought ashore.

The English maintained two forces in the area: the East Kent Reserves – just over 2,000 men – were stationed in the vicinity of Canterbury, while a larger force of 4,000 foot and 700 cavalry were encamped on the Downs, some 12 miles south of Ramsgate. These were the troops who would have had to contest the landing, as the main army at Tilbury was too far away to intervene. Dr Geoffrey Parker has argued that the English Militia of this period was an under-rated force, and that they were more efficient and more willing than most historians give them credit for. Of these 6,700 men, 5,000 were militiamen. Regardless of their enthusiasm, they would have been hard pressed to hold their ground against 18,000 veteran Spanish troops. In fact, many militiamen had started to desert when the Armada reached Calais, which suggests that they would have been less than reliable troops on the battlefield.

We can assume that the Duke of Parma might have taken casualties during the landing operation – possibly losing as many as a thousand men. However, he would have almost certainly have succeeded in dispersing the English sent against him.

The Last Fight of the *Revenge*, 1591. In the summer of 1591, the *Revenge*, commanded by Sir Richard Grenville, took part in an English expedition to the Azores. Lord Howard's fleet was surprised by a much larger Spanish force, and while most of the English ships managed to escape, the *Revenge* was overhauled and quickly surrounded by Spanish galleons, pouring shot into her at close range. The fight lasted for around 16 hours, the English crew repulsing numerous boarding attempts, while their ship lay battered and helpless. With the *Revenge* unable to fight back, and most of his men killed or wounded, the dying Grenville finally surrendered his ship. The plate shows the action soon after dawn, when the Revenge was surrounded by three Spanish galleons: the *San Barnabe* on her port side and *La Asuncion* and *La Serena* pinning her bow. Having just driven off a fourth galleon pinned to her stern, the *Revenge* is exchanging fire with the rest of the Spanish fleet, massed in the darkness off her starboard beam (Tony Bryan).

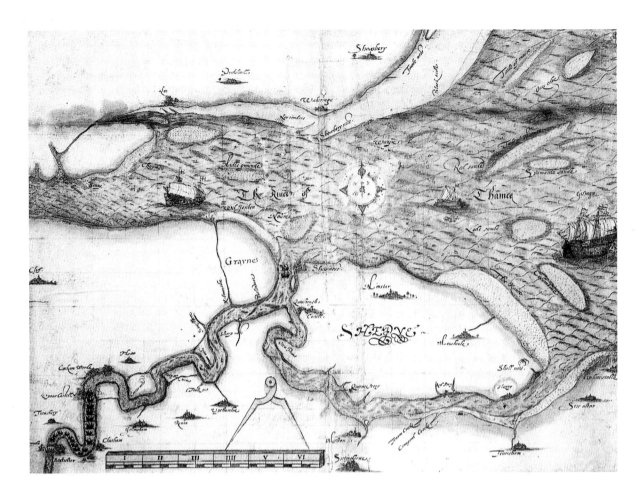

A chart of the Medway and the Thames Estuary, c.1580. This was the sheltered haven where the Duke of Parma hoped the Armada's ships could anchor in safety, and support his army as it marched on London. It also represented the last hope of a safe anchorage for the Duke of Medina Sidonia's fleet after it was driven from the coast of Flanders (Hatfield House Collection, Hertfordshire).

He would then have set about establishing a fortified camp in the vicinity of Ramsgate or Margate, although if his defeat of the Kent Militia had been decisive, he might well have been able to follow up his success by occupying the fortifications along the Kent coast, at Sandown, Deal, Walmer and Dover. With his rear secure, he would have then contemplated his advance on London, some 70 miles away to the west.

His line of advance would have taken him through the fortified town of Faversham, then on to the line of the River Medway, which would have presented him with a formidable natural obstacle. He would have realized this, and would have begun his march westward as soon after securing his base as he could – ideally before the main English army could reach the area. It was three days' march to the river, and he would have been hard pressed to reach it before the Earl of Leicester arrived with his main army. We have to assume that the 2,800 men of the East Kent reserves who held the river line would have been joined by the main English army, creating a force of just under 20,000 men. Parma would therefore have had to conduct a river crossing against an enemy who enjoyed parity in numbers with him.

Parma was under orders to 'take some enemy port', which would allow the Armada a place where it could seek haven and repair its damage. The mouth of the River Medway would have been just such a haven, and the defences there were rudimentary enough to present little problem to the Duke of Medina Sidonia, and to his own small army of 5,000 soldiers. The nearest fortification of any note was at Upnor, which still allowed the Armada to seek shelter in the mouth of the estuary. The presence of the fleet there would also give Parma the opportunity to make another landing, this time on the west side of the estuary, on the Isle of Grain. Without the fleet, he would have had two military options. One was to march south, and attempt a river crossing in the vicinity of Maidstone. The second was to launch a frontal attack, and trust in the fighting ability of his veterans. Parma was well aware that even a badly trained militiaman could fire a musket, arquebus or bow in a defensive battle, and consequently it is more likely he would have tried to turn the English flank.

This would have been a tricky operation, but then Parma had the experienced commanders and men he needed to make it work. This means that the decisive land battle which would have decided England's future would have taken place in the vicinity of Maidstone and Aylesford. The armies might have been equal in numbers, but the Spanish had a decided edge in troop quality. Parma's veteran German, Italian, Spanish and Walloon troops would have been difficult to stop. We cannot really tell who would have won, with the advantages of troop quality on one side and of terrain on the other. However, the odds were heavily in favour of the Spanish.

Of course, even if the Duke of Parma had defeated the Earl of Leicester's army, he still had to march on to London. The capital was the gathering place for a second army – known as the Queen's Bodyguard. Her own 2,000 household troops would have formed the core of this army, and their ranks would have been swelled by upwards of 16,000 militiamen. Then there were the militiamen of the 'maritime counties' of the South Coast, who had been shadowing the Armada as it sailed up the Channel. They might well have been available to reinforce this last royal army. Could these troops have stopped the Spanish at the gates of London?

The Spanish certainly had a lot of hurdles to cross. The fleet had to transit the English Channel safely – a task it performed admirably. It had to remain off the Flanders coast until the Duke of Parma's army was ready to embark – something it signally failed to do. Then it had to transport this army to Kent, where the Duke of Parma was to take charge of the land operations. Without sea communications the invasion was doomed, however successful Parma might have been against the English militiamen. If Lord Howard had managed to drive the Armada away from the Kent coast, the contrary winds meant that it would have been unable to return to support Parma. Links between Flanders and Kent would have been severed, and Parma's men would have been in real trouble.

There are probably too many imponderables, and too many 'what-ifs' to predict what might have happened. However, an invasion would have humiliated Elizabeth, and even if her army had managed to contain Parma, the Spanish might have been able to use their presence on English soil to force the English queen to the conference table. A limited victory could have been claimed, resulting in a major propaganda coup for the Spanish. Philip could have forced concessions such as the tolerance of Catholicism in England, the recognition of the claim of Mary Queen of Scots to the English throne, and even the surrender of all Dutch towns held by English troops. Whatever the result of a successful landing that August, one thing remains certain. Instead of being seen as a failure, the 'Great Enterprise' and the great Armada would have been a crowning achievement for Philip II – real proof that he was indeed the master of all Europe.

Bibliography

Although it would be impossible to list all of the printed works consulted in the production of this book, a selection of the many available works is listed below, and is recommended for further reading. These works are either still in print or readily available through second-hand book outlets or through inter-library loan.

In addition, numerous relevant articles have appeared in the *International Journal of Nautical Archaeology*, the *Mariner's Mirror* and other specialist publications.

Andrews, Kenneth R, *Elizabethan Privateering: English Privateering during the Spanish War, 1585–1603*, Cambridge University Press (Cambridge, 1964)

Arnold, J. Barto & Weddle, Robert S., *The Nautical Archaeology of Padre Island: The Spanish Shipwrecks of 1554*, Academic Press (New York, NY, 1978)

Bass, George F., *The History of Seafaring*, Thames & Hudson (London, 1974)

Bass, George F. (ed.), *Ships & Shipwrecks of the Americas: A History Based on Underwater Archaeology*, Harper & Row (New York, NY, 1979)

Caruana, Adrian, *The History of English Sea Ordnance, 1523–1873: Vol. 1: The Age of Evolution, 1523–1715*, Jean Boudriot Publications (Rotherfield, 1994)

Davis, Ralph, *The Rise and Fall of the Atlantic Economies*, Cornell University Press (Ithaca, NY, 1973)

Elliot, J.H., *Imperial Spain, 1469–1716* St Martin's Press (London, 1964)

Gardiner, Robert (ed.), *Cogs, Caravels and Galleons: The Sailing Ship, 1000–1650*, Conway Maritime Press (London, 1994)

Glete, Jan, *Warfare at Sea, 1500–1650: Maritime Conflicts and the Transformation of Europe*, Routledge Press (London, 2000)

Guilmartin, John F., Jr, *Galleons and Galleys*, Cassell (London, 2002)

Haring, C.H., *Trade and Navigation Between Spain and the Indies at the Time of the Hapsburgs*, P. Smith Publishing (Gloucester, MA, 1964)

Hattendorf, John B. & Unger, Richard W. (eds), *War at Sea in the Middle Ages and Renaissance*, Boydell Press (Woodbridge, Suffolk, 2002)

Howard, Frank, *Sailing Ships of War 1400–1860*, Conway Maritime Press (London, 1979)

Howarth, David, *The Voyage of the Armada: The Spanish Story*, Collins (New York, 1981)

Kelsey, Harry, *Sir Francis Drake: The Queen's Pirate*, Yale University Press (New Haven, CT, 2000)

Kirsch, Peter, *The Galleon: Great Ships of the Armada Era*, Naval Institute Press (Annapolis, MD, 1990)

Konstam, Angus, *The History of Shipwrecks*, Lyons Press (New York, NY, 1999)

Konstam, Angus, *Sovereigns of the Seas: The Quest to Build the Perfect Renaissance Battleship*, Wiley (Hoboken, NJ, 2008)

Laughton, J.K. (ed.), *State Papers Relating to the Defeat of the Spanish Armada*, 3 volumes, Navy Records Society (London, 1905)

Loades, David, *The Tudor Navy: An Administrative, Political and Military History*, Scolar Press (Aldershot, 1992)

McKee, Alexander, *From Merciless Invaders: The Defeat of the Spanish Armada*, Souvenir Press (London, 1963)

Martin, Colin, *Full Fathom Five: Wrecks of the Spanish Armada*, Viking Press (London, 1975)

Martin, Colin & Parker, Geoffrey, *The Spanish Armada*, Hamish Hamilton Publishing (London, 1988)

Mathewson, R. Duncan III, *Treasure of the Atocha*, E.P. Dutton (New York, NY, 1986)

Mattingly, Garrett, *The Armada*, Cape Publishing (Boston, 1959)

Nelson, Arthur, *The Tudor Navy: The Ships, Men and Organisation, 1485–1603*, Conway Maritime Press (London, 2001)

Oppenheim, M., *A History of the Administration of the Royal Navy from 1509 to 1660*, (London, 1896; reprinted Aldershot, 1988 by Gower Publishing)

Oppenheim, M., *The Naval Tracts of Sir William Monson*, Vol. I, Navy Records Society (London, 1903)

Parry, John H., *The Spanish Seaborne Empire*, Knopf Publishing (New York, NY, 1966)

Pérez-Mallaina, Pablo E., *Spain's Men of the Sea: Daily Life on the Indies Fleet in the Sixteenth Century*, Johns Hopkins University Press (Baltimore, MD, 1998)

Phillips, Carla Rohn, *Six Galleons for the King of Spain*, Johns Hopkins University Press Baltimore, MD, 1986)

Rodríguez-Salgado, M.J. (ed.), *Armada 1588–1988*, Exhibition Catalogue, National Maritime Museum, Greenwich (London, 1988)

Sténuit, Robert, *Treasures of the Armada*, E.P. Dutton (London, 1974)

Stradling, R.A, *Europe and the Decline of Spain: A Study of the Spanish System, 1580–1720*, George Allen & Unwin (London, 1981)

Sugden, John, *Sir Francis Drake*, Touchstone Books (New York, NY, 1990)

Unger, Richard W. (ed.), *Cogs, Carvels and Galleons: The Sailing Ship, 1000–1650*, Conway Maritime Press (London, 1994)

Usherwood, S. (ed), *The Great Enterprise: The History of the Spanish Armada as Revealed in Contemporary Documents*, Folio Society (London, 1982)

Wagner, Henry R., *Sir Francis Drake's Voyage Around the World*, (San Francisco, 1926. Reprinted 2006 by Martino Publishing)

Wagner, Kip, *Pieces of Eight: Recovering the Riches of a lost Spanish Treasure Fleet*, E.P. Dutton (New York, NY, 1966)

Walker, Bryce, *The Armada*, Seafarers Series, Time Life (Amsterdam, 1982)

Walton, Timothy R., *The Spanish Treasure Fleets*, Pineapple Press (Sarasota, FL, 1994)

Waters, D.W., *The Elizabethan Navy and the Armada of Spain*, National Maritime, Monograph Series No.17, Greenwich (London, 1975)

Williams, Neville, *The Sea Dogs: Privateers, Plunderers and Piracy in the Elizabethan Age*, Weidenfeld & Nicolson (New York, NY, 1975)

Wood, Peter, *The Spanish Main*, Seafarers Series, Time Life (Amsterdam, 1979)

✤ Index